Podcasting For Dummies, 2nd Edition

Cheat Sheet

iTunes Podcast Catalog: Artwork Parameters

- 600 × 600 pixels, both in width and height
- 8-bit channel, RGB Mode
- JPEG (`.jpg`) format

Suggested Settings for MP3 Compression

- Bit rate: 128 Kbps (best quality for both voice and music)
- Sample rate: 44.100 kHz / 44,100 Hz
- Joint Stereo

ID3 Tags Defined and Implemented

- **Name:** The name or number of this particular podcasting episode. For example, *Technorama* Ep 204: The Data Compost Heap.
- **Artist:** Your name or the name of your podcasting team. For example, Grant Baciocco and Doug Price, Grammar Girl, Scott Sigler.
- **Album:** The name of your show or your show's Web site. For example, ChuckChat.com, Vobes, Gmail Podcast.
- **Track Number:** (Optional) The sequential order of the podcast. For J.C. Hutchins's *7th Son* and Tee's *MOREVI* podcast, the track numbers are chapters.
- **Year:** The year the episode was produced.
- **Composer:** (Optional) Your engineer's name or the originators of the material. For example, in Tee's podcast, *MOREVI*'s artist is listed as Tee Morris, but the composers are Tee Morris and Lisa Lee because the original work was cowritten.
- **Genre:** We recommend Podcast for most, but choose appropriately and be consistent.
- **Comments:** A quick two or three lines of show notes for your podcasts. This is similar to comments you leave in your XML. It's a good idea to include your contact information here also.

D0783416

For Dummies: Bestselling Book Series for Beginners

Podcasting For Dummies, 2nd Edition

Cheat Sheet

Popular Audio-Editing and Recording Software

Program	Where to Find More Info	Mac or PC
Audacity	audacity.sourceforge.net	PC, Mac
Ambrosia	www.ambrosiasw.com/utilities/wiretap	Mac
Audition	www.adobe.com/products/audition	PC
Pyro	www.cakewalk.com/Products/AudioCreator	PC
GarageBand	www.apple.com/ilife/garageband	Mac

Tips for Preparing for an Interview

- Know who you're talking to and what you want to talk about. It's a good idea to visit guests' Web sites and do research. You don't have to be an expert on their subject matter, but you should be familiar with it.
- Have your questions follow a logical progression.
- Prepare twice the number of questions that you think you'll need. Then if your guest gives brief answers, you have a stockpile of questions to call upon.
- Never worry about asking a stupid question. Chances are, your audience has never heard it *answered* before.

Popular Blogging Software

Program	Where to Find More Info
WordPress	wordpress.org
LibSyn	libsyn.com
Blogger	blogger.com

Finding a Podcast

Site Name	URL
iTunes	apple.com/itunes
Podcast Pickle	podcastpickle.com
Podcast Alley	podcastalley.com

For Dummies: Bestselling Book Series for Beginners

Podcasting

FOR

DUMMIES®

2ND EDITION

by Tee Morris, Chuck Tomasi, and Evo Terra

Foreword by Kreg Steppe

WILEY

Wiley Publishing, Inc.

Podcasting For Dummies®, 2nd Edition

Published by
Wiley Publishing, Inc.
111 River Street
Hoboken, NJ 07030-5774

www.wiley.com

Copyright © 2008 by Wiley Publishing, Inc., Indianapolis, Indiana

Published by Wiley Publishing, Inc., Indianapolis, Indiana

Published simultaneously in Canada

For general information on our other products and services, please contact our Customer Care Department within the U.S. at 800-762-2974, outside the U.S. at 317-572-3993, or fax 317-572-4002.

For technical support, please visit www.wiley.com/techsupport.

Wiley also publishes its books in a variety of electronic formats. Some content that appears in print may not be available in electronic books.

Library of Congress Control Number: 2008930831

ISBN: 978-0-470-27557-3

Manufactured in the United States of America

10 9 8 7 6 5 4 3 2 1

WILEY

About the Authors

Tee Morris is an instructor at EEI Communications, based out of the Washington DC/Virginia/Maryland metro area, and he teaches various applications in graphic design and video editing; he also teaches Podcasting for Government and Corporate Business. When he isn't working as a freelance artist and instructor, Tee writes science fiction and fantasy. Tee's writing career began with his 2002 historical epic fantasy, *MOREVI The Chronicles of Rafe & Askana*, published by Dragon Moon Press. His other works include MOREVI's highly anticipated sequel, *Legacy of MOREVI: Book One of the Arathellean Wars*, and *Billibub Baddings and The Case of The Singing Sword*, a spoof of both fantasy and hard-boiled detective novel that received an Honorable Mention for ForeWord Magazine's Book of the Year and was a finalist for the Independent Publisher's Best Science Fiction and Fantasy. It was the podcast of his debut novel that led to this team-up with Evo Terra in *Podcasting For Dummies*.

Find out more about Tee Morris at www.teemorris.com.

In "real life," **Chuck Tomasi** is an IT Manager for Plexus Corp., a contract electronics company headquartered in Neenah, Wisconsin. He's also a devoted husband and proud father of two beautiful girls. As for his alter ego . . . Chuck was bitten hard by the podcasting bug (there's an understatement). He was so eager to get started in late 2004 that he made a few tweaks to his self-written blog software and had the feed ready to go. Since then, one podcast has grown to four distinctly different shows. Freestyle, a personal insight in to the podcaster's life, Gmail Podcast, a collection of short tips on Google's mail application, Radio Yesterday, a collection of old time radio shows, and Technorama, a light-hearted geek show that was named a finalist in the 2007 Parsec Awards in two categories. All of Chuck's productions can be found at www.chuckchat.com. As if he weren't busy enough, he graciously offers his talents to other podcasters in the form of audio production, technical assistance, writing for Podcast User Magazine (podcastusermagazine.com), and speaking engagements such as podcaster meetups, multimedia classes, and the New Media Expo. When people talk about podcasting with passion, Chuck's enthusiasm comes to mind. To top things off — by strange coincidence — both Chuck and Evo have license plates in their respective states that read PODCAST.

Learn more about Chuck at his Web site: www.chucktomasi.com.

Evo Terra is the poster child for Type A personalities the world over. Evo is a washed-up musician, tree-hugging herbalist, heretical-but-ordained minister, talk-radio personality, advertising executive and technology innovator, all wrapped up in one single-serving package. In the podcasting world, Evo tends to infect others with the podcasting bug, from budding show hosts to the people behind the scenes finding new uses for podcast technologies.

He is the man behind helping authors podcast their works to the masses at Podiobooks.com.

Evo currently resides in Phoenix, Arizona with his wife Sheila and his son NJ. Neither of which have a podcast. Yet.

Authors' Acknowledgments

Due to the complexity of the issue and the incredible growth in the community, it would be impossible to properly express our thanks to all the parties who were of great help with this book. So with that . . .

To our wives, Donna, Sheila, and Natalie: Thanks for not strangling us for our constant "Oh! We've got to add that to the book!" moments. We deeply appreciate the averted gazes of death when we answered that no, unfortunately we would not be coming to bed and that yes we did realize it was three o'clock in the morning.

To the podcasters that provided not only inspiration, but also camaraderie and friendship along the way. Through listening to you all and talking to many, you served as a constant reminder of why we were pouring our hearts and souls into this text.

Finally, a special nod to Michael R. Mennenga for passing along that e-mail on October 12, 2004, that opened a door to a world of time-shifting, kick ass mystic ninjas, and science fiction and fantasy geeks around the world interested in what we have to offer.

Publisher's Acknowledgments

We're proud of this book; please send us your comments through our online registration form located at www. dummies.com/register/.

Some of the people who helped bring this book to market include the following:

Acquisitions and Editorial

Project Editor: Rebecca Senninger
   (Previous Edition: Kim Darosett)

Executive Editor: Steven Hayes

Copy Editor: Virginia Sanders

Technical Editor: Stephen Eley

Editorial Manager: Leah Cameron

Editorial Assistant: Amanda Foxworth

Sr. Editorial Assistant: Cherie Case

Cartoons: Rich Tennant
   (www.the5thwave.com)

Composition Services

Project Coordinator: Katie Key

Layout and Graphics: Reuben W. Davis,
   Melissa K. Jester, Ronald Terry,
   Christine Williams

Proofreaders: John Greenough, Lisa Stiers

Indexer: Potomac Indexing, LLC

Publishing and Editorial for Technology Dummies

   Richard Swadley, Vice President and Executive Group Publisher

   Andy Cummings, Vice President and Publisher

   Mary Bednarek, Executive Acquisitions Director

   Mary C. Corder, Editorial Director

Publishing for Consumer Dummies

   Diane Graves Steele, Vice President and Publisher

   Joyce Pepple, Acquisitions Director

Composition Services

   Gerry Fahey, Vice President of Production Services

   Debbie Stailey, Director of Composition Services

Contents at a Glance

Table of Contents

Foreword

So you want to start a podcast? Well, good news! Everyone that has ever started a podcast has found fame, fortune, and success. Hollywood calls with infinite interest, ad nauseam, at all the new and original projects that are out there. Celebrities fall all over themselves to make appearances on podcasts, just waiting for the beckon call of the shows' hosts. Awards are awarded, parties are partied, and recognition and praise are rained down on you daily.

Really? No, it isn't really like that, but we can dream can't we?

I'll be the first to tell you that it isn't all cotton candy clouds and graham cracker streets, but what you can expect is, if you stick with it and make something that is interesting or entertaining, people will come. It takes time to build, but a podcast can be much more than just a cold or stoic mp3 and an RSS feed sitting on a server. They are seeds, seeds for a community.

Podcasting introduced me to individuals, cultures, and personal experiences from all over the world as a podcaster and as a listener. People that I wouldn't have otherwise met, from online friends to others I have met in person and consider true friends (starting with the guys that wrote this book), all wound up connecting with me through this exciting medium.

Also expect your venture into podcasting to be a personal learning experience, not just a social one. I have found that by being yourself, being honest, and opening up to your listeners that these complete strangers will relate to you and become engaged. Those listeners will (generously) give you feedback. When you do start to get feedback from listeners, they will routinely present you with a new perspective on subjects you talk about, confirm things you already know, and even take you into directions you never considered.

There is a lot that you will not expect in your new podcasting adventure and that is where this book comes in. *Podcasting For Dummies* is written by three lovable and knowledgeable dummies who have been down that long and winding road. They will help you side step and overcome hurdles that will ultimately enable you to have fun podcasting . . . and that is what it's all about. That, you can expect.

* Personal Note: As is evident in the pages that follow, I have taught Tee, Evo, and Chuck a lot about podcasting, and it shows. Wax on, Wax off.

by Kreg Steppe

Introduction

Maybe you've been casually surfing the Web or perusing your newspaper when the word podcasting has popped up. Steadily, like a building wave that would make champion surfers salivate with delight, the term has popped up again and again — and your curiosity continues to pique as the word podcasting echoes in your ears and remains in the back of your mind as a riddle wrapped in an enigma, super-sized with a side of fries and a diet soda to go.

Podcasting For Dummies, 2nd Edition, is the answer to that super-sized riddle-enigma combo, and it even comes complete with a special prize. Beginning with the question at the forefront of your mind — *What is podcasting?* — this book takes you through the fastest-growing technological movement on the Internet. By the time you reach the end of this book, the basics will be in place to get you, your voice, and your message heard around the world — and you can even have a bit of fun along the way.

About This Book

"So what are you up to, Tee?"

"I'm currently making a podcast of my first novel, a swashbuckling tale that carries our heroes . . ."

"Uh . . . what is a podcast?"

Asked by best friends and lifetime technologists, this question continues to crop up over and over again, immediately after the word *podcast* lands in a casual conversation. Just the word *podcasting* carries an air of geekiness about it — and behold, the habitual technophobes suddenly clasp their hands to their ears and run away screaming in horror lest they confront yet another technical matter. Too bad. If they only knew how technical it really isn't. When you peel back the covers and fancy-schmancy tech-talk, it's a pretty simple process to make your own podcast. You just need someone pointing the way and illuminating your path.

This is why we're here: to be that candle in the dark, helping you navigate a world where anyone can do anything, provided they have the tools, the drive, and the passion. You don't need to be a techno-wizard or a super-geek — you need no wad of tape holding your glasses together, and your shirt tail need not stick out from your fly. Anyone can do what we show you in this book.

Anyone can take a thought or an opinion, make an audio file expressing that opinion, and distribute this idea worldwide. Anyone can capture the attention of a few hundred — or a few thousand — people around the world through MP3 players hiding in computers, strapped around biceps, jouncing in pockets, or hooked up to car stereos.

Anyone can podcast.

Podcasting, from recording to online hosting, can be done on a variety of budgets, ranging from frugal to Fortune 500. You can podcast about literally anything — including podcasting for its own sake. As blogging gave the anonymous, the famous, the almost-famous, and the used-to-be famous a voice in politics, religion, and everyday life, podcasting adds volume and tone to that voice.

Podcasting is many things to many people — but at its most basic, it's a surprisingly simple and powerful technology. What it means boils down to a single person: you. Some liken it to radio (at least online radio), but it can do — and be — so much more. Podcasting is a new method of communication, transmitting your voice and its message around the world without using public airwaves, connecting the Global Village in ways that the creators of the Internet, RSS, and MP3 compression would probably never have dreamed. It is the unique and the hard-to-find content that can't find a place on commercial, college, or public access radio.

You're about to embark on an exciting adventure into undiscovered territory, and here you will find out that podcasting is all these things and so much more.

How to Use This Book

Podcasting For Dummies, 2nd Edition, should be these things to all who pick up and read it (whether straight through or by jumping around in the chapters):

- ✔ A user-friendly guide in how to listen, produce, and distribute podcasts
- ✔ A terrific reference for choosing the right hardware and software to put together a sharp-sounding podcast
- ✔ The starting point for the person who knows nothing about audio editing, recording, creating RSS feeds, hosting blogs, or how to turn a computer into a recording studio
- ✔ A handy go-to "think tank" for any beginning podcaster who's hungry for new ideas on what goes into a good podcast and fresh points of view
- ✔ A really fun read

There will be plenty of answers in these pages, and if you find our answers too elementary, we give you plenty of points of reference to research. We don't claim to have all the solutions, quick fixes, and resolutions to all possible podcasting queries, but we do present to you the basic building blocks and first steps for beginning a podcast. As with any *For Dummies* book, our responsibility is to give you the foundation on which to build. That's what we've done our level best to accomplish: Bestow upon you the enchanted stuff that makes a podcast happen.

This book was written as a linear path from the conceptualization stages to the final publication of your work. However, not everyone needs to read the book from page one. If you've already gotten your feet wet with the various aspects of podcasting, jump around from section to section and read the parts that you need. We provide plenty of guides back to other relevant chapters for when the going gets murky.

Conventions Used in This Book

When you go through this book, you're going to see a few ⌘ symbols, the occasional ⇨, and even a few things typed `in a completely different style`. There's a method to this madness, and those methods are conventions found throughout this book.

When we refer to keyboard shortcuts for Macintosh or Windows, we designate them with (Mac) or (Windows). For Mac shortcuts, we use the funky cloverleaf symbol, (found on the Command key) and the corresponding letter. For Windows shortcuts, we use the abbreviation for the Control key (Ctrl) and the corresponding letter. So the shortcut for Select All looks like this: ⌘+A (Mac) / Ctrl+A (Windows).

If keyboard shortcuts aren't your thing and you want to know where the commands reside on menus, we use a command arrow (⇨) to help guide you through menus and submenus. So, the command for Select All in the application's menu is Edit⇨Select All. You first select the Edit menu and the Select All.

When we offer URLs (Web addresses) of various podcasts, resources, and audio equipment vendors, or when we have you creating RSS feeds for podcatchers such as iTunes, iPodder, or iPodderX, we use `this particular typeface`.

Bold Assumptions

We assume that you have a computer, a lot of curiosity, and a desire to podcast. We could care less about whether you're using a Mac, a PC, Linux, Unix, or two Dixie cups connected with string. (Okay, maybe the two Dixie cups connected with string would be a challenge; a computer is essential.) In podcasting, the operating system just makes the computer go. We're here to provide you tools for creating a podcast, regardless of what OS you're running.

If you know nothing about audio production, this book can also serve as a fine primer in how to record, edit, and produce audio on your computer, as well as accessorize your computer with mixing boards, professional-grade microphones, and audio-engineering software that will give you a basic look at this creative field. You can hang on to this book as a handy reference, geared for audio *in podcasting.* Again, our book is a starting point, and (ahem) a fine starting point at that.

With everything that goes into podcasting, there are some things this book is not now, nor will ever be, about. Here's the short list:

- ✔ We're not out to make you into an übergeek in RSS or XML (but we give you all you need to make things work — even get you iTunes-ready).
- ✔ We figure that if you get hold of Audacity, GarageBand, Audio Hijack Pro, Soundtrack, or Audition, you can take it from there (but we give you overviews of those programs and a few basic editing examples).
- ✔ We're not out to teach you how to use an MP3 player such as an iPod, an iRiver, or a Zen Micro product.

For that matter, to dispel one of the biggest misconceptions of podcasting, you will not be told to run out and get an iPod. *You do not need an iPod to podcast — or to listen to podcasts for that matter.*

If you are looking for a terrific start to the podcasting experience, then — in the words of the last knight guarding the Holy Grail in *Indiana Jones and the Last Crusade* — "You have chosen wisely."

How This Book Is Organized

The following sections give you a quick overview of what this book has to offer. And yeah, we're going to keep the overview brief because we figure you're anxious to get started. But the fact that you're reading this passage also tells us you don't want to miss a detail, so here's a quick bird's-eye view of what we do in *Podcasting For Dummies.*

Part I: Podcasting on a Worldwide Frequency

Part I goes into the bare-bones basics of how a podcast happens, how to get podcasts from the Internet to your computer, and how to host a podcast yourself — ending up with a few places online that offer podcast feeds you can visit to sample the experience and (later on) to let the world know "Hey, I've got a podcast, too!"

Part I also helps you pick out the best hardware and software you need to start podcasting.

Part II: The Hills Are Alive with the Sound of Podcasting

Consider this part of the book *Inside the Actor's Studio* — part Tech TV, and part WKRP (with your host, Dr. Johnny Fever . . . *booooouuugaaar!!!*). This is where we offer some techniques the pros use in broadcasting. Podcasting may be the grass-roots movement of homespun telecommunications, but that doesn't mean it has to sound that way (unless, of course, you *want* it to sound that way). From preshow prep to setting your volume levels to the basics of audio editing, this is the part that polishes your podcast.

Part III: So You've Got This Great Recording of Your Voice. Now What?

The audio file you've just created is now silently staring at you from your monitor (unless you're listening to it on your computer's music player, in which case it's just defiantly talking back at you!), and you haven't a clue what your next step is. We cover the last-minute details and then walk you through the process of getting your podcast online, finding the right Web-hosting packages for podcasts, and getting a good working handle on the RSS and XML used in podcast feeds.

Part IV: Start Spreadin' the News about Your Podcast

"I wanna beeee a part of it. Podcasting, babeeeee . . .
If I can get on Daily Source,
Then I'll have no remorse for pod—cast—in . . . podcasting . . ."

Sorry. Sinatra moment.

Anyway, you have the podcast recorded, edited, and online, but now you need to let people know you have this great podcast just waiting for them — and that's what we explore in Part IV. With the power of publicity — from free-of-charge word-of-mouth (arguably the most effective) to investment in Google AdWords (arguably the most coverage for your dollar), you have a wide array of options to choose from when you're ready to announce your presence to the podcasting community.

Part V: Pod-sibilities to Consider for Your Show

The question of *why* one should podcast is as important as *how* to podcast. We cover some basic rationales that many folks have for sitting behind a microphone, pouring heart, soul, and pocket change into their craft each and every day, week, or month. These questions have no right or wrong answers, but our hope is that this part offers pointers to convey you safely through the thought process behind podcasting.

Part VI: The Part of Tens

Perhaps the toughest chapters to write were these: the *For Dummies* trademark Part of Tens chapters. So don't skip them because we'll be über-miffed if you fail to appreciate how hard we busted our humps to get these chapters done!

Right — so what do we give you in our Part of Tens? We give you a list of the ten people who made (and/or currently make) podcasting the hottest communications trend to come down the pike since the invention of the Internet. We also offer suggestions for the beginning podcaster — such as what kind of podcasts should be on your MP3 player, just to give you an idea of what's out there, how they sound, and how you can benefit from them. Finally, our Part of Tens closes with the great debate: Podcasting versus Radio. Is radio dead? Is podcasting just another fad? Read . . . and then *you* decide.

About the Companion Podcast

In some cases, a _For Dummies_ book comes with a companion Web site hosted by the good people at www.dummies.com. This book comes with a companion _podcast._ Go to your browser and surf to www.dummies.com/go/podcasting fd and follow the instructions to get free weekly audio commentary from Tee Morris and Chuck Tomasi about concepts in this book explored in greater detail, from the difference between good and bad edits, when too much reverb is too much, and the variety of methods you can use to record a podcast.

Icons Used in This Book

So you're trekking through the book, making some real progress with developing your podcast, when suddenly these little icons leap out, grab you by the throat, and wrestle you to the ground. (Who would have thought podcasting was so action-packed, like a Connery-Bond movie, huh?) What do all these little drawings mean? Glad you asked.

When we're in the middle of a discussion and suddenly we have one of those _"Say, that reminds me . . ."_ moments, we give you one of these tips. They're handy little extras that are good to know and might even make your podcast sound a little tighter than average.

If the moment is more than a handy little nugget of information and closer to a _"Seriously, you can't forget this part!"_ factoid, we mark it with a Remember icon. You're going to want to play close attention to these puppies.

Sometimes we interrupt our train of thought with a _"Time out, Sparky . . ."_ moment — and this is where we ask for your completely undivided attention. The Warnings are exactly that: flashing lights, ah-ooga horns, dire portents. They're reminders not to try this at home because you'll definitely regret it.

These icons illuminate the _"So how does this widget_ really _work . . . ?"_ moments you may have as you read this book. The Technical Stuff icons give you a deeper understanding of what the wizard is doing behind the curtain, making you all the more apt as a podcaster. But if you want to skip the nitty gritty details, that's perfectly fine, too.

Where to Go from Here

At this point, many *For Dummies* authors say something snappy, clever, or even a bit snarky. We save our best tongue-and-cheek material for the pages inside, so here's a more serious approach. . . .

We suggest heading to where you're planning to record your podcast, or just plant yourself in front of a computer, and start with Chapter 1 where you're given a few links to check out, some suggestions on applications for downloading podcasts, and directories to look up where you can find Tee's and Chuck's (many) podcasts, and other podcasts that can educate, inspire, and enlighten your ears with original content.

Where do we go from here? Up and out, friends. Up and out . . .

Part I
Podcasting on a Worldwide Frequency

The 5th Wave   By Rich Tennant

"Hold on, Barbara. I'm going through my old episodes of the 'I Love Boas' podcast."

In this part . . .

Depending on who's describing it, podcasting is either taking the world by storm or providing an interesting diversion. If neither of those, it falls somewhere in between. Whatever it is, we like it, and we think you will too. In this first part, we peel back the covers and go beyond the hype to talk about what this technology is and exactly what you need to do to become involved with it — from soup to nuts.

Chapter 1

Getting the Scoop on Podcasting

In This Chapter
▶ Finding out what podcasting is
▶ Creating a podcast
▶ Finding and subscribing to podcasts

*S*ometimes the invention that makes the biggest impact on our daily lives isn't an invention at all, but the convergence of existing technologies, processes, and ideas. Podcasting may be the perfect example of that principle — and it's changing the relationship people have with their radios, music collections, books, education, and more.

The podcasting movement is actually a spin-off of another communications boom: personal Weblogs, commonly referred to as *blogs*. Blogs sprang up right and left, providing non-programmers and designers a clean, elegant interface that left many on the technology side wondering why they hadn't thought of it sooner. Everyday people could chronicle their lives, hopes, dreams, and fears, and show them to anyone who cared to read. And oddly enough, people did care to read — and still do.

Podcasting combines the instant information exchange of blogging with audio and video files that can be played on a computer or portable media device. When you make your podcast publicly available on the World Wide Web, you are exposing your craft to anyone with a computer and a broadband Internet connection. To put that in perspective, some online sources report the global online population is over 1.2 billion users. In the United States, broadband connections are now more popular than dialup among the 235 million Internet users. And to top it all off, portable players are surging in popularity, with over 22 million adult owners.

This chapter is for the consumers of the content (the audience) and those who make the content (the podcasters) alike. We cover the basic steps to record a podcast and lay out the basics of what you need to do to enjoy a podcast on your media player.

If you're starting to get the idea that podcasting is revolutionary, ground-breaking, and possibly a major component of social upheaval, great. But not all podcasts are so deep. In fact, many of them are just plain fun!

Deciding Whether Podcasting Is for You

Technically speaking, *podcasting* is the distribution of specially encoded multimedia content to subscribed personal computers via the RSS 2.0 protocol. Whew! Allow us to translate that into common-speak:

> Podcasting allows you to listen to stuff you want to hear, whenever and wherever you want.

Podcasting turns the tables on broadcast schedules, allowing the listener to choose not only what to listen to, but also when. And because podcasts are transferred via the Internet, the power to create an audio program isn't limited to those with access to a radio transmitter.

The simplest reason to podcast is that *it's just plain fun!* We've been podcasting since the beginning, and we're still having a blast, continuing to get out messages to our worldwide audiences and challenging ourselves with new tricks and techniques in creating captivating media. So, yeah, for the fun of it. Heck of a good reason.

The following sections cover other reasons podcasting is probably for you.

You want to deliver audio content on a regular basis

Sure, you can include audio content in your blog if you have one. Many bloggers record audio segments and insert them as links into the text of their blog posts. Readers of the blog then download the files at their leisure. However, audio blogs require the readers to manually select the content they want to download. What sets podcasting apart from blogging is that podcasting automates that process. A listener who subscribes to your podcast is subscribed to all of your content, whenever it's available. No need to go back to the site to see what's new!

You want to reach beyond the boundaries of radio

In radio, the number of people who can listen to a show is limited by the power of the transmitter pumping out the signal. Podcasting doesn't use radio signals, transmitters, or receivers — at least not in the classic sense. Podcasts use the World Wide Web as a delivery system, opening up a potential audience that could extend to the entire planet.

No rules exist (yet, anyway) to regulate the creation of podcast content. In fact, neither the FCC nor any other regulatory body for any other government holds jurisdiction over podcasts. If that seems astounding, remember that podcasters are not using the public airwaves to deliver the message.

Just because the FCC doesn't have jurisdiction, you're not exempt from the law or — perhaps more importantly — immune to lawsuits. *You're personally responsible for anything you say, do, or condone on your show.* Additionally, the rules concerning airplay of licensed music, the distribution of copyrighted material, and the legalities of recording conversations all apply. Pay close attention to the relevant sections in Chapter 4 to avoid some serious consequences. When it comes to the legalities, ignorance is not bliss.

What's in a name, when the name is podcasting?

As with most items that make their way into the conventional lexicon of speech, the precise origins and meaning behind *podcasting* are somewhat clouded. Although the domain podcast.com was originally registered back in 2002 (nothing was ever done with it, as far as we know), and Ben Hammersley suggested that and many other terms in February 2004 (www.guardian.co.uk/media/2004/feb/12/broadcasting.digital media), it's generally accepted in the podcast community that the first person to use the term as a reference to the activity we now know as podcasting was Dannie Gregoire on September 15, 2004 (http://groups.yahoo.com/group/ipodder-dev/message/41).

Although some assert the name has connotations to the popular iPod device created by Apple, Dannie didn't have that in mind when the phrase was coined. Regardless of the intentions, the term has been *backronymed* (that is, treated like an acronym and applied to a variety of plausible existing meanings). Of all the possibilities, we prefer *Programming On-Demand casting* (not *broadcasting*), which shortens nicely to *podcasting*. But of course, you can choose whichever one makes sense to you.

Granted, the podcasting phenomenon was in part fueled by the wildly popular iPod portable media device, but no evidence suggests that the two were related when the name was coined.

Narrowcasting (the practice of delivering content to a select group) distinguishes podcasting from traditional forms of broadcast communication, such as radio. Where a radio station *broadly* casts its signal to anyone who happens to be within the radius of the signal, podcasts *narrowly* cast content to people who have made the overt decision to listen.

You have something to say

As a general rule, podcasters produce content that likely holds appeal for only a select group of listeners. Podcasts start with an idea, something that you have the desire and knowledge, either real or imaginary, to talk about. Add to that a bit of drive, do-it-yourself-ishness, and an inability to take no for an answer. The point is to say what you want to say, to those who want to hear it.

Podcasts can be about anything and be enjoyed by just about anyone. The topics covered don't have to be earth-shattering or life-changing. There are a few rules and guidelines in common practice, but there may be times when you find it necessary to bend the rules. (That can be a lot of fun in itself!)

Some of the most popular podcasts are created by everyday people who sit in front of their computers for a few nights a week and just speak their minds, hearts, and souls. Some are focused on niche topics; others are more broad-based.

You want to hear from your listeners

We've heard more than one podcaster comment on the fact that they get, well . . . comments. Podcast listeners are more likely to provide feedback for the podcasts they listen to than radio show listeners are likely to e-mail their thoughts to the show host. That's probably traceable to the personal nature of a podcast. Podcasts offer their listeners — and makers — more control, options, and intimacy than traditional broadcast media can. Of course, the radio is much harder to talk back to than a computer with an Internet connection and e-mail.

When you ask for feedback, you're likely to get it — and from unusual places. Because geography doesn't limit the distance your podcast can travel, you may find yourself with listeners in faraway and exotic places. And this feedback isn't always going to be "Wow, great podcast!" Listeners will be honest with you when you invite feedback.

Creating a Podcast

There are two schools of thought when it comes to creating a podcast: The *"I need the latest and greatest equipment in order to capture that crisp, clear sound of the broadcasting industry"* school of thought, and the *"Hey, my computer came with a microphone, and I've got this cool recording software already installed"* school of thought. Both are equally valid positions, and there are a lot of secondary schools in-between. The question is how far you're willing to go.

But allow us to dispel a few misconceptions about podcasting right off the bat: You're not reprogramming your operating system, you're not hacking into the Internal Revenue Service's database, and you're not setting up a wireless computer network with tinfoil from a chewing gum wrapper, a shoestring, and your belt — regardless of whether MacGyver showed you how. Podcasting, as mentioned earlier, is not rocket science. In fact, here's a quick rundown of how you podcast:

1. Record audio and convert it to a download-friendly format.
2. Create a simple but specialized text file that describes your audio file.
3. Upload everything to the Web.

Yes, yes, yes, if it were that simple, then why is this book so thick? Well, we admit that this list does gloss over a few details, but a podcast — in its most streamlined, raw presentation — *is* that simple. The details of putting together a podcast start in Chapter 2 and wrap up in Chapter 7; then Chapters 9, 10, and 12 walk you through all the geek-speak you need to accomplish the podcast.

Looking for the bare necessities

You need a few things before starting your first podcast, many of which you can probably find on your own computer:

✔ **A microphone:** Take a look at your computer. Right now, regardless of whether you have a laptop or desktop model, Windows or Macintosh, your computer probably has a microphone built into it — or a jack for plugging in an external mic, and maybe even an included external mic packaged somewhere with the manuals, cables, and such.

Position the microphone in a comfortable spot on your desk or table. If you're using a laptop, it should be somewhere on your desk that allows for best recording results without hunching over the computer like *Young Frankenstein*'s Igor (That's *EYE*-gor.) Check the laptop's documentation to find out where the built-in microphone is located in the unit's housing.

Usually the built-in microphone in a laptop is located close to the edge of the keyboard or near the laptop's speakers. Some models tuck it in at the center point of the monitor's base.

✔ **Recording software:** Check out the software that came with your computer. You know, all those extra CDs that you filed away, thinking, "I'll check those out sometime." Well, the time has arrived to flip through them. You probably have some sort of audio-recording software loaded on your computer, such as RecordIt (PC) or GarageBand (which comes pre-installed with many new Macs).

If you don't already have the appropriate software, here's a fast way to get it: Download the version of Audacity that fits your operating system (at `http://audacity.sourceforge.net`), shown in Figure 1-1. (Oh, yeah . . . it's free.)

✔ **An audio card:** Make sure your computer has the hardware it needs to handle audio recording and the drivers to run the hardware — unless, of course, you have a built-in microphone.

Some desktop computers come with a very elementary audio card built into the motherboard. Before you run out to your local computer vendor and spring for an audio card, check your computer to see whether it can already handle basic voice recording.

For tips on choosing the right mic and audio accessories, be sure to check out Chapter 2. Chapter 3 covers all the software you need.

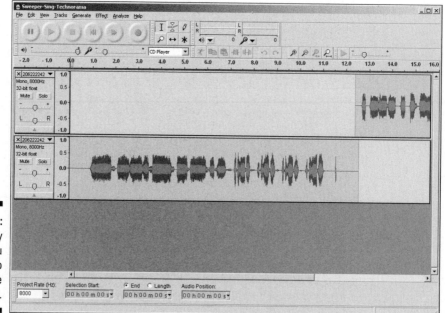

Figure 1-1:
Audacity allows you to edit audio and create MP3 files.

Recording your first podcast

When you have your computer set up and your microphone working, it's time to start recording. Take a deep breath and then follow these steps:

1. **Jot down a few notes on what you want to talk about.**

   Nothing too fancy — just make an outline that includes remarks about who you are and what you want to talk about. Use these notes to keep yourself on track.

   All this — checking your computer, jotting down notes, and setting up your recording area — is called *preshow prep,* discussed in depth in Chapter 4 by other podcasters who have their own ways of approaching preshow prep (all of which can give you some starting points).

2. **Click the Record button in your recording software and go for as long as it takes for you to get through your notes.**

   We recommend keeping your first recording to no more than 20 minutes. That may seem like a lot of time, but it *will* fly by.

3. **Give a nice little sign-off (like "Take care of yourselves! See you next month.") and click the Stop button.**

4. **Choose File⇨Save As and give your project a name.**

   Now bask in the warmth of creative accomplishment.

Compressing your audio files

Nearly all portable media devices and computers can play MP3 files as a default format. Some play many other formats, but MP3 is used as a common format. If your recording software has the ability to output straight to MP3 format, your life is much simpler. In Audacity's case, you need to download an add-on file. If you can't export directly to MP3, check out Apple iTunes at `www.apple.com/itunes`. (The iTunes window is shown in Figure 1-2.) It does many things for the podcaster, including converting a wide variety of audio file formats to MP3. Yes, it's from Apple, but the Apple folks made sure to create a version for Windows also.

After you install iTunes, follow these steps to convert your audio file:

1. **Choose File⇨Add File to Library.**

   Or you can press ⌘+O (Mac) or Ctrl+O (Windows).

2. **Browse for the audio file you want to convert and then click Open.**

   Your file is now in the iTunes Library.

Figure 1-2:
Apple
iTunes,
available
for both
Mac and
Windows
platforms,
can create
MP3 files
from a
variety of
audio
formats.

3. Find the audio file in the iTunes Library and click to select it.

4. Choose Advanced⇨Convert Selection to MP3.

Your file is converted to the MP3 format. Figure 1-3 shows the progress screen that indicates your file is being converted.

The default file format for iTunes file import is AAC. If your menu doesn't have a Convert Selection to MP3 option, go to iTunes Preferences (File⇨Preferences on a Mac, or Edit⇨Preferences in Windows), under the Advanced tab, Importing tab, and change the Import Using option to MP3 Encoder. The Settings should be at least Good Quality (128 kbps). Now your files will be imported and converted to MP3.

Congratulations — you just recorded your first audio podcast! Easy, isn't it? This is merely the first step into a larger world, as Obi-Wan once told Luke.

Transferring your audio to the Web

An audio file sitting on your desktop, regardless of how earth-shattering the contents may be, is not a podcast. Nope, not by a long shot. You have to get it up on the World Wide Web and provide a way for listeners' podcatcher software to grab that tasty file for later consumption.

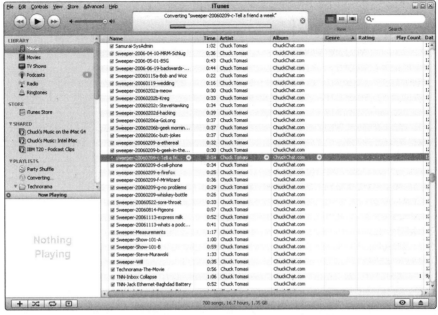

Figure 1-3:
While compressing audio files, Apple gives a progress report on the conversion process.

If you already have a Web server for your blog, company Web site, or personal site, this process can be as easy as creating a new folder and transferring your newly created audio file to your server via your FTP client of choice.

If that last paragraph left you puzzled and you're wondering what kind of mess you've gotten yourself into . . . relax. We don't leave you hanging out in the wind. Chapter 10 covers everything you need to know about choosing a Web host for your podcast media files.

Note that we called your audio a podcast *media* file. Podcasting isn't just about audio. On the contrary, you can podcast any sort of media file you like, even video. Although this book focuses on audio files, you can use all the tips we give here to handle other types of media files.

After you post the media file, you need to create a specially formatted text file, known as an RSS file (*Really Simple Syndication*), explained in detail in Chapter 12, and move it up to your Web server. This file describes where to find the media file you just placed on your Web server. This is your *podcast feed*. People who listen to your podcast can subscribe to your show by placing a link to this podcast feed in their podcatching client.

Yes, we know . . . this sounds really complicated. But we assure you it's not. Some hosting companies such as LibSyn (www.libsyn.com) specialize in taking the technological "bite" out of podcasting so you can focus on creating your best-sounding show. With LibSyn (shown in Figure 1-4), moving your audio files to the Web server is as simple as pushing a few buttons, and the creation of the RSS 2.0 podcast feed and even the accompanying Web page are automatic.

If you want to take more control over your Web site, podcast media files, and their corresponding RSS 2.0 feed, look at Chapters 10 and 12. In those pages, we walk you through some essentials — not only how to upload a file but also how to easily generate your RSS 2.0 file using a variety of tools.

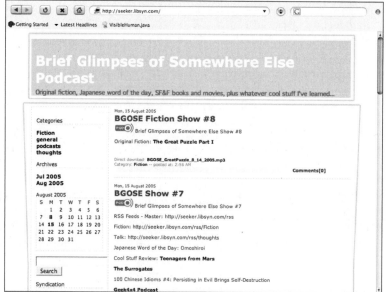

Figure 1-4:
LibSyn
handles
many of the
technical
details of
podcasting.

Grabbing listeners

With media files in place and an RSS 2.0 feed ready for podcatcher consumption, you're officially a podcaster. Of course, that doesn't mean a lot if you're the only person who knows about your podcast. You need to spread the word to let others know that you exist and that you have something pretty darn important to say.

Creating show notes

Before you pick up a bullhorn, slap a sandwich board over yourself, and start walking down the street (virtually, anyway), you have to make sure you're descriptive enough to captivate those who reach your Web site. First, you're going to want to describe the contents of your show to casual online passers-by in hopes of getting them to listen to what you have to say.

You can easily glance at a blog and get the gist of a conversation, but an audio file requires active listening to understand, and it's quite difficult to skim. In effect, you're asking people to make an investment of their time in listening to you talk, read a story, or play music. You need some compelling text on a Web page to hook them.

Descriptions of podcast episodes are called *show notes,* and they're designed to quickly showcase or highlight the relevant and pertinent contents of the audio file itself. A verbatim transcript of your show isn't a good idea, but we do recommend more than simply saying "a show about my day." Chapter 11 discusses ways to create your show notes and offers tips and tricks to give them some punch. (Refer to Figure 1-4 for an example of what show notes look like on a Web browser.)

Getting listed in directories

When you have a ready media file and a solid set of show notes, you're ready to take your podcast message to the masses. You can get listed on some directories and podcast-listing sites, such as iTunes, Podcast Alley, Podcast Pickle, Zune Marketplace, and Digg.com (explained later in this chapter). Potential listeners visit literally dozens of Web sites as they seek out new content, and getting yourself listed on as many as possible can help bring in more new listeners to your program.

A huge listener base is a double-edged sword: More demand for your product means more of a demand on you and the resources necessary to keep your podcast up and running. We recommend working on your craft and your skills, as well as getting a good handle on the personal and technological requirements of podcasting, *before* you embark on a huge marketing campaign. When you're ready, Part IV has more details about marketing.

Part IV spends a lot of time talking about the various ways you can attract more listeners to your show and ways to respond to the ideas and feedback that your listeners inevitably provide. Many podcasters are surprised at the sheer volume of comments they receive from their listeners — but when you consider how personal podcasting is (compared to traditional forms of media distribution), that's really not surprising at all.

Catching a Cast with Your Podcatching Client

So you have the MP3 file, some XML, and accompanying show notes. You're all set, but ask yourself, "How do podcasts get from the Web to my computer?" To access all this great, new content, you need a *podcatcher,* an application that looks at various RSS feeds, finds the new stuff, and transfers it from the

Internet to your computer automatically. In this section, we take a look at some of the different podcatching clients available for your listening/viewing needs.

You may think you need an iPod for all kinds of reasons, but you really don't need one to podcast. Allow us to state that again: *You do not need an iPod to listen to or create a podcast.* As long as you have an MP3 player — be it an application on a Mac, an application on a PC, or a portable device you can unplug and take with you — you possess the capability to listen to podcasts. Depending on the MP3 player, you may even be able to create your podcast on the device as well — but to listen, all you need is a device that can play audio files.

The catcher that started it all: Juice

Juice (shown in Figure 1-5) started life as a product called iSpider, then was branded as iPodder, and later became iPodder Lemon. In November 2005, as if searching for a new identity in the community, the package was rebranded as Juice. It was inspired by a script written by Adam Curry (yes, the former MTV VJ and no, we're not kidding). It promotes itself as an *open-source* (free to use) application that downloads audio files from RSS feeds of your choice directly to your Mac or PC. You can then sync your portable player with your computer's media player, and now you're podcasting-on-the-go.

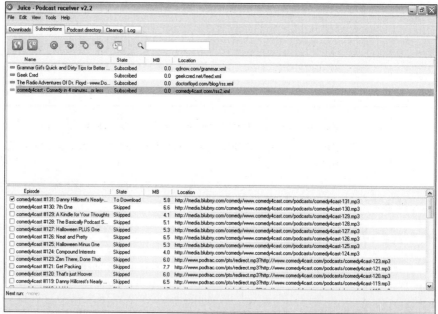

Figure 1-5:
The ground-breaking, trendsetting, and all-around-first podcatching client — Juice.

Download Juice from `http://juicereceiver.sourceforge.net`. After you install it, subscribing to feeds is a simple process. Follow these steps if you don't have a specific podcast in mind:

1. **Click the Podcast Directory tab.**

   Juice comes preloaded with a variety of the more popular directories of podcasts.

2. **Navigate through the directory structure.**

   Click the name of the directory to see the choices offered. In some cases, you may need to click through to a subdirectory to see additional podcasts.

3. **Double-click the name of a podcast.**

   You can also single-click the name of the podcast and then click the Add button near the top.

4. **Click Save.**

That's it! You've just subscribed to your first podcast with Juice.

Of course, you don't have to navigate through the list of podcasts. Follow these steps if you have a specific podcast in mind:

1. **Click the Subscriptions tab.**

2. **On the Subscriptions panel, click the little green button with a plus symbol on it.**

   The Add a Feed window opens.

3. **On your favorite podcast Web site, look for a small icon, typically orange, that says RSS, RSS 2.0, or something similar.**

    The icon may not even say RSS, but simply be a symbol like the one in the margin.

4. **Right click the icon to copy the link location.**

5. **Paste the copied information into the URL field of the Add a Feed window.**

   Or, type it in — just be very careful with your typing! If you get it wrong, you won't get your downloads.

Congrats! You now know how to use Juice to subscribe to any podcasts you happen to come across in the future.

The 800-pound gorilla called iTunes

With the launch of iTunes version 4.9 in June 2005, podcasting went from what the geeks were doing in the basement of the Science Building to the next wave of innovation on the Internet (which was, of course, developed by the geeks in the basement of the Science Building). As always, a step into the mainstream market brought some dismay; the hardcore, independent pod-casters considered this a sad day for podcasting as corporate entities (sponsored by Disney, ESPN, BBC, and so on) dominated the iTunes Music Store podcast directory (shown in Figure 1-6). What about the indie podcasts — the ones that started it all? Would they be forgotten? Go unnoticed? Languish unsubscribed? Well, at first, it seemed that many of the original groundbreak-ers that the podcasting community knew and loved (*The Dawn and Drew Show, Career Opportunities, The Catholic Insider, GrammarGirl*) might get lost in the stampede. But not yet, as it turns out.

Apple's iTunes (available for download at `www.itunes.com`) works as a pod-catching client. It lends an automatic hand to people who don't know where to find aggregators, where to find blogs that host podcasts, and which pod-cast directories list the shows that fit their needs and desires — now they too can enjoy a wide range of podcast choices.

Figure 1-6:
The Apple
iTunes
Music
Store's pod-
cast feature.

With iTunes, podcasting reached into the mainstream markets around the world. (And if that doesn't make you go "Wow!" consider this: On August 4, 2005, iTunes launched in Japan. Within four days, the iTunes Music Store had *1 million downloads.* Sony's own MP3 download service averages less than 500,000 downloads a month.) Instead of dealing with third-party applications, Apple iTunes is a one-stop shop for all your podcasting needs.

It gets even better: Subscribing to a podcast with iTunes is just as easy, if not easier than with Juice. Follow these steps to do so:

1. **In the iTunes Music Store, click the Podcasts link located in the top section of the left column.**

   You can also click the Podcasts icon on the top left of the main iTunes screen and the Podcast Directory icon in the lower right. Or search for a podcaster or a podcast using the Search bar in the upper-right of the iTunes interface.

2. **Find the podcast of your choice.**

   You can do that by

   • Clicking the Browse link to browse through all the podcasts in iTunes

   • Searching by clicking the Power Search link

   Both of these links are located in the Quick Links section on the right side of the Podcasts page in the iTunes Music Store.

3. **When you get to the podcast page (and available podcasts) in iTunes, click the Subscribe button.**

   If you're using iTunes for the first time to subscribe to a feed, you get a confirmation message. You can select the Do Not Ask About Subscribing Again option to avoid this message.

After your podcast finishes downloading, you can find the new episodes by going to the Podcasts section in the left column of iTunes. The new episodes are marked to let you know that you have fresh content waiting for you, and iTunes remembers where you left off in a podcast if you pause or zip over to another podcast or playlist.

Options, options, and more options

Of course, everyone's tastes and styles are different, and there are plenty more options for podcatching clients. Maybe you're using Mac, Windows, or an entirely different operating system. Maybe you don't want to install any new software on your system, or maybe you just like to be different. Hey, that's okay! You too can be a podcast listener:

- **Doppler:** Designed exclusively for the Windows platform, Doppler (`http://dopplerradio.net`) has a strong contingent of dedicated users who are perfectly happy with the features it offers. Additionally, it seems to be a pretty rock-solid piece of software, and it's available for free.

- **Songbird:** Songbird (`www.softpedia.com/get/Multimedia/Audio/Audio-Players/Songbird.shtml`) is another Windows-only application that takes an interesting approach to podcatching (and music) with its Web browser look and feel. The default interface is a bit dark, but it can be customized if you have a little savvy with that sort of thing. Although the software is stable, it was a bit confusing at first to subscribe to podcasts — a little digging through the help provides two options. The product idea is sound, but needs a little maturity as of this writing.

- **Podcast Ready:** In some ways, Podcast Ready (`http://podcastready.com`) is similar to iTunes. It combines simple-to-use software and an easy-to-use Web interface to find and download podcasts. Using a book-marked link, you can quickly subscribe to podcasts via Podcast Ready's site from any Web page with an RSS feed. Using MyPodder software, you can sync your Podcast Ready subscription list with your iPod. MyPodder is available for Windows, Mac OSX, Linux, and more, and is available to download right from the Podcast Ready site.

- **Zune Marketplace:** Zune Marketplace (`http://zune.net`) is the companion software to the Zune portable media device. The marketplace contains lots of choices for music and podcasts. It is currently available only for Microsoft Windows — which makes sense because Microsoft makes the Zune. Using categories or a search, you can quickly find content that interests you. Many podcasters have the Zune icon on their Web sites to make it easy to get their content with a single click of the mouse.

- **PodNova:** PodNova (`http://podnova.com`) is a service that tracks podcast content, yet doesn't require you to download any software to your desktop. You have the option to download some software so files can be transferred to your MP3 player, but it's nice to know that some services don't require this step. The service is pretty intuitive with a decent search and allows you to set up lists of your favorite shows so you can keep them handy.

This is only a starting point for getting access to podcasts. Any attempt at a comprehensive list here would be instantly obsolete. Podcasting continues to grow in popularity, and new podcatching clients and players are coming out all the time. Don't think podcast listening is limited to your computer or MP3 player — you can even listen to podcasts on your phone or TiVo.

For more information and product comparisons, we suggest heading over to PodcatcherMatrix (`http://podcatchermatrix.org`) and exploring more podcatching clients. Bottom line: At this point, you should easily be able to subscribe to the podcasts of your choice.

Quest for Podcasts

Now that you have your podcatching client, it's time to take a good listen to what's happening in the podcasting community. If you're going to podcast (and with you picking up this book, it's a safe assumption that the interest is strong), it's a good idea to take a look around the podcasting community and see what other podcasters are doing.

Many podcatching clients have internal directories of podcasts, and you can access their listings from another directory or listing site maintained elsewhere on the Internet. Other aggregators maintain their own lists based on how many listeners have used their podcatcher to subscribe to particular shows.

We give you a few other places to get started in the following sections — directories, podcast-listing services, and even podcast-specific search engines. (Check out the various sources mentioned in Chapter 18 as well.) So where are these directories? Fire up your browser and, as Edgar Winter says, "Come on and take a free ride. . ."

There are so many directories for podcasts that Rob Walch of Podcast411 has put together a "directory of directories" (`http://podcast411.com/page2.html`). As of this writing, 161 different directories are listed!

iTunes

For the time being, iTunes is king of the hill when it comes to podcast directories. The directory includes not only show information, searchable in a myriad of ways, but also the ability to listen to specific episodes, subscribe to a podcast with one click, visit the show's Web site, leave comments, and see the podcast picks of other people who share an interest in the show you're viewing — and all that is tied in to the same free, friendly software you use to sync your iPod! When your podcast gets legs and starts running, and it comes time to post your name in the directories, make sure you put iTunes near the top of the list. From a public relations standpoint, it's pretty impressive to say "My podcast is listed in Apple iTunes." Many Web sites even have a link directly to their iTunes podcast page and one-click subscription. You have to admit, the people at Apple are always trying to make things simpler.

Podcast Pickle

Gary Leland and the crew at Podcast Pickle (http://podcastpickle.com) take a slightly different approach for listeners to find the podcasts they're looking for. Their best innovation, in our opinion, is the Favorites listing. Rather than rely on voting as a measure of popularity, the Pickle allows registered members to mark as many shows as they like as their favorites. The more people who have marked a show as Favorite, the higher up on the Favorites list a podcast is. And unlike Podcast Alley's fairly unwavering top 10 list, Podcast Pickle periodically takes its top ranked podcasts and moves them to the "Hall of Fame" to allow others to show up in the top listing. A neat idea!

Yes, it's a lot like a popularity contest; you have no way to judge how well *you* might like a show just because a bunch of other people do. That's why Podcast Pickle also allows you to browse by category or search for relevant keywords that mean something to you. Like Podcast Alley, it also has an active forum section where you can see what other folks are saying about a particular podcast before you subscribe.

Podcast Alley

Podcast Alley (http://podcastalley.com) quickly became the first place to boast, brand, and generally beat your chest about your show. With incredibly active forums, detailed descriptions of podcasts, and individual episodes — plus the majority of all podcasters clamoring to get their listeners to "VOTE FOR ME ON PODCAST ALLEY THIS MONTH!" — it's no wonder that Podcast Alley is one of the most active podcast listing and ratings service to date.

Zune

Apple has the iPod and Microsoft has the Zune (www.zune.net). Like many things before, Microsoft wasn't the first to the table when it came to podcasting. The company took a "wait and see" approach for the first couple years, but eventually got on board with its Zune product family. As of now, the Zune is supported only on Windows platforms.

Like the iPod, the Zune supports audio — including podcasts — and video. Although you can't search for podcasts from the main Web page, you can search from within the Zune software. Click the Podcasts link in the Marketplace section in the upper left of the screen to get started searching and subscribing.

Digg.com

Digg.com is a site originally known for its innovative way of getting news to the masses by having its news stories get noticed by peer selection, a process they call *digging*. In 2006, a podcast directory was added to the mix (www.digg.com/podcasts). As more people digg a show (or episode), the more popular it gets and the higher it moves in the digg.com list. That's right, Gracie — another popularity contest. Like other sites, digg.com has its share of "fanboys" of certain shows that garner the lion's share of the diggs that can leave some pretty good content unnoticed. As a directory, its information is well laid out and pretty easy to find.

Other Podcast Resources

It goes without saying that this book is a snapshot in time, and you will likely want to keep up on the latest news and information of the podcasting world. We have a few suggestions to get you started. Perhaps, as you gain experience in podcasting, you'll share some of your pearls of wisdom with the community by contributing back to the vast universe of podcasting that many people like to call the *podosphere*. We recommend trying out these:

- ✔ **Blogger and Podcaster Magazine:** If you're looking for a great resource of information from the people who live and breathe new media, look to Blogger and Podcaster Magazine (http://bloggerandpodcaster.com). Founded in 2007, the online magazine uses a graphical reader application that makes you feel like you're reading a real magazine! You can also pick up audio clips — and yes, it's even available in a print version sent to your door.

- ✔ **Podcast User Magazine:** Podcast User Magazine (http://podcastusermagazine.com) is a monthly PDF publication exclusively about podcasting. As producer Paul Nichols says, "[it] is precisely what it says on the tin — a magazine about podcasting." The publication is targeted at everyone from the professional producer to the complete novice. Topics cover a wide spectrum, including business, education, news, reviews, tips, and tricks from the veteran podcasters.

- ✔ **New Media Expo:** Some have compared podcasting to a religion. As in many religions, podcasters are drawn to a central gathering place. The New Media Expo (www.newmediaexpo.com), or NME, is the annual "Mecca" for podcasters and one of our favorite podcast gatherings. Started by Tim and Emile Bourquin in 2005, the expo is a great way to network with other podcasters, vendors, and attend focused conference sessions.

If you're watching your budget, there's a fee to attend the conferences, but the expo floor is free of charge. Of course, like many cons and expos, a lot of the fun happens after hours. In 2008, the New Media Expo moved from sunny southern California to "sin city," Las Vegas. (Just remember — what happens at the NME, stays at the NME.)

Chapter 2

Getting the Gadgets That Make a Podcast Go

In This Chapter

▶ Choosing the microphone that's best for you

▶ Getting the right mixing board

▶ Accessorizing your studio

*N*ow that you're effectively hip as to what podcasting is and what it's all about, you need to start building your studio. This studio can come in a variety of shapes, sizes, and price tags. What you're thinking about doing — podcasting — is like any hobby you pursue. If it's something to pass the time, then keep your setup simple. A modest setup with little to no investment is ideal if you want to see whether you like playing with audio. If, on the other hand, you find yourself tapping into a hidden passion or (even better) talent, you might want to upgrade to the audio gear that's bigger, better, and badder than the basics.

If you suddenly decide you — yes, you — have a message you want to share, your next plan of action will be one of two options: picking up a digital recorder, reading the instruction manual, and then downloading some free audio-editing software; or watching the DIY Network for methods of sound-proofing the basement and looking at industry-standard equipment that might require some extra homework to master.

This is the beauty of podcasting. In the long run, it doesn't matter whether your podcasting studio is an iPod with a plug-in microphone or comprised of the latest mixing boards, audio software, and recording equipment. Both approaches to podcasting work and are successfully implemented on a variety of podcasts.

So which one works best for what you have in mind? That's what we take a look at in this chapter, discussing the options, advantages, and disadvantages of each setup.

Finding the Right Mic

It's easy and affordable to make your computer podcast-capable. Your first order of business is to find the right mic. If you already have a microphone built into your laptop (and you don't mind starting out basic), you can just download Audacity (described in Chapter 3) and take advantage of the fact that it's free. That's all there is to it! (For openers, anyway.)

However, if your desktop computer didn't come with a mic (or you're just not happy podcasting Quasimodo-style), you're going to want to shop around. While microphone shopping, consider the following criteria:

- **What's your price range?** In many cases, especially with "cheap" mics, you get what you pay for in quality of construction and range of capabilities. You want the most affordable model of microphone that will do the job for you and your podcast.

- **Do you plan to use the mic primarily in the studio or on location?** A high-end shockmounted model isn't the best choice for a walk in the park, and a lapel mic might not provide you with the quality of sound expected for an in-studio podcast. Before you purchase your mic, consider your podcasting location needs.

There are many different types of microphones and microphone connections (or jacks). Some mics are meant to plug in to mixers, some directly to your computer's USB port, and still others to portable recorders. If you're thinking of starting with an inexpensive mic, you may not be able to plug it in to your "upgraded" rig later on. Depending on your needs, you may find yourself upgrading more than just your microphone down the road.

- **What do you want this mic to do?** Record sound? Yeah, okay, but what kind and in what surroundings? Some mics offer ease of handling for interviews. Some are good at snagging specific outdoor sounds. Others may be better at capturing live music. You need to consider multipurpose mics, guest mics, and on-location recording devices, or any kind of condition your podcast provides for you.

Even after narrowing your options, there are so many microphones on the market. After a while, the manufacturers, makes, and models all start to give you that kind of brain-freeze you get when you eat ice cream too quickly. The sections that follow give you the lowdown on the mic that's right for your budget and even make a few *sound* recommendations along the way.

Say, did you know there's a companion podcast for this book? Yeah, it's *Podcasting For Dummies: The Companion Podcast.* In Season Two, Tee hosts several episodes concerning microphones, including one where he and podcaster Phil Rossi (`http://philrossi.net`) test four mics, comparing and contrasting the sound of each. To find out more about microphones, gadgets, and concepts, listen to *Podcasting For Dummies: The Companion Podcast* available at www.dummies.com/go/podcastingfd.

Mics on the cheap

Most of the economical microphones on the market use USB (Universal Serial Bus) hookups. Figure 2-1 shows two types of USB plugs, which you may have used for attaching a digital camera or an MP3 player. You can go online to any of the computer equipment retailers and type **USB microphones** in their respective search engines. Make sure you include **USB**, because a search for microphones can bring up many more alternatives, including video cameras, high-end mics (which we talk about next), and other devices that might be way out of your budget.

You don't have to sacrifice your retirement fund to get started with a USB microphone. Prices start under $20 for a simple desktop microphone. The phase "you get what you pay for" doesn't always apply in podcasting either. We've heard some pretty amazing sounds out of very inexpensive microphones.

When shopping for microphones, you'll hear a lot of terminology like *omnidirectional* and *unidirectional*. These multisyllabic words may look cool to type and are impressive to say, but when you read them or they're spoken to you, they can be a little intimidating. In the next two sections, we demystify these terms and explain how effective these various mic types are for podcasting.

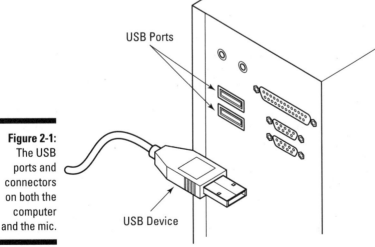

USB Ports

Figure 2-1:
The USB ports and connectors on both the computer and the mic.

USB Device

Omnidirectional mics

Most microphones that come preinstalled in laptops are *omnidirectional* — they pick up sounds from all directions at once. The iPod accessory iTalk Pro (from Griffin Technologies, priced at around $50 on `www.griffin technology.com/products/italkpro`) is an omnidirectional microphone. Omnidirectional mics pick up your voice, along with the television in the background, the traffic outside, the rustling of clothes, the ceiling fan . . . basically, if it makes noise and is within range of the mic, it's recorded.

Although omnidirectional mics are ideal for *sound-seeing tours* such as *Tokyo Calling* (`http://tokyocalling.org`) or *CitizenReporter.org with Bicyclemark* (`http://citizenreporter.org/category/audio/`), they may not be ideal for all in-studio podcasting because they don't capture your sound in detail — even when your mouth is so close that your lips brush against the mic's screen. They tend to add a sharp, tinny quality to your voice and cut out on harsh, sudden sounds such as consonants (especially *p*s and *t*s). That's partly because basic omnidirectional mics vary widely in quality and partly because of the limits imposed by their construction. The built-in models, for instance, are sometimes crammed into leftover nooks in their devices, where they're awkward to use and can pick up internal noise.

One omnidirectional desktop mic that we recommend is the eMic (`www.gembird.us/html/emic.htm`). It currently retails for about $16 and is compatible with both Mac and Windows platforms. There are also omnidirectional mics that come with headphones. Logitech's ClearChat Pro (headset), priced at $50, offers you the ability to record and monitor yourself as you do so.

One advantage headsets have over a desktop microphone is that your mouth is always the same distance away from the actual part of the microphone that picks up sound. If you're an animated podcaster like your authors, this may be useful. On the other hand, they can be very sensitive to breathing sounds. If the mic boom is in the wrong position, the slightest breath from your mouth or nose will sound like an F5 tornado.

Although purchasing a USB headset is a monetary plus because you're getting both headphones and mic together with one purchase, this isn't all you need to monitor yourself as you record. To self-monitor your recording, you need software that offers you an on-screen mixer, a mixing board, or the option to monitor the incoming audio signal.

Installation for these inexpensive investments is a breeze. Find a USB port on your Mac or PC, plug in your new headset or microphone, and set up your audio preferences in your recording software. You're ready for recording.

Unidirectional mics

Unidirectional mics, unlike their omnidirectional brethren, pick up sound from only one direction: the direction they're pointing in. What makes unidirectional mics a good choice for podcasting is in how they by design filter out surrounding sounds, reproducing only the sound directed to it. For in-studio podcasting, interviews, and quality recording, unidirectional microphones are the best option.

If you want to know exactly what a unidirectional mic is and what it can do, take a look at the Brian DePalma film, *Blow Out.* John Travolta plays a Foley Artist, a guy who collects random sound effects and then enhances them for particular moments in whatever film he's working on. One night, he takes a stroll through the park with a *gun microphone,* a unidirectional mic that picks up only sounds located where it is pointing. This microphone is so particular that it concentrates on recording along the line of sight — so it records not only the sound of a tire blowing out, but also the gunshot that causes it to happen.

If you're out shopping for a unidirectional microphone, watch for the term *cardioid.* It relates to the pattern and sensitivity of the microphone. It's also one of those buzzwords that will make you sound more intelligent!

Investing in a high-end mic

Say, however, you really want a cleaner sound for your podcast, and the $50 (or cheaper) microphones just aren't cutting it for you. As you shop, you see mics ranging in price from an inexpensive $70 and reaching up to $3,600! (No, you're not seeing a typo involving an extra zero.) So what defines a microphone? Price? Manufacturer? Look?

What truly defines a microphone is how you sound in it and how it reproduces the sound coming in. Based on how mics work, prices vary, but as you can see from our recommendations, plenty of high-quality microphones that are out there can pick up nuances and details and still remain in the range of affordability.

When you purchase a higher-end microphone, keep in mind that you probably will receive no additional cables for hook up, a jack that does not fit into your computer, and no stand. That's because you're upgrading to professional equipment. The manufacturer is assuming that you already have the tools, bells and whistles, and extra do-dads to make this mic work for you. For the lowdown on what accessories you need to hook up your new mic to your computer, check out the "Accessorize! Accessorize! Accessorize!" section later in this chapter.

Remember those three questions a few pages back? Question #2 — *Do you plan to use the mic primarily in the studio or on location?* — helps narrow your search even more for the microphone that's the right investment for you. At this level, there are two kinds of mics you will hear people talk about: *dynamic* and *condenser* mics.

Although dynamic microphones are marketed more for on-location recording and condenser mics are considered best for in-studio recording, these aren't fast-and-hard rules for what mics should be used where. Sometimes, podcasters use condensers in outdoor settings, and some podcasters prefer the sound of dynamic mics in studio over condensers. When picking a microphone, you want a mic that not only suits your needs but also makes you sound good. *Really* good.

Dynamic mics

Dynamic mics are what you see everywhere from speaking engagements to rock concerts. In fact, when someone mentions the word "microphone," the image that comes to mind is probably a dynamic microphone. These mics work like a speaker in reverse. Sound entering a dynamic mic (by speaking directly into it) vibrates a *diaphragm* (a small plate) attached to a coil. This is located within proximity of a magnet, and the vibrations that this Wile E. Coyote setup makes create a small electric current. When this signal runs through a preamp or mixer, the original sound is re-created. This system sounds complicated (and if you've ever looked inside of a microphone, it is), but the internal makeup of dynamic microphones is such that they can take a lot of incoming signal and still produce audio clearly. They're also rugged in build so they can be manhandled.

If you have a podcast that's "out in the field" or if you're recording on the street and want to be able to surrender the mic to guests and subjects without worry, look no further than the *Shure SM58* (pictured in Figure 2-2). This mic has been in use for over 40 years and is considered the industry standard for its durability and reliability. Podcasters picking it up for $100 love it for its affordability.

Condenser mics

When podcasting happens in studio and you're looking for the subtleties and nuances of the human voice in your recording (the more detail you get, the better!), you may want to shop for studio *condenser* microphones. The anatomy of a condenser microphone is very different from a dynamic one. In the condenser, a diaphragm (similar to the dynamic's) is suspended in front of a stationary plate that conducts electricity. As a signal enters the microphone, the air between the diaphragm and the plate is displaced, creating a fluctuating electrical charge. Once given a bit more power (*phantom power,* which is explained later in this chapter), the movement becomes an electrical representation of the incoming audio signal.

A Shure-fire investment

Remember the opening of *The Blues Brothers?* Jake (John Belushi) turns to Elwood (Dan Aykroyd), after looking over the "new used" car his brother is driving, and asks him what happened to their Cadillac. "I traded it," Elwood replies, "for a microphone." Jake leans forward, a little stunned. "You traded the Bluesmobile *for a microphone?!?*" Then, on reflection, he nods. "All right, I can see that." There are differences between the economic $20 USB microphones and the more expensive dynamic and condenser microphones, and there are even bigger differences between the $100 microphones and the $700 microphones.

The Shure SM7B was the first *industry* microphone Tee ever had in *Imagine That!* Studios. This was a microphone that, for its price, could easily cover two mixers and two high-end microphones, and this was a *dynamic* microphone, a kind of microphone that Tee wasn't accustomed to working with in studio. He had recorded with this mic before though, in locations such as the Washington D.C. WJFK and NPR affiliates in the DC-metro area. Now, it was in his studio, and after his first recording project, Tee understood — with the mic's clarity and exceptional performance — exactly why Shure microphones are referred to as "the industry standard" when it comes to recording equipment, be it in-studio or on location recording.

Microphones can definitely be an investment, worth the trade-in of a car in Jake and Elwood's case. What you invest in a microphone will reflect in the quality of its sound. For Tee, the investment was the right one. But is such an investment right for you? Be sure that you and your podcast are ready for this kind of studio asset. Ask other podcasters what they use, try out microphones if vendors allow for such test drives, and take your time before making such an investment.

Figure 2-2:
Christiana Ellis, creator of the *Space Casey* comedy podcast, relies on the Shure SM58 for her recording needs.

This set-up sounds very delicate, doesn't it? Guess what — it is! This is why condenser mics are transported in padded cases; they're not really built for hand-held use and are best used in a studio application (as shown in Figure 2-3) versus an on-location kind of podcast. If manhandled or jostled around, plates can be knocked out of whack or damaged, causing problems in the pick-ups.

The advantage to this delicate setup is that condenser mics are far more sensitive to sound, and they pick up a wider spectrum of audio. These microphones are so sensitive to noise around them that some come with *shockmounts* — spring-loaded frames that "suspend" the mic when attached to a microphone stand, providing better reception while reducing any noise or vibration from your microphone stand. Think of a shockmount as a shock absorber for your mic.

Tee is a big fan of the AKG Perception Line. Shown in Figure 2-3 as part of Farpoint Media's Draco Vista Studios' setup, the Perception 100 is a fantastic investment for $100, and it can also come bundled with *mixer boards* (discussed later in this chapter) and even in economical two-packs from online vendors like BSW (www.bswusa.com). With each higher model of Perception, cost and features go up, but the quality sound that the AKG line captures remains the same.

Figure 2-3:
Farpoint Media founder Michael R. Mennenga uses an AKG Perception 200 in Draco Vista Studios, assuring studio quality sound from home.

Studio condenser mics

Microphone vendors are noting the popularity of podcasting, and now *USB Studio Condenser* microphones are becoming more and more prevalent. Samson Technologies (www.samsontech.com) was the first to produce such a microphone — the *C01U*. For less than $90, podcasters can now record studio condenser microphone quality audio and need only a USB port to power and connect the mic. The C01U (and the all-encompassing Recording Pak shown in Figure 2-4) was the predecessor to other USB condenser mics like the Blue Snowball, and the Marshall MXL 990 USB.

The phantom (power) of the podcast

You might notice that condenser mics (such as the Perception 100 described in this chapter) are *phantom powered* — their connection to the mixer provides them with all the power they need. Portable condenser mics use batteries to get their kick, but when they start to die, so does your recording quality. (A word to the wise: Always check your mic's battery level before you interview and have fresh batteries on hand.) Because phantom power comes from the mixing board (in the studio) through the cable connecting to the mic, it supplies a constant boost. No battery worries.

Figure 2-4:
Samson
Tech-
nologies
offers
everything
you
need for
portable
podcasting
with
the C01U
Recording
Pak.

The clear advantage of working with USB microphones is you no longer need the audio card, the mixer, or any of the go-betweens once considered essential for connecting audio gear to a computer. With USB condenser microphones, the audio signal now has a direct connection to the computer. It makes your podcast production extremely portable.

Two drawbacks of USB microphones are in their latency and expandability:

- **Latency** is the slight echo you hear in your voice as you record. This is your computer trying to re-create the signal in real time for monitoring purposes. The recording itself will sound fine, but as you're monitoring yourself, you may hear yourself echoing, and the echo may progressively get worse the longer you record one session, depending on your computer's performance. A faster computer can reduce the latency but likely not resolve it completely. You can side-step the latency problem by disabling the recording application's monitor.

- The other problem is **expandability**. Hooking up four C01Us to a hub *can be* possible for multitrack recording, but doing so requires fairly advanced multitrack recording software which is beyond the scope of this book. USB condenser microphones are great for solo podcasters, especially ones who travel a lot, and USB condensers are quick and easy to set up and figure out.

High end is relative. Professional recording studios can spend hundreds of dollars on a single microphone. Fortunately, the MP3 format isn't so finicky. For this book, we're defining *high-end* microphones as those ranging from $100 to $150.

Podcasts Well with Others: The Mixing Board

If you're looking to have more people in studio or you want to entertain guests on your podcast, you need more than just a really good microphone. (Otherwise there will be the passing back and forth of a mic, and that'll get distracting after a while.) You also need inputs for more microphones and full control over these multiple microphones.

Along with a good microphone (and probably a *microphone stand,* discussed later in the "Accessorize! Accessorize! Accessorize!" section), you will want to invest in a *mixing board.* What a mixing board (or *mixer*) does for your podcast is open up the recording options, such as multiple microphones, recording acoustic instruments, and balancing sound to emphasize one voice over another or balance both seamlessly.

You see mixers at rock concerts and in "behind the scenes" documentaries for the film and recording industry. They come in all shapes and sizes; Figure 2-5 shows the Alesis MultiMix8 FireWire. At $300, you might feel like you're sinking a sizable chunk of change into it. (Other Multimix USB options include the sans-iPod option MultiMix8 for $150.) After doing the math, this mixer does compare to others, so you might be coming out ahead in the financial investment.

Before you take your mixer out of its packing, make sure you have room for it somewhere on the desk or general area where you intend to podcast. Something you'll want to consider is how close you want to be to the mixer. An ideal reach for your mixer is a short one. Whether it's you recording yourself or balancing the levels of those around you, clear off a section within a relaxed reach. You'll be happier because of it.

The anatomy of a mixing board

The easiest way to look at a mixing board is as if you're partitioning your computer into different recording studios. But instead of calling them *studios,* these partitions are called *tracks*.

Figure 2-5:
The Alesis
MultiMix8
FireWire
Mixer, a
reliable and
fantastic
mixing
board for
podcasting.

A mixing board provides mono tracks and stereo tracks, and you can use any of those tracks for input *or* output of audio signals. No matter the make or model, mixing boards are outrageously versatile. If you're podcasting solo or with a friend, you can hook up two mics so you won't have to huddle around the same microphone or slide it back and forth as you take turns speaking — nobody wants that. Multiple microphones are the only way to go when you and your friends gather around to record. The real advantage of the mixer is that it allows you to adjust the audio levels of those multiple inputs independently so they sound even.

You may also be wondering about all those wacky knobs on a mixing board. Some of the knobs deal with various frequencies in your voice and can deepen, sharpen, or soften the qualities of your voice, and perhaps even help filter out surrounding *ambient noise* (which is the sound of an empty room because even in silence, there is noise). The knobs on the mixing board that are your primary concern are the ones that control your volume or *levels,* as the board labels them. The higher the level, the more input signal your voice gains when recording. If one of your tracks is being used for output, the level dictates how loud the playback through your headphones is.

Heavy-metal legends Spinal Tap may prefer sound equipment that "goes to 11," but cranking your mixing board way up and leaving it that way won't do your podcast much good. The best way to handle sound is to set your levels before podcasting. That's what's going on when you see roadies at a concert do a mic check. The oh-so-familiar "Check One, Check Two, Check-Check-Check . . ." is one way of setting your levels, but a better method is just rambling on as if you were podcasting and then adjusting your sound levels according to your recording application's volume unit (VU) meter. For more on setting levels, hop to Chapter 6 for all the details.

Hooking up a mixer to your computer

Now that you have your desk cleaned off (mind the dust bunnies!) and a perfect place for the mixer, set your mixer where you want it. And then make certain you can see the following items:

- ✔ Your USB or FireWire mixer
- ✔ A power supply
- ✔ A USB or FireWire cable
- ✔ A CD of drivers

Before hooking up the new mixer, check the manufacturer's Web site for any downloads (new drivers, upgrades to firmware, patches, and so on) needed to make your digital mixing board work. The drivers on the CD — if a CD is included or if drivers are needed — may be out of date. If you do see any recent updates on the manufacturer's Web site, download them and have them on standby.

USB and FireWire mixers are so similar in setup that we can give the same steps for both kinds of mixers. Regardless of where you fall in the Mac/PC debate, you can follow these steps to hook up your mixer board:

1. **Shut down your computer.**

2. **Connect the power supply to the back of the mixer and to an available wall socket or power strip.**

3. **Find an available USB or FireWire port and plug your mixer-appropriate cable into the computer.**

   If your computer's ports are maxed out, we recommend investing in a PCI card that gives your computer additional USB or FireWire ports. We recommend against running your digital mixer through a hub because that might create latency issues and/or affect the quality of the audio.

   A direct connection between your mixer and computer is the best.

4. **Plug the USB or FireWire cable into the back of your mixer.**

5. **Connect your input devices (microphones, headphones, monitors, and the like) to the mixer.**

Analog versus digital

So you decide to go mixer shopping and you see a lot of these mixers going for $40 or $50, and in some cases offering more inputs than the $300 Multimix we recommend here at half the cost. What gives?

Before making this "too good to be true" deal, check the details of this inexpensive mixing board. The model may be an *analog* mixer as opposed to Alesis' MultiMix models, Behringer Xenyx series, or Yamaha's MW-USBs, which are *digital* mixers. Digital mixers connect directly to the computer either via FireWire or USB ports. The inexpensive analog mixers connect with a computer through another audio interface, most commonly an *audio card*. Almost all computers have an audio input that you can plug your analog mixer into. If you don't have one or if you want a little better quality, you can find audio cards starting around $100. Admittedly, add-in cards have to be installed, which you can either do yourself or pay someone to do for you. Once the card is working, you need RCA cables to plug into the audio card, as well as adapters for the RCA cables to connect to the right mixer board inputs. Now comes the time investment in figuring out how everything (audio card, mixer, and cables) hooks up.

With digital mixers, you plug it into an available USB or FireWire port. That's it.

In the case of mixers, you *do* get what you pay for. Cheaper mixers often have inferior audio output because of cheap pre-amps or other components. They often are poorly constructed and don't last as long. For something that sits on the desk, it's amazing how much abuse a mixer can take. That's not to say *all* analog mixers are cheap or that you can't find a quality analog mixer, just that digital mixers are considerably less hassle to install and offer some enhanced functionality like recording multiple inputs to multiple tracks in your recording software — trust us here, that's powerful stuff when it comes time to edit.

We mention that digital mixers can be attached with either USB or FireWire. Choices, choices, choices . . . is there no end to this podcasting buffet? FireWire, or IEEE 1394 as the geeks call it, is generally a bit more expensive, but is less error-prone and tends to put less load on your computer's CPU than USB. On the other hand, your computer may not come with a FireWire port, requiring an add-in card — yes, more money to consider.

6. **Power up your mixer by turning on the Main Power and the Phantom Power switches. See Figure 2-6.**

7. **Start your computer.**

8. **From the manufacturer's CD, install any drivers your USB/FireWire mixer may need.**

   Follow the instructions according to the manufacturer's enclosed documentation. Restart your computer if necessary.

   Most USB and FireWire audio hardware works just fine on Macs without the need for driver installation, but check your audio hardware manuals just to be safe.

Figure 2-6:
Power switches (both for the board and for phantom power) can be found on the backs of the mixing boards.

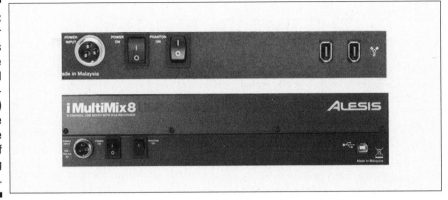

And that's it! You're ready to record with your USB or FireWire mixer. Now with headphones on your head and some toying around, you can set levels on your mixer good for recording.

Before filing away the reference manual that came with your mixer, be sure you know how things work. Buttons like the "Mix to Control Room" suddenly make sense to you as opposed to being "that button that needs to be down when I record". Getting a grasp of how things work on your mixer only makes you a better podcaster, so keep that reference manual close by and set aside a few pockets of time to clock in some reading time with it.

Accessorize! Accessorize! Accessorize!

A microphone and a mixing board are just the beginning when it comes to putting together your audio suite. You now need to add the final touches, as Martha Stewart would no doubt tell you if she were helping you with this process. Now when it comes to accessories, Martha might make suggestions like a doily for the mic stand or a sweet, hand-knitted cover for the mixer. When we talk about accessories, we have something different in mind. Here are some optional add-ons that can help you produce a rock solid podcast:

> ✔ **Headphones:** Some of the best advice in podcasting comes from our Technical Editor, accomplished podcaster and producer Steve Eley (www.escapepod.org): Invest in a nice pair of headphones. Headphones help you monitor yourself as you speak. That may seem a little indulgent, but by hearing your voice, you can catch before playback any odd trip-ups, slurred words, or missed pronunciations.

The G-Track: The best of both worlds

So far we've been talking about microphones and mixers as being two separate entities, but Samson Technologies — the same people behind the ultra-portable C01U Recording Pak — decided to take the audio equivalent of chocolate and peanut butter and combine them into one sweet device: *The G-Track,* shown in the figure.

This microphone is a lot more than just a studio condenser mic. The G-Track has inputs *built directly into the mic* for an additional audio source (labeled as "Instrument" but it can really be for any audio input) and for headphones. With the mic's basic interface, you can now mix in secondary audio with little to no crossbleed from whoever is on the mic. All this, and the microphone is completely USB-powered, the latency kept at a minimum as the headphone jack is closer to the signal than a computer's or mixer's headphone jack. The G-Track is a completely portable studio condenser mic solution; and for a podcaster into music, mixing, or simply on-the-go, this mic's potential can really get the audiophile's creative juices going. To hear the G-Track in action, listen to the second season of *Podcasting For Dummies: The Companion Podcast,* featuring Phil Rossi on guitar and his opinion on this mic's potential from the musician's perspective.

We suggest you invest in good headphones before you spend a lot of money on a better mic, or else you won't know how good the microphone is. Good headphones are nice to have for monitoring, but really show their value during the editing and mastering process.

Another advantage with headphones is they have better sound quality than your computer's speakers as well as reduce ambient noise around you if you purchase what are called *closed-ear headphones.* Keep it simple for your first time out with a pair of the *Sennheiser HD202* closed-ear headphones for around $20. These headphones end in a $\frac{1}{8}$-inch jack but come with an adaptor that makes them a $\frac{1}{4}$-inch stereo male jack (as shown in Figure 2-7), plugging directly into your mixing board. For more on headphones, how to shop for them, and the different kinds out there, check out *Expert Podcasting Practices For Dummies,* by Tee Morris, Evo Terra, and Ryan Williams.

There are those Bose Noise Cancelling stereo headphones you see advertised on television for $300, promising the highest quality for audio listening. Note, we say *listening.* Not *recording* and *editing.* Any headphones you see listed as noise-cancelling are going to be terrific for listening to audio, but those headphones aren't the best for recording and editing. You want to be able to hear the noise that these headphones cancel out so that you can eliminate it before a word is recorded. The best noise reduction and elimination happens before and during recording, not afterward. For podcast production, stick with closed-ear headphones sans the noise-cancelling feature.

✔ **Cables:** As mentioned in the "Investing in a high-end mic" section earlier in the chapter, your newfangled microphone may arrive without any cable — and buying the wrong cable can be easy if you don't know jack (so to speak). So check the mic's connector before you buy. With many high-end mics, the connectors aren't the typical RCA prongs or the $\frac{1}{4}$-inch jack shown in Figure 2-7; instead, you use a three-prong connection: a 3-pin XLR male plug. It connects to a 3-pin XLR *female* plug, as shown in Figure 2-8.

Figure 2-7:
A $\frac{1}{4}$-inch male connection, which is needed to connect headphones to a mixing board.

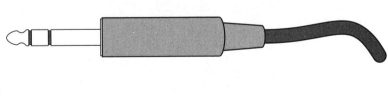

Zoom H2: Podcasting-on-the-go

The idea of "portable podcasting" had a lot of limits hemming it in at one time, ranging from how mobile the studio could be to figuring out the ideal conditions for a small, built-in condenser mic to the audio's overall quality. Then in 2006, Samson Technologies (www.samsontech.com) introduced the Zoom H4, an impressive (if not intimidating-looking) portable recorder-player-mixer that raised the bar for portable podcasting. It was thought nothing could beat it . . . until Samson rose to this challenge in 2007 with the Zoom H2 — a lightweight, unobtrusive, all-in-one solution for portable-podcast recording.

As the iRiver was considered the must-have portable recording device in 2005, so now is the H2 Zoom, seen everywhere at the 2007 Podcast & New Media Expo. It comes as no surprise this device is from Samson that, since the unveiling of the C01U, has aggressively targeted podcasters looking to keep their productions portable. At $200, the H2 records directly to SD Media (up to 4GB) or to your computer with its built-in microphone, a microphone capable of 90°, 180°, or full 360° Surround Sound pickup. The H2 can record directly to MP3 format (in a variety of bitrate compressions), to WAV format (also in a variety of bitrate settings), and in a multi-track format.

Fitting in the palm of your hand, the recorder also offers a Line In and External Mic Input and an easy USB interface with your computer. This unit makes a great portable rig or startup unit for the beginning podcaster.

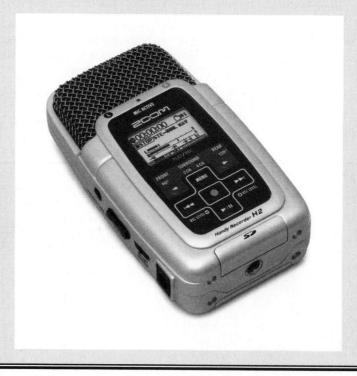

Figure 2-8:
XLR male
and female
plugs,
standard
plugs for
phantom-
powered
micro-
phones.

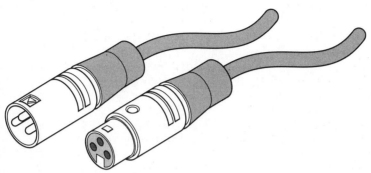

To plug a microphone into your mixer, you want to specify a *3-pin XLR-to-XLR male-to-female* cord; the female end connects to the mic, the male end to the mixer. These cables begin at $9 and work their way up, depending on the length of the cord and quality of the inputs.

✔ **Microphone stands:** On receiving the microphone and possibly its shockmount, you may notice the attachment for a mic stand . . . but no mic stand comes with your new mic. It's your responsibility to provide one, and although that may sound like an easy buy, your options for mic stands are many, each with their advantages.

A simple *desktop mic stand* can run you around $10 and is the most basic of setups. When shopping for the right height and make, you'll notice other stands like a *boom mic stand* around the $100 range.

The type of mic stand that is best for you depends on what you want it to do and how you want to work around it. With the inexpensive desktop stand, you're all set and ready to go without the extra hassle of positioning and securing a boom stand to your desk. The boom stand, though, frees up space on your desk, allowing for show notes and extra space for you to record and mix in. Consult your budget and see what works for you.

✔ **Pop filters and windscreens:** Go to any music store (Radio Shack, Guitar Center, and so on) and ask for *pop filters* and *windscreens,* which are both shown in Figure 2-9. Both devices can help soften explosive consonants (percussive ones like *B* and *P*) during a recording session. A windscreen can also reduce some ambient room noise. Using both on one mic could be overkill, but these are terrific add-ons to your microphones.

Figure 2-9:
Wind-
screens
(left) and
pop filters
(right) help
you
control
unwanted
noise and
percussive
consonants
(such as
P and *B*)
during
recording.

Chapter 3

Building Your Podcast's Digital Workstation

After you have your recording equipment in place, plugged in, and running, it's time to take a look at audio-editing software packages. These are the applications that help you take that block of audio marble and chisel the podcast that is hidden within it.

As with digital photo editors, DVD-authoring software, and word processors, software for audio comes in all sizes and all costs, ranging from free to roughly an entire paycheck (or three). Like any software package, the lower the cost, the simpler the product and the easier it is to understand, navigate, and use for recording. However, as the software grows more complex (and expensive), the features that offer advantages for pro-level work become abundantly clear. In this chapter, we run down some of the audio recording/editing software that might be right for you.

For when you have your show recorded and cleaned up, we also explore options for you to share your masterpiece with the rest of the rest of the world. The real power of podcasting is the ability for listeners to subscribe to a "feed" and get your show automatically delivered to their computer rather than download it manually from your Web site. The piece that makes all this magic happens is the RSS feed. We introduce you to some software to help you manage your feed here and dig into the details in Chapter 12.

When you have software and hardware in place, test your setup to make sure everything works. Take a look at your application's preferences so that your sound input and output are going through your mixer, bring up the volume on the channel on the mixing board that your microphone is connected to, and then listen to yourself through your headphones.

Budget-Friendly Software

Whoever said "you can't get something for nothing" didn't know about podcasting. It's amazing what kind of product you can turn out with little or no monetary investment.

Audacity: Who says you can't get something for nothing?

Audacity (shown in Figure 3-1) is a piece of software that quickly became a podcaster's best friend. It's easy to see why: It's free and simple to use. It's available for downloading at `http://audacity.sourceforge.net`.

Designed by volunteers who simply wanted to "give back to the Internet" something cool, Audacity is designed for a variety of audio capabilities such as importing, mixing, editing, and exporting audio. For podcasters, it's become the must-have tool for recording voice straight off a computer. It's also compatible with Windows, Macintosh, *and* Linux. (We want to send a big thank you to the volunteers who went out of their way to show that yes, software can be made available for *any* platform, provided the creators are driven enough to make it happen!)

But what can a free piece of software do? Well, for openers, Audacity . . .

- Records live audio through microphones or mixer channels
- Can record up to 16 channels at once
- Imports various sound formats for editing and remixing
- Exports final projects to WAV, AIFF, AU, and MP3s
- Grants the user unlimited Undo and Redo commands
- Can create an unlimited number of audio tracks
- Removes static, hiss, hum, and other constant background noises
- Offers a wide variety of effects to manipulate your audio (and these effects are expandable via third-party plug-ins)
- Records at an audio quality of up to 96 kHz

Make sure you access the right URL. Remember that the Web site for Audacity is `http://audacity.sourceforge.net` and *not* `www.audacity.com`. If you happen to enter the latter address in your browser, you find yourself at Audacity, Inc., a Seattle, Washington–based janitorial service.

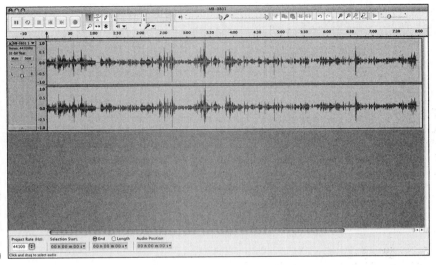

Figure 3-1:
Audacity is
a freeware
application
that allows
you to edit
audio and
create MP3
files.

Cakewalk's Pyro for the PC: Podcasting is so HOT!

Audacity is an excellent piece of software for the basics, but what if you desire more control over the capabilities and features of your audio-editing package? Are you looking for more recording options, additional audio filters, built-in multitrack recording, and pre-recorded music loops? (Gads, what some people will do to set a mood or a tone for a podcast.)

Pyro (http://cakewalk.com/Products/Pyro) is part of the consumer line of audio software offered by Cakewalk. If your computer has the horse-power and the hard drive space, you can buy Pyro and directly download it for around $20. If you prefer a hard copy of the software, though, you can also make that happen for a few dollars more (around $30, if you're counting). And just so you know, Pyro is available only for Windows.

Pyro (shown in Figure 3-2) offers its users some serious goodies:

✔ Record audio from a microphone or other media (CD, LP, cassette, or Internet audio stream).

✔ Display and edit beat-by-beat with audio waveform displays.

✔ Pro-grade audio engineering tools included: DeClicker, DeClipper, DeNoiser, Loudness Maximizer, Reverb, and other post-production effects.

✔ Support for MP3, WAV, and WMA files.

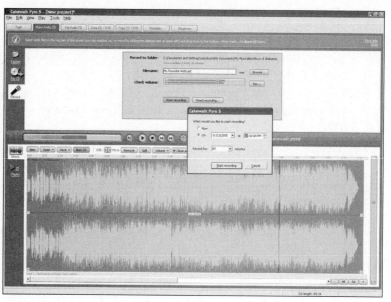

Pyro allows users to record, edit, mix, and produce audio compositions, whether it is an original score for your podcast, a continuous music mix, or just you and your own personal soundtrack. Between its easy audio-editing features and Cakewalk's collection of original audio samples (called *Cakewalk Loops*), it's a breeze to set your own themes and special effects.

GarageBand: Moby in your Mac!

Pyro is an economic audio package for the PC user looking to go beyond Audacity, but what about Mac users? For people in the minority of the computer world, it's always a frustration to hear software developers say, "No, we won't be making this product available for Mac users." Sometimes Mac users seem to be denied the coolest toys and utilities because they just aren't offered for the Mac operating system (maybe a penalty for thinking differently, but still . . .).

Apparently Steve Jobs and his crew heard about this injustice, and shortly after the iPod took off, there came a gem that made it more than cool to be a Mac user — especially one who's into podcasting. Mac-using podcasters call this gem *GarageBand*.

With hundreds of music loops that can easily switch from one instrument to another, GarageBand (shown in Figure 3-3) makes royalty-free music easy to compose. Many of the loops are editable and, with a bit of tweaking, can set the right mood for your podcast. With the release of iLife '08, GarageBand has a few new additions (and one blessed repair) to enhance its initial version:

✔ Multitrack recording supports simultaneous tracks recording independent audio sources all in one recording session.

✔ With the Multi-Take feature, you can now do multiple readings or segments and save them as separate files. Then you can pick which one you want for the final.

✔ You can see a display of the music, with actual notation, in real time.

✔ You can choose to record your podcast as a Music Composition (Old School podcasting with GarageBand) or take advantage of the extra features available in the Podcast mode; note the extra track at the top in Figure 3-3.

✔ You can save the recordings as loops in the GarageBand library.

Upgrading from older versions of GarageBand means purchasing the complete iLife package, starting at $79.99. There is no separate upgrade for GarageBand, but the good news is that the new GarageBand also includes the latest versions of iPhoto, iTunes, iMovie, iWeb, and iDVD, each of which is a terrific application in its own right.

Figure 3-3: GarageBand (pictured here in the Podcast mode) is easy to use and easy to have a blast with.

GarageBand's most appealing asset is its hundreds of sampled instruments available in loops. You can easily edit and splice together these loops with other loops to create original music beds of whatever length you choose. Prerecorded beds range from Asian drum ensembles to Norwegian Folk Fiddles to Blues Harmonica; these ensembles are easily incorporated with editable loops of Classic Rock piano, Southern Rock, or Emotional Piano reminiscent of films like *Love Story* and *Sense and Sensibility*.

GarageBand also provides a capability — with many (not all) of the samplings — to create your own musical theme. Sure, some instruments may sound better than others, but you might — with a bit of trial and error — create an original melody that serves as the best royalty-free intro and exit for your podcast.

If you're planning to do a bit of composing in GarageBand, be warned. Much like working with video in Final Cut, GarageBand is a lot of fun but can easily soak up free time that you would normally dedicate to recording. So if you need to get in touch with your inner Mozart, set aside a good-size pocket of time to put together your desired riffs. You have many options to choose from; as with podcasting, it's best not to rush the process.

GarageBand is easy to tinker with, navigate, and understand within a short span of time. Plenty of terrific books are available for mastering all the nuances of GarageBand. We cannot praise this application enough — and with expansion packs from Apple (called Jam Packs) that add instruments, riffs, and loops to your GarageBand and start at $100 each and other loops and special effects available from other software vendors (and usually stocked online or at your local Apple Store), this unassuming software offers a lot to the podcaster.

WireTap Studio Pro: Recording and editing made easier

If you're not interested in the musicality of GarageBand (or any of the other applications offered in iLife), Mac users have another handy application for recording podcasts and it comes with a few features not found in Audacity. This renegade of audio software is called WireTap Studio Pro (`www.ambrosia sw.com/utilities/wiretap`).

What makes WireTap Studio Pro (shown in Figure 3-4) unique is its ability to record audio from nearly any source — not only coming in from microphones and musical instruments, but also from Internet audio streaming and live audio chats from Skype and iChat. WireTap even allows you to mix in music from your iTunes libraries!

Figure 3-4:
WireTap
Studio Pro
makes a
podcast
happen with
only a few
clicks.

WireTap sports the familiar features that Audacity, GarageBand, and Pyro possess — such as converting analog music to digital; preparing MP3 files specifically for podcasting (by adding ID3 tags, setting bandwidth, and so on); and supporting audio formats such as WAV, AIFF, and MP3. The latest version of WireTap offers some appealing capabilities:

✔ Records incoming audio from microphones or other input devices.

✔ Records and encodes audio into a wide variety of file formats including all the popular ones needed for podcasting (AIFF, WAV, MP3, AAC).

✔ Simultaneously records two sources of incoming audio (on a per-application basis) into separate tracks.

✔ Provides lossless/non-destructive waveform editor.

✔ Provides Apple and Camel Audio digital effects for post-production.

✔ Provides basic MP3 and MPEG-4 Audio ID3 tag editor.

✔ Offers automated options for scheduling recordings.

Retailing for about $70, WireTap Studio Pro is a reliable application for Macintosh podcasters and prides itself in being a one-stop shop for podcasting needs. It's a non-Apple product that can record in Apple's audio-compression formats, easily records streaming audio signals that tend to elude other audio-recording and -editing software, and also offers editing tools for both audio and ID3 tags so you can create the podcast from beginning to end, making it ready for upload. Keep a sharp eye on this new player; it's carving a niche for itself in the podcasting community.

Sharing with the rest of the class

We're particularly keen on GarageBand's Preferences, which let you organize your final AIFF files in an iTunes playlist. When you're done with that particular recording session (what GarageBand refers to as a "song" as you're using the "Old School" approach to podcasting), choose Share➪Send Song to iTunes.

The file is then exported in AIFF and immediately dropped into the playlist you named in GarageBand, where it's tagged with your name (or podcasting ID) and the "album" (which can be anything from the show title itself to the air date of the show). See Chapter 9 for details on adding ID3 tags.

The Sky's the Limit: Big-Budget Software

If you're lucky enough to have unlimited funds and resources to build your podcasting studio, this section on software is for you. A majority of podcasts are working on the bare-bones plan, and so far the investment in the equipment we've recommended (in Chapter 2) is for a budget of under $500 — provided you feel like making an investment in a professional microphone, mixing board, or software.

You may hear podcasters say "content is king," meaning it doesn't matter how good you sound if you don't have anything to say. What makes a good podcast is the same whether you're on a budget of $0, $500, or $Ridiculous.

The difference is in the sound you can get. For the corporate entity, government agency, or professional organization venturing into podcasting, sound quality is crucial as your reputation and experience are now being "socially tested." Do you not bother with the details, or do you raise the quality bar? Commercial podcasting demands nothing less than the best in audio quality. Depending on your budget and the future of your podcast, you can purchase and set up the higher-end audio hardware.

Podcasting is still a new media, but if you want to push its envelope and have the bucks, high-end audio software gives you full control over every aspect of the audio you're recording.

Adobe Audition

At one time, a favorite software application was CoolEdit. But when Adobe Systems purchased it and repackaged the software as Adobe Audition (shown in Figure 3-5), it got even better. Audition (www.adobe.com/products/audition) is offered as an upgrade (provided that you meet the upgrade eligibility) at $99 or a full stand-alone version is available at $349. Audition's features are nothing short of awesome:

- ✔ 128 tracks available to the user

- ✔ Can record 32 different sources simultaneously

- ✔ Offers 50 digital sound effects to enhance your audio tracks

- ✔ Provides 5,000 royalty-free loops that can be easily edited and compiled to create your own music beds

- ✔ Offers Surround Encoder for 5.1 surround sound mixing for audio only or integration into an Adobe Premiere Pro project

- ✔ Offers audio restoration tools like Click/Pop Eliminators and Noise Reduction that can restore recordings from vinyl and cassette recordings; remedy pops, hisses, hums; and fix clipped audio

- ✔ Offers integrated CD burning for audio

What makes Audition so appealing to heavily engineered productions such as *Slice of SciFi* (http://sliceofscifi.com) and *Murder at Avedon Hill* (http://pgholyfield.com/maah) is the complete control users have over the audio. Audition gives you dominion over pitch, wavelength, time-stretching, background-noise removal, and Dolby 5.1 stereo output, making it a staple in the digital audio industry.

Audition runs exclusively on the Windows platform, but fret not, Mac users. There's an Audition equivalent for you called Soundtrack Pro, and since its upgrade to version 2, it's out to make itself a must-have tool for the professional podcaster.

Figure 3-5:
Adobe
Audition
(formerly
CoolEdit)
is the PC/
Windows
software for
editing and
engineering
audio that
gives the
podcaster
complete
control.

Apple Soundtrack Pro

Apple Soundtrack Pro (http://apple.com/finalcutstudio/sound trackpro) is the up-and-coming software in the industry and one of many incredible applications that make up the Apple Final Cut Suite. In its latest incarnation, Soundtrack Pro (shown in Figure 3-6) has been given features built for Mac-based podcasters:

✔ Supports multitrack recording.

✔ Displays multiple audio takes in a single window. After you select your desired takes, Soundtrack Pro compiles them for a final composite — complete with *crossfades* (the simultaneous fading from one audio source into another) — creating seamless playback for the end result.

✔ Copies audio effects and EQ settings from another clip — setting them on an audio clipboard for quick access and application or saving them as a preset for future use.

✔ Features specific functions for producing podcasts, including audio-only, enhanced, and video podcast formats, such as chapter, artwork, and URL markers.

✔ Outputs multitrack audio projects into 5.1 surround sound.

✔ Automatically updates any changes made in Final Cut Pro.

Soundtrack Pro sounds like a dream come true, but here's the reality check: It's no longer a stand-alone purchase. It's bundled with the Logic Studio for around $500 and the Final Cut Suite for a whopping $1,300.

Figure 3-6:
Apple
Soundtrack
Pro is a
fantastic
tool for
podcasters
aiming for a
professional
polish to
their
production.

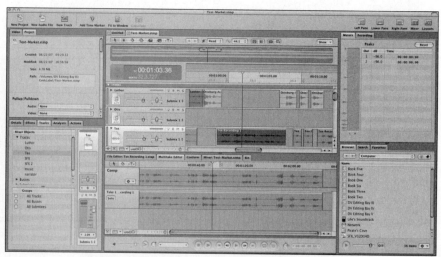

A more economic option for podcasters who want to go beyond GarageBand is *Logic Express* (priced at $200), a digital workstation geared for the modern musician. Many of the higher functions of Logic Express focus on composition and music arrangement, and the interface is very different from GarageBand and Soundtrack Pro (which share enough in common that you can make the jump). For its price, though, you can accomplish a lot with it.

Gluing It Together with RSS

The hardware (mics and mixers) and the software (GarageBand and Audacity) are necessary to record audio and create the podcast media file. That's the fun and creative part. But to make your recording a podcast, you need to get your hands dirty on the tedious and technical parts and add two more three-letter acronyms to your vocabulary: *XML* and *RSS.*

RSS is a "flavor" of XML. Chapter 12 plunges rather deeply into RSS 2.0, but here we give a fast overview of where the RSS 2.0 feed fits into the podcasting equation.

It's all about the <enclosure>, baby

If you already have a blog, you're probably already generating an RSS feed — or have the ability to do so. Although podcatching clients can read this existing RSS feed, the feed needs to include the <enclosure> tag in order for podcasting to work.

Dave Winer invented the <enclosure> tag in early 2001 for the purpose of embedding links to large audio, video, or other "rich media" elements into an RSS feed. At the time, Dave and Adam Curry were trying to solve the click-and-wait problems inherent in big files such as audio and video. Typically, if a user clicked a link to a 30MB file, several minutes would drag by before the file was completely downloaded to the user's hard drive and was usable. Not a good user experience, regardless of what's in the file.

With the advent of the <enclosure> RSS element, users could subscribe to places where they expected large files as a regular occurrence and move the downloading of those files to the early hours of the morning, when the users were snug in bed and a ten-minute download was no big deal.

Of course, users back then had to be technically savvy to take advantage of this new RSS element. It wasn't until the summer of 2004 that Adam Curry wrote what most consider the first podcatching client — a simple, user-friendly desktop program that extracted enclosed media files from RSS 2.0 feeds called RSS2iPod. And behold! Podcasting was born.

We've helped dozens of podcasters get started — and in nearly every case, the XML/RSS step is the biggest source of confusion. So, to get the basics out of the way, XML (eXtensible Markup Language) is a *language,* and RSS (Really Simple Syndication) is a file format built on XML. XML's purpose is to allow systems such as computers, network devices, and other gadgets to exchange information in a structured format. The RSS file is that bit of information that the podcaster publishes so others can use their podcatching software to check for new content automatically.

If that explanation doesn't do it for you, try this analogy about *Star Trek* geeks and trained monkeys. Consider this: *Star Trek* geeks (or just STG) know everything about their passion in life — *Star Trek.* Perhaps you've seen other forms of geekiness expressed toward other public icons — say, Apple computers, the Boston Red Sox, or The Beatles. But you know the type of person we're talking about, right?

As a podcaster, you need a program that acts like a *Star Trek* geek. Your virtual STG has a single job: To boldly know everything there is to know about your podcast — and to flip happily into data-dump mode every time someone drops by to see what's new.

And the trained monkey? Well, listeners don't have time to drop by and check on each and every podcaster they want to hear. So the podcast listener employs a trained monkey to tell him exactly which *Star Trek* geeks to check with — and how often. When an STG has something new to say, the trained monkey comes back to his owner with the specifics. (And they said nobody could tie *Star Trek,* monkeys, and podcasting together. Ha!)

Here the role of the STG is filled by the RSS 2.0 file created by the podcaster — and the trained monkey is actually the podcatching client (iTunes, for example) used by the listener.

As a podcaster, your job is not only to create your RSS 2.0 file, but also to make sure you keep that file updated and current each time you post a new podcast media file. Lucky for you (and us too), plenty of software solutions make this step a breeze.

Simplify the process and get a blog!

If you're looking to spend the least amount of time dinking around with your RSS feed, look no further than the popular blogging software solutions. Blogs are easy to set up, are often free, and ease the process of generating and updating of RSS feed by doing it automatically.

You can choose from dozens of blog software packages, each with a variety of bells and whistles that are designed to make your updates (including your RSS feed) as easy and/or customizable as possible. For a crash course, check out _Syndicating Web Sites with RSS Feeds For Dummies_ and _Blogging For Dummies_ (both published by Wiley); they can help you choose which blog software might be right for you. Meanwhile, here are a few options:

- **WordPress (`http://wordpress.org`):** Perhaps the most popular blogging solution in the writers' eyes, WordPress has many advantages over other free blogs. Not only is it easy to install and get running, but it also supports podcasting out of the box. When you incorporate the PodPress plug-in (available at `www.mightyseek.com/podpress`), podcasting takes on a whole new level of "user friendly" options as podcasts can be distributed via RSS or played directly through the blog. There are also thousands of WordPress and user-developed templates that can be used as is or customized (with a bit of knowledge on how HTML and PHP work) to fit your specific look and feel for your podcast. Oh, and it's free. To make incorporation into your Web site seamless, many hosting companies like DreamHost (`http://dreamhost.com`) offer packages that have WordPress preinstalled. Figure 3-7 shows the WordPress signup page.

There are two basic options where to put your blog. Unless you're an _ubergeek,_ run your own server farm, load operating systems, handle patches, and have a hefty Internet connection, you're likely to let someone else do all that work for you. Prices and products vary. For the podcaster, there are two varieties — the _non-hosted model_ blog, where you get to choose the blog software, and the _hosted model_ where the choice is made for you. In the non-hosted model, sure you get to choose what blog software to use, but there is a little more work involved with setting it up and maintaining it. In the hosted model, you generally give up some of the flexibility for ease-of-use.

- **Blogger (`www.blogger.com`):** Blogger holds the distinction of being one of the most widely used blogging systems. It's available only in a hosted model and is still the de-facto standard for most of the blogging world. While free from cost and any setup confusion, Blogger is somewhat limited in functionality, customizability, and ease in troubleshooting when something goes wrong. (In other words, if something does go "boom," you're at the mercy of Blogger's tech support.) Although it does allow you to create an RSS 2.0 template, it won't allow you to include the podcast media file as WordPress does. Several workaround solutions exist, but your Blogger account won't allow you to podcast without some work.

- **LibSyn (`http://libsyn.com`):** Don't be surprised if Liberated Syndication turns up quite a lot in this book. LibSyn is a combined blog/hosting company specifically designed for podcasting. Although it may not address all your needs, its ease of use and all-in-one nature should not be passed up. Some podcasters choose to use LibSyn as their hosted solution, others use it to store their podcast files while their blog is on a non-hosted solution somewhere else. Either way, we think LibSyn's pricing is quite reasonable, starting at $5 per month.

Figure 3-7:
WordPress
is a popular,
user-friendly
blogging
option that
helps pod-
casters get
their shows
out into the
world.

[Screenshot: WordPress.com signup page]

WordPress.com

http://wordpress.com/signup/

WORDPRESS.COM

Preferred Language: English

Sign Up   Features   Support   Story   Advanced

Get your own WordPress.com account in seconds

Fill out this one-step form and you'll be blogging seconds later!

Username:

(Must be at least 4 characters, letters and numbers only.)

Email Address:

(We'll send your password to this address, so triple-check it.)

Legal flotsam: ☐ I have read and agree to the fascinating terms of service.

⦿ Gimme a blog! (Like username.wordpress.com)
○ Just a username, please.

Next »

Terms of Service   Privacy   Support   Stats | Copyright 2007 Automattic, Inc.   AN AUT⦿MATTIC CREATION

Fine. Do it without a blog.

Blogs are great if you want to include text and other information along with
your podcast. But if you're enough of a purist that you want your podcast to
stand on its own without a supporting Web site, that's okay, too.

A place to put your show notes — and a home for your podcast, where folks
can get your e-mail address or other pieces of data they may not catch on the
show — is a really good idea. If you're confident that you prefer your podcast
to stand on its own and exist only as an RSS 2.0 file, these options may be
what you're looking for. If you're not sure, we suggest avoiding this route.

Take a closer look at some of these Web sites to provide a home for your
podcast, sans blog. With these services, your podcast is simply an RSS file
and an accompanying MP3 file, making show notes, additional comments,
and hyperlinks a bit of a challenge; but you can podcast without a blog if you
please, and here's where you do that:

✔ **Hipcast (`www.hipcast.com`):** For $9.95 per month, Hipcast lets you
record, host, and publish MP3 files, generating a custom RSS 2.0 file
for you automatically. No blog or hosting company is required. In fact,
these folks even came up with a way to record and upload your audio

file right in your browser — no recording software required. This is a great option if you want to test the waters of podcasting without making a huge investment of time or money.

✔ **Podcastamatic (http://kenwardtown.com/podcastamatic):** Podcastamatic automates the creation of an RSS 2.0 file based on the contents of a folder on a Web server. It's not for the technical neophyte, but if you already have a Web server and don't really want to run blogging software of any flavor, this is a solid free option.

Once installed and configured on your server, Podcastamatic watches a particular folder for new MP3 files you upload. When it detects changes to the folder, it generates a new RSS 2.0 file. It even creates or populates an HTML page if you so desire.

✔ **Feeder (http://reinventedsoftware.com/feeder):** Feeder provides a simple interface that gives a lot of flexibility to podcasters who already maintain an active site. You fill it out, and it cranks out an RSS 2.0 file that's ready to be uploaded to the server. Very easy, full featured, and self-contained, it's popular among many podcasters. It's for Macs only, and it's a steal at $29.95.

FeedBurner turns any blog into a podcast

Rick Klau and the folks at FeedBurner deserve a nod for their dedication to a podcasting approach that's 100 percent *For Dummies*-friendly. With a free FeedBurner account, you can convert an existing RSS, Atom, or other syndication feed to a podcast-ready feed in three simple steps:

1. **Sign up for a free FeedBurner account at www.feedburner.com.**

2. **Burn your existing feed.**

   Enter the URL of your blog's feed into the easy-to-use interface and select the I Am a Podcaster option. Then click the Next button.

3. **Confirm your feed title and address and then click the Activate Feed button.**

   FeedBurner then converts any podcast media file links into an embedded `<enclosure>` element in a new feed, provided you link the podcast episode to the blog post. (Remember to provide a link to the MP3 in the post.)

That's it! You now have a new podcast-ready RSS 2.0 feed.

FeedBurner is now watching your original blog feed. The next time you make a post and include a link to a media file (MP3, M4V, PDF, . . . whatever), your new FeedBurner feed automatically does the behind-the-scenes magic necessary to get the `<enclosure>` tag pointing at the file you referenced in your post. Although your original feed (maybe `www.fishingalaska. com/index.xml`) doesn't change, your new FeedBurner feed (perhaps `http://feeds. feedburner.com/FishingAlaska`) is now podcast-friendly and ready to be served to podcatching clients.

Doing it by hand

What's this about podcasting by hand? Are you crazy? No, seriously — generating an XML file in RSS 2.0 format isn't overly difficult, but it's extremely easy to mess up! Sure, you could open Notepad, TextEdit, or any text editor, download a few examples, and generate your own code, but we advise against it.

However, some code warriors — in the same vein of hand-coding HTML, JavaScript, and other markup languages — insist on composing their own code from the ground up (you glutton for punishment, you). You'll want to jump ahead to Chapter 12 for an in-depth look at writing a simple RSS 2.0 feed. We also recommend getting *extremely comfortable* with *Syndicating Web Sites with RSS Feeds For Dummies* or *Beginning XML,* 4th Edition (or at least keeping a copy of each under your pillow); those books go into more detail on these topics.

When you finish putting together your home-spun, handmade RSS feed, you're going to want to make sure your *i*s are dotted, *t*s are crossed, and open statements are closed. Go to Feed Validator at `http://feedvalidator.org` and enter your feed's URL (not the host blog or site, but the feed itself) and then click the Validate button. Feed Validator tells you whether your feed is airtight. You can also find the full technical specifications for RSS 2.0 and a few answers to questions you may have about RSS.

Finding a Host for Your Podcast

Unless you already have hosting taken care of, you're going to need a place on the Web to put your stuff. You know — your podcast media files, RSS feed, and show notes for your podcast. You also need a way to get them up there.

Getting a hosting provider is a breeze, with hundreds of companies all vying for your precious, hard-earned money each month. The good news is that all this competition has brought down the cost of hosting packages significantly. The bad news is that you have to go through a lot of clutter to reach the right selection.

This section covers the basic needs for most beginning podcasts and mentions a few pitfalls to watch out for. In Chapter 10, we get into the process of actually moving your files to your host.

Don't rush into a hosting agreement just yet. We suggest reading the rest of this chapter as well as Chapter 10 before forking over your credit card. We cover lots of good information that can help you narrow your choices.

When you're comparing hosting plans, try not to get bogged down in the number of e-mail addresses, MySQL databases, subdomains, and the like. All of those features have their own purposes, but as a podcaster, you have only two worries: how many podcasts the site can hold and how much bandwidth you get.

Size does matter

Podcast media files are big. Unlike bloggers, podcasters eat up server space. Where simple text files and a few images take up a relatively small space, podcast media files tend to be in the 5MB to 50MB range. And that's just for audio. For video, the size can double.

Here some suggestions for zeroing in on what you need storage-space-wise:

- ✔ Think about how many podcasts you want to keep online and plan accordingly. If you have a plan that isn't constrained by storage space, then you don't need to worry about it.
- ✔ Consider the amount of server space you'll need to host your blogging software, databases, text, and image files. For example, Tee is using well over 3GB of space for just one of his podcasts, and not all of that covers his media files! Of course, he's been building his Web site since 2001 and didn't get to that level overnight. (Podcasting did help quite a bit though.)

Podcasters should look for hosting plans that include at least 3GB of storage space. As of this writing, several host providers charge less than $10 per month for that much space, and more.

Bandwidth demystified

Of equal importance to storage space is bandwidth, an elusive and often-misunderstood attribute of Web hosting that is critical to podcasters. *Bandwidth* refers to the online space needed to handle the amount of stuff you push out of your Web site every month. The bigger the files, the more bandwidth consumed. Compounding the problem, the more requests for the files, the more bandwidth consumed.

For instance, the bandwidth for Farpoint Media's *Slice of SciFi* is over 10 terabytes a month — that's pretty impressive. At the initial launch, the amount of information exchanged (read: downloads) was modest, but then people started talking. With the rise in popularity (thanks to interviews with people like Bruce Campbell, *Stargate's* Amanda Tapping, Grant Wilson of *Ghost Hunters,* and star of *Star Trek:TNG* and Web 2.0 Wil Wheaton), the downloads increased.

So did the demands on bandwidth. Web hosts, in situations like this, must consider when it's time to allocate a larger bandwidth package to handle a show — and that means more cash outlay for you.

And therein lies the double-edged sword of success. Most podcasters want more listeners — and that means more podcatching clients requesting the podcast media files. Bottom line: The more popular your show gets, the more bandwidth is being consumed every month.

To simplify, pretend that you produce one show each week, and your show requires 10MB of bandwidth. You publish the show on Monday, and your 100 subscribers receive your show that evening. You've just consumed 1,000MB of bandwidth (100 × 10MB) for that week. But next week, more people have found out about your incredibly amazing show, and now you have 200 sub-scribers. Next Monday, your bandwidth increases to 2000MB, which gets added to your previous week's total to bring you up to 3,000MB. The new lis-teners were so happy, they also download the previous week's show, tacking on an extra 1,000MB. You've just consumed 4,000MB (or 4GB) of bandwidth for the month. You still have two weeks to go in the month, and if your num-bers continue to climb like this, you will be burning through bandwidth (and your Web host budget) quickly!

If you want even more detailed math on figuring out bandwidth needs, take a look at Chapters 10 and 14. Both offer real-world tips on figuring out what your bandwidth requirements might be. As a general rule, though, the longer your podcast episodes are, the more bandwidth you will need. If you find a plan that offers unlimited bandwidth, the problem is solved. Otherwise, you'll want to try and find a plan that's high in the gigabytes. If you have a podcast that's both long and popular, start looking at plans that offer 1TB (that's *tera-bytes*) or more.

You have ways to avoid the issue of bandwidth, or at least make it less of a concern even if you have large ambitions — as well as files. Chapter 10 talks about some podcast-specific and some advanced hosting options. Even if you don't think you'll have to worry about bandwidth, it's a section to pay close attention to because you'll likely be more popular — and perhaps more wordy — than you think.

Part II
The Hills Are Alive
with the Sound
of Podcasting

The 5th Wave   By Rich Tennant

"You ever notice how much more streaming media
there is than there used to be?"

In this part . . .

A podcast starts with a simple audio recording. Whether you're recording your voice or splicing together various audio clips to create a show, every podcaster needs to know the ins and outs of the recording process. In this part, we help you figure out what to record, how to record it, and how to avoid some pitfalls along the way.

Chapter 4

Before You Hit the Record Button . . .

*T*une to a classical radio station (and when we refer to "classics" here, we mean Beethoven and Haydn, not the Beatles and Hendrix) and listen to the DJs — oh, sorry, the on-air personalities — featured there. You'll notice that they're all speaking slowly and articulately, mellowed and obviously relaxed by the melodic creations of greats such as Mozart, Wagner, and Joel. (Yes, Billy Joel has a classical album — a pretty good one, too!) Although the on-air personalities of your local classical music station all sound alike, they sound dramatically different from the wacky Morning Zoo guys on your contemporary hits radio station who sound as if they're on their eighth cup of espresso.

When you hear people talk about *finding your voice* in broadcasting, that's what they mean. You come to an understanding of what your average audience wants (and to some degree, expects), and then you meet that need. This chapter helps you develop the voice and personality you want to convey when podcasting.

After you discover your voice, you will want to get ready for the show. This chapter shows you what to do to prepare for smooth and easy podcasts that (one can hope) will be glitch-free during the recording process. Preshow prep is not only important, but also essential in making a feed worth catching. Even the most spontaneous of podcasts follows a logical progression and general direction, remaining focused on the podcast's intent.

Choosing a Unique Topic for Your Podcast

Before you can think about putting together a podcast, you need to decide what topic you want to cover. At the time of this writing, a sample of what people were podcasting (according to PodcastAlley.com) — listed by genre from most to least common — looked like this:

Topic	Number of shows
General	7,982
Music	6,891
Technology	3,854
Comedy	2,807
Religion & Spirituality	2,421
Business	1,816
Society & Culture	1,744
Education	1,558
Sports & Recreation	1,266
Video Podcasts	1,148
TV & Film	998
News & Politics	991
Health	977
Arts	952
Travel	514
Food & Drink	264
Environment	163
Games & Hobbies	110
Kids & Family	46
Science & Medicine	28
Government & Organizations	10

That's a total of 36,540 podcasts — an increase of 30,000 since the first edition of this book was published in 2005. This averages out to roughly 50 new podcasts going online every day.

The first thing to understand about podcasts is that this activity isn't all about being "number one" in your chosen podcast genre. Granted, some podcasts do vie for top honors on various polls. But instead of worrying about garnering ratings (a topic that's covered in Chapter 13), think about what will make your podcast uniquely worth your effort and your listeners' time. Here are some ways you can create a unique podcast:

- ✔ **Study other podcasts.** Before you can figure out what will make your podcast unique, check out some other podcasts. The best way to find out what makes a podcast worthwhile is to subscribe to a few feeds that pique your curiosity.

  Listen to these feeds for a few weeks (provided they're weekly) and jot down what you like and don't like about them. From the notes you take, you might find your angle. Keep in mind that downloading and listening to other podcasts should be educational and constructive, not a raid for fodder for your own show.

  Don't steal content, special effects, or content structure from another podcast. Approach others' podcasts as you would someone's Web site. It's okay to be inspired, as long as you don't make your podcast a carbon copy of your inspiration's work. When you have your podcast up, avoid criticizing another podcast in your own; criticizing someone else's work is no way to better yours. Stay on the pod-sitive side.

- ✔ **Pick a topic you know.** Whether you've decided to take on the topic of music, religion, or technology, the best way to make your podcast unique is to find an angle you're comfortable with (Polka: The Misunderstood Music, Great Travesties of Sports History, Forgotten Greats of Science Fiction). There's also the possibility that your initial show may inspire an additional angle so unique that you'll have to start another podcast specifically to address that audience.

The content you bring — regardless of what genre it's in — is unique because it is *your* podcast. It's your voice, your angle, and your approach to whatever intent you pursue. Provided you maintain a high confidence level and genuinely enjoy what you're doing, people will tune in and talk to other listeners about what you're podcasting.

Finding Your Voice

The broadcasting industry might not want to admit to this, but podcasting and commercial radio share a lot in common. In the early days of what is now a major radio genre, talk shows were reserved for National Public Radio and news stations. In general, they were pretty dry and lackluster, bringing their listeners the news, weather, and daily topics that affected the world — but nothing particularly unusual or exciting.

Then a guy named Howard Stern came along and changed everything in this once-tiny niche! You can love him, you can hate him — you can claim to hate him when secretly you love him — but Stern completely turned around what was considered AM-only programming. Now talk radio is big business. Some personalities are just out to entertain (Don & Mike, Ron & Fez); others use it to voice their political viewpoints (Rush Limbaugh leaning to the right stereo channel while Al Franken favors the left); and then you have the bottom-of-the-barrel personalities (insert your least favorite on-air loudmouths here) who turn you off radio and on to podcasting!

A majority of podcasting is just that: talk radio. Actually, a more accurate description would be "*homespun* talk audio" because radio is *broad*cast whereas podcasting is *narrow*cast. Each podcast has a different personality and appeals to a different market. Finding your voice is one of the most challenging obstacles that you (as a once-and-future podcaster) must clear.

Even if your podcast's aim is entertainment, you have a message you want to convey. That message will influence the voice you adopt for your podcast. If you're podcasting an audio blog about life, its challenges, and the ups and downs that you encounter, then maybe a soft tone — relaxed and somewhat pensive — would be appropriate. But if you decide to go political — say you're the Angry Young Man who's fed up with the current bureaucracy — then it's time to fine-tune the edginess of your voice. That's what you need for a podcast of this nature.

After you discover the passion your podcast is centered around (see the preceding section for tips on how to do that), here are some ways to *find your voice:*

✔ **Record your voice and then listen to what it sounds like.** It astounds us how many people hate listening to their recorded voice. It's a fear akin to getting up in front of people and speaking. When finding your voice, though, you need to hear what your current voice sounds like. Write a paragraph on your show's subject. Then read it aloud a few times and find a rhythm in your words. Expect the following:

  • Talking too fast

  • Swallowing small, one-syllable words like *to, in*

  • Ignoring commas, thereby creating one long, run-on thought

  • Lip-smacking, heavy breathing, and the unavoidable *ahs* and *ums*

You can edit out some of these problems (see Chapter 7), but you should grow accustomed to hearing your own voice because you'll hear yourself again and again . . . and again . . . during the editing process. The more familiar you are with how your voice sounds, the easier time you'll have editing your podcasts before publishing them online.

✔ **Play around with the rhythm of your speech.** You don't have to be an actor to podcast, but you can apply some basics of acting when you're recording. One of these basics, as one of Tee's acting professors told him, is to "Make a meal of your words." This means to play around with the rhythm of your speech. When you want to make a point, slow down. If you're feeling a tad smarmy, pick up the pace. Above all, be relaxed and make sure you don't sound too contrived or melodramatic.

✔ **Speak clearly.** Another simple trick from the acting world to add to your arsenal is to open your mouth wider. Many people talk with their mouths mostly closed, but by opening up your mouth, you can gain clarity. So, when making a meal of your words, it *is* good manners to chew with your mouth open.

✔ **Speak with confidence.** Speak confidently about your topic. No one is going to believe in what you have to say if you don't believe in yourself. It may take a few podcasts to find a groove, or you might hit the ground running and have a podcast that immediately takes off. Just speak with conviction and allow yourself to shine.

✔ **Develop your podcasting personality.** After you know what you sound like when you record, here's where you develop your podcasting personality. Is your persona going to be light, fun, and informal, or something a little edgy, jaded? Is your message taking an angle of marketing, politics, or religion? Or are you podcasting a love of music, science, or your Macintosh? Your persona should generally match the theme of your show. If you're doing a show on classical music, a persona of a morning radio DJ probably isn't going to work. If you're taking a light-hearted look at politics, you may want to have a little more levity in your tone and pace than a funeral director.

Deciding Whether You Need an Outline or Script

What method works best for you? A full script and hours of prep time, or a single note card and two clicks of the mouse — one for *Record* and another for *Stop?* Both approaches work, depending on the podcaster's personality. It could be said that there's little difference between a writer and a podcaster: Some writers prefer to use an outline when putting together a short story or novel; others merely take an idea, a few points, and a direction, and then let their fingers work across the keyboard.

If you decide to work with a script, it's a good idea to invest some time into *preshow prep,* simple preparation for what you're going to say *and* how you're going to deliver it. Depending on your podcast, though, prep time may vary. Here are a couple of examples of how dramatically different prep time can be for different podcasting situations:

✔ For his podcast *Speaking of Beer,* "Charlie the Beer Guy" does very little prep — usually just enough to get accurate numbers for the alcohol content of his subject. After he does minimal orientation with the guest panel, he's ready to record. You really need to know your subject and have good chemistry with your show participants to make a minimal plan like this turn in to a good show, but it can work.

✔ On the other side of the spectrum is *The Radio Adventures of Doctor Floyd,* a 10-minute show in the style of old-time radio with a modern, educational, comedic spin. Grant Baciocco and Doug Price (see Figure 4-1) have every show carefully scripted. Depending on the historical research required, Grant can spend anywhere from 1 to 3 hours doing preshow prep. The careful scripting comes in real handy when "Doctor Floyd" has celebrity actors playing a part in the show.

Figure 4-1:
The Radio Adventures of Doctor Floyd's Grant Baciocco (left) and Doug Price (right) take their comedy seriously, and that means plenty of preshow prep!

Preshow prep can range anywhere from jotting a few notes on a napkin to writing a complete scripted with full sound effects — regardless of show length. So how far should your prep go technically? That depends on what your podcast needs. Outlines and scripts will keep you on track with what you want to say, serving as roadmaps you use to keep moving smoothly from Point A to Point B.

Whether you're a napkin scribbler, a script writer, or somewhere in between, if you've never done any kind of planning like this, the secret to efficient pre-show prep can be boiled down to three disciplines:

✔ **Habit:** Many podcasters, especially podcasters emerging from corporate offices, prepare for podcasts in the same manner as business presentations. They jot down essential points on note cards to keep the podcast on track, but the points are the only material they write beforehand.

You can easily apply your organizational skills from the workplace to the podosphere. For example, C.C. Chapman eats, breaths, and sleeps marketing in his day job. He has been able to take this "PowerPoint mentality" of speaking for 30–60 minutes based on a few bullet items, and apply it to his show. His entire preshow prep for his podcast *Managing the Gray,* is to take listener suggested topics or questions, jot down a few bullet items, and run with it. With a collection of ideas and topics gathered between podcasts, he begins his one-take recording with a handful of points serving as a guideline.

✔ **Talent:** Some podcasters are truly the Evel Knievels of the podosphere, firing up their mics and recording in one take. These podcasters tend to have backgrounds in live entertainment, deciding in a moment's time when a change of delivery is required. This is a talent of quick thinking, and although it keeps material spontaneous and fresh, it's a talent that must be developed with time.

For example, Dan Klass is the demented mind behind the sharp and sarcastic podcast, *The Bitterest Pill.* His show is completely improvised. No prep time. Not a list of key points in sight. How can he do this? Dan's is a special breed of bravery: He's a professional stand-up comedian.

✔ **Passion:** Passion is a driving force with a majority of podcasters that keeps their podcasts spur-of-the-moment. With enough drive, inspiration, and confidence in their message, they keep their prep time to a minimum because podcasting isn't a chore but a form of recreation.

For example, *Doctor Who Podshock* by Ken Deep, Louis Trapani, James Naughton, and a cast of others, is all centered around the *Doctor Who* television series. Their preshow prep can be as much as a couple hours of research or as little as five minutes of topic overview and then they let their passion for The Doctor, the TARDIS, the Daleks, and more carry them through more than an hour of show.

Determining a Length for Your Show

If you've been using this chapter to develop your podcast, you've made serious progress by this point in getting your preshow prep done. Now you're ready to podcast, right?

Well, no. Have you thought about how long your show's episode is going to run? No? Okay then, check out the following sections.

The hidden value of the short podcast

There are many podcasts that run under ten minutes where hosts deliver their message and then sign off only moments after you thought they signed on. On average — and this is more like an understood average, not really a scientific, detailed study of all the podcasts out there — a podcast runs from 20 to 30 minutes per episode. So what about these 10-minute vignettes? Does size matter? Does time matter? (Woah. Deep.) Is there such a thing as too short a podcast?

Here are some advantages in offering a short podcast:

- **Shorter production time:** Production time is reduced from a week-long project to a single afternoon of planning, talking, editing, and mixing. With a quick and simplified production schedule, delivering a podcast on a regular basis — say, every two weeks, weekly, or twice a week — is easier.

- **Fast downloads:** You can be assured — no matter what specs you compress your audio file down to — that your podcast subscribers will always have fast and efficient downloads.

- **Easy to stay on target:** If you limit yourself to a running time of less than ten minutes, you force yourself to stick to the intent (and the immediate message) of your podcast. There's no room for in-depth chat, spontaneous banter, or tangents to explore. You hit the red button and remain on target from beginning to end, keeping your podcast strictly focused on the facts. Shakespeare said, "Brevity is the soul of wit." Considering his words, ol' Bill would probably have podcast under 15 minutes if he were alive today.

Nothing's wrong with keeping a podcast short and sweet. In fact, you might gain more subscribers who appreciate your efficiency.

A little length won't kill you

Now with that quote from the Bard about brevity, you might think, "Shakespeare said *that?!* Before or after he wrote *Hamlet?*" That's a good point because Shakespeare did have a number of his characters say, "My lord, I will be brief . . ." and then launch into a three-to-four-page monologue.

So what if Shakespeare decided to be brief in his podcast? Would he get any subscribers if his show ran longer than half an hour? What if he broke the 60-minute ceiling? Would the Podcast Police shut down his show?

Podcatchers (such as iTunes, Juice Receiver, and Songbird) and subscribers, on reading your show notes and descriptions, should be able to figure out the average running time of your show. On a particular topic, some podcasts can easily fill two or even three hours. It's hard to believe even avid podcast audiences would want to sit and wait for such a mammoth download, but huge productions have some definite advantages:

- ✓ **If the show is an interview, you have anywhere from two to three hours with an authority.** It's something like having a one-on-one session stored on your computer or MP3 player. From marketing shows like *G'day World* or science/tech shows like *Technorama,* if a guest or authority is part of the podcast, you can rest assured your podcast will go a little longer than 30 minutes — and sometimes it should.

- ✓ **You're allowed verbal breathing room.** Discussion stretching past the 30-minute mark allows you and your co-hosts or guests to break off into loosely related banter, widening your podcast's focus and sparking discussion that can lead in other directions.

   Be careful with this one. Shows and interviews that ramble aimlessly run the risk of losing audience attention. We talk more about good interview practices in Chapter 5.

The cost of podcasts longer than 30 minutes is in bandwidth and file-storage — issues that smaller podcasts rarely, if ever, have to deal with. See Chapter 10 for a discussion of the bandwidth demands on your server.

Finding that happy medium

Is there such a thing as middle ground in the almost-completely undiscovered territory that is podcasting? How can you find a happy medium if podcasters can't agree on a standard running time?

The happy medium for your podcast should be a sense of *expectancy* or *consistency.* For example, in Tee's podcast of *Billibub Baddings and The Case of the Singing Sword,* the running times for each chapter are across the board —

the shortest is just over 30 minutes, and the longest weighs in at a whopping 1 hour, 15 minutes. His audience, however, understands this is a *podiobook,* an audiobook in serialized format. Readers understand that chapters vary in size with a printed book, so it's no surprise when a podiobook follows suit. Some of the podcasts are short, sweet, and a quick bridge between one plotline and another. Other chapters reveal a new plot twist or introduce new characters, meaning that some length is in order.

Podiobooks aren't the only genre that variable length works well for. If your podcast deals in do-it-yourself home improvement, explaining the construction of a bookshelf will be a far shorter show than one about adding an extension to your deck.

Give yourself some time to develop your show, your voice, and your direction. If you build some consistency and expectation for your audience, it's easier to introduce a little variation or even a happy medium into your running time.

I Hear Music (And It Sounds Like Police Sirens!)

In creating your own podcast, something that will give your show an extra punch or just a tiny zest is the right kind of music. We're all musicians, and although our skills and tastes range from classical to rock 'n' roll, we all

Podcast *Galactica*

The SciFi channel has struck gold with an innovative approach on an old favorite from the '70s: *Battlestar Galactica.* With a new cast, a new look, and some gender-bending on the characters Boomer and Starbuck, the successful series rounds off a solid night of science fiction. *Galactica* takes delight in taking chances and challenging boundaries. In the spirit of taking chances (as well as being interested in reaching new audiences), Executive Producer Ronald D. Moore and SciFi.com decided to host a podcast: hour-long episodes, similar to director commentaries on DVDs, providing an inside look at what went into the season's most recent episode.

An hour inside Ron Moore's head? That's a sci-fi geek's dream come to life. Season one of *Battlestar Galactica* was so successful that its premiere, "33," won Science Fiction's highest honor — the Hugo — for Best Short Form Dramatic Presentation. The companion podcast of *Battlestar Galactica* was so successful that SciFi brought it back for repeat episodes and has now broadened its scope to include scriptwriting sessions and guest appearances from cast members. Moore's casual chats last an hour (well beyond the average running time for a podcast . . . not that anyone subscribing cares) and provides inside stories on how improvisational the actors can be on the set, delves into the decision process behind shooting schedules, and even grants a more personal look at the production, such as referring to über-intense actor/director Edward James Olmos as "Eddie." Keeping the production values to the basics, *Galactica's* companion podcast adds a new dimension to the military SciFi epic by taking fans behind the scenes and into the imagination of its creator.

appreciate and understand the power of music and what it can bring to a podcast.

We also understand and appreciate the law. Although you may think it's cool to "stick it to the man" and thumb your nose at Corporate America, the law is the law, and there are serious rules to follow when featuring that favorite song of yours as a theme to your podcast.

We want to make this clear as polished crystal — we are not lawyers. We're podcasters. We've looked up the law on certain matters so we know and understand what we're talking about, but we are *not* lawyers. We can tell you about the law and we can give a few simple definitions of it, but we are *not* giving out legal advice. If you need a legal call on a matter concerning your podcast — whether it concerns the First Amendment, copyright issues, or slander — please consult a lawyer.

The powers that be

The government still regards the Internet as a digital Wild West, an unknown territory that's avoided regulation for many years, granting those who use it a true, self-governed entity where ideas, cultures, and concepts can be expressed without any filtering or editing, unless it comes from the users themselves.

Does this mean we podcasters are free to do as we please? Well, no, not by a long shot. There are some rules and regulations that even podcasts must follow. There are also organizations that both broadcasters and podcasters *must* pay attention to.

The following organizations all have influence on the destiny of podcasting, and it's only going to benefit you as a podcaster to understand how their legislation, activities, and actions are going to affect you.

The Federal Communications Commission (FCC)

The Federal Communications Commission, or FCC (www.fcc.gov), is the watchdog of anything and everything that gets out to the public via mass communications. The FCC keeps an eye on technology development, monopolies in the telecommunications industry, and regulating standards for telecommunications in the United States and its territories. They are most commonly known for enforcing decency laws on television and AM/FM radio.

For podcasters, the FCC can't regulate what is said (yet) because it doesn't consider the Internet a broadcasting medium. However, given existing legislation to reduce *spam* (junk e-mail) and the growing popularity of podcasting among mainstream broadcasters (such as Clear Channel, Oprah Winfrey, and the SciFi Channel), it may not be long before the law catches up with technology.

The Recording Industry Association of America (RIAA)

Sean Fanning. Does that name ring a bell? Sadly, it was Fanning who lost his battle against the Recording Industry Association of America, also referred to by their more common acronym RIAA (www.riaa.com), when he contested that his file-sharing application, Napster, in no way infringed on copyright laws and was not promoting music piracy. The RIAA led the charge in shutting down the original Napster and continues to protect property rights of its members — as well as review new and pending laws, regulations, and policies at the state and federal level.

The RIAA will have a definite say as to why you cannot use a selected piece of music for your podcast. Simply put, it's not your music. Sure, you own that CD, but the music you listen to is under the condition that you use it for listening purposes only. (Didn't realize there were conditions involved, did you?) This means you can't use it as your own personal introduction that people will associate with you. And, no matter how appropriate your favorite song is, you cannot use it as background music. Unless you're granted licenses and you pay fees to the record labels and artists, you're in copyright violation when playing music without permission.

One way of getting music for themes, background beds, and segues is to look into what musicians and podcasters refer to as *podsafe music.* This is professionally produced music from independent artists who are offering their works for podcasting use. The demand for podsafe music has been so high that the Podsafe Music Network Web site (see Figure 4-2) was launched (www. mevio.com/music/), offering a wide array of genres, artists, and musical works. Today several other sources of podsafe music exist including Garage Band.com (www.garageband.com) and Magnatune (www.magnatune.com). Find out more about podsafe music, the conditions of using it, and how it can benefit your podcast.

Figure 4-2:
The Podsafe Music Network: professional music that is podcast friendly and waiting for your patronage.

The Electronic Frontier Foundation (EFF)

In addition to the big dogs who are passing the laws and legislations to restrain your podcasting capabilities, a group is looking out for you, the podcaster, with Science Fiction author and tech guru Cory Doctorow stepping forward as one of its more outspoken members. The Electronic Frontier Foundation, or EFF (www.eff.org), is a donor-supported organization working to protect the digital rights of the individual; to educate the media, lawmakers, and the public on how technology affects their civil liberties; and uphold said civil liberties if they're threatened.

A good example of EFF's mission is its involvement in various legal cases concerning URL domain registration and *cybersquatters* (individuals who buy desired domains and then hold on to them, waiting for the highest bidder). The EFF stands for the rights of legitimate Web site owners who happen to own a domain that a larger corporation would desire to use.

The EFF, provided you have a strong case to contradict the findings of the RIAA and the FCC, will stand up for you and give your voice a bit of power when you're standing up to a corporate legal machine.

Creative Commons (CC)

Founded in 2001, Creative Commons (CC) is a nonprofit corporation dedicated to helping the artist, the copyrighted material, and the individual who wants to use copyrighted material in a constructive manner but may not have the resources to buy rights from groups like the RIAA.

Copyright protection is a double-edged sword for many. On the positive side of a copyright, your work is protected so that no one can steal it for their own personal profit, or if someone makes the claim that you're ripping off their work, your copyright is proof that your egg came before their chicken. That's the whole point of the copyright — protection. The downside of this protection is that people now must go through channels for approval to feature your work in an educational or referential manner; and although you're given credit for the property featured, there's still a matter of approvals, fees for usage, and conditions that must be met. Also, many contributors just want to share their work with others on no other terms but to contribute and share with the world. Copyrights complicate this.

This complication of the digital copyright, protections, and desire to exchange original creations brought about Creative Commons (http://creative commons.org), shown in Figure 4-3. It's dedicated to drafting and implementing via the Internet licenses granting fair use of copyrighted material.

Figure 4-3:
Creative Commons offers free licenses for use of original content in podcasting.

In the case of the podcaster, you want to offer your audio content to everyone, not caring whether listeners copy and distribute your MP3. As long as the listeners give you credit, that's all fine and good for you. CC can provide you with licenses that aid you in letting people know your podcast is up for grabs as long as others give credit where credit is due. CC provides these same licenses for artists and musicians who would not mind at all if you used their music for your podcast.

CC licenses are made up of permission fields:

- **Attribution:** Grants permission for copying, distribution, display, and performance of the original work and derivative works inspired from it, provided credit to the artist(s) is given.

- **Noncommercial:** Grants permission for copying, distribution, display, and performance of the original work and derivative works inspired from it *for noncommercial purposes only.*

- **No Derivative Works:** Grants permission for copying, distribution, display, and performance of the original work only. No derivative works are covered in this license category.

- **Share Alike:** Grants reproduction of the original work and also allows derivative works *if* they are also released under a similar Creative Commons license.

These four fields can be used as stand-alone licenses or can be mixed and matched to fit the needs of the podcaster or the artist offering content for the podcast.

The CC and its Web site give details, examples, and an FAQ page that answers questions concerning the granting of licenses for use of protected content. Just on the off-chance you don't find your answer on the Web site, it gives contact information for its representatives. CC is a good group to know and can open opportunities for you to present new and innovative ideas and works in your podcast.

I can name that tune . . . I wrote it!

Using almost anyone else's music for your podcast can be an open invitation for the RIAA to shut it down. This is primarily to protect the artist's rights. Think about it — how would you feel if you were producing a popular podcast, receiving praise from all over the world, and while you're thinking about ways of taking the podcast to the next level, you turn on your radio and hear your podcast being broadcast on a top-rated radio station. Soon, your podcast is all the rage on the broadcasting airwaves — and you haven't made dollar one.

The same thing can be said for artists and their music. They work hard to produce their work, and now podcasters are using their music to brand their shows, not bothering to compensate the artists for their efforts. Artists love to say that they "do what we do for the love of the craft" but in the end, it's their *work,* and artists have to pay the bills too.

So how can you use a piece of music without suffering the wrath of the RIAA or FCC? Ask permission of the artist? Only if the artist owns the rights to the music and the recordings. Otherwise, you also need to get written permission from artists, musicians, record labels, producers . . .

The best way to avoid the legal hassles is to avoid copyrighted material that is not your own.

If you want to use published pieces that aren't royalty-free, ask the artist directly (if you can) for permission to use that music on a regular basis. Compensation to the artist may come in the form of a promotion at the beginning or end (or both) tags of the podcast. As long as you have written permission from the artists and the artists have the power to grant it (that is, they haven't signed the power over to their label or publisher), you should be able to use their work to brand your show or feature them on your podcast. (If you're not sure whether you have the appropriate permission, you may want to consult an attorney.) This is usually acceptable with independent artists because, in many cases, they also own the record label. Confirm this with artists. Otherwise, you run into the same legal issues if you were to use music recorded by Queen, Switchfoot, or U2.

You can always offer your podcast as a venue for the musician to sell his or her work. Dave Slusher of *Evil Genius Chronicles* (www.evilgeniuschronicles. org) has written permission from the Gentle Readers to use its music as intro, exit, and background music for his podcast; in return, Dave promotes its CD *Hi, Honey*. This promotion works well for the Gentle Readers as well as artist Michelle Mallone (www.michellemalone.com). After her music was featured on Dave's podcast, her sales spiked — both through her Web site and on iTunes!

I'll take the First: Free speech versus slander

Words can (potentially, at least) get you in just as much trouble as music. The legal definition of *slander* is *a verbal form of defamation, or spoken words that falsely and negatively reflect on one's reputation.*

So where does podcasting fit into all this? Well, the Internet is a kind of public space. Think about it — before you open your mouth and begin a slam-fest on someone you don't like in the media or go on the personal attack with someone you work alongside, remember that your little rant is reaching MP3 players around the world. Be sure — *before* you open your mouth to speak — that you aren't misquoting an article or merely assuming that your word is gospel. When expressing jaded opinions, have real evidence to back up what you say — and put up or shut up!

Chapter 5

Interview-Fu: Talk to Me, Grasshopper

- -

In This Chapter

▶ Getting prepared for interviews

▶ Recording your interviews with Skype

▶ Approaching an in-person interview

▶ Making sure your interviews are trouble-free

- -

*P*odcasting is empowering. There's something about a microphone in your hand that gives courage. Suddenly, you're not afraid of anything. Oh yeah, you're "running with the big dogs" now, and like Charlie Rose, Larry King, or Mike Wallace, you're asking the questions to find out what makes your guest tick.

What sets you apart from those big dogs, though, is skill. James Lipton of *Inside the Actor's Studio* may make interviewing look easy, but make no mistake: Interviews are not easy. It takes skill to host an interview, and hosting a great interview is an art. The good news is these luminaries possessing the gift of gab all had to start somewhere. Podcasting is an excellent venue to hone your interviewing skills, but you're going to want a solid foundation to build your skill set on.

Along with helping you schedule an interview, we help you get ready for it by looking at hardware and software tried and true for us, asking good questions to keep the conversation lively and engaging, and giving you examples of bad questions best avoided. Finally, we impart those always-valuable behind-the-scenes technical tips that make the interview go smoothly.

I'll Have My People Call Your People: Interview Requests

The courage to submit an interview request comes simply from your interest in the interview subject. Script or compose an e-mail to ask your favorite author, actor, sports celebrity, podcaster, or whomever you want for an interview. You may need to submit the request multiple times, and sometimes you may have to work through numerous people simply to get a "no" as your final reply. That happens. It doesn't mean that individual is mean, a rude person, or otherwise. They just don't do interviews. For every "no," you will find ten others who will enthusiastically say "yes."

Here are some other things you should keep in mind when working on the interview request:

- ✔ **Market yourself and your show:** A good deal of marketing is involved with podcasting. Your interview request needs to sell your services to the prospective interviewee. If you're part of a podcasting network, be sure to mention that. Large listenership numbers are always helpful. Have you done interviews before? If so, do some name dropping. If not, a good place to start might be with other podcasters. They're looking to get their names out and grow their listenerships also.

- ✔ **What can I do for you?** The person (or the person's agent) is going ask "What's in it for me (or my client)?" You need to ask yourself questions like: Does he or she have a new book coming out? Perhaps he or she is about to launch a special product? Find an angle and work with it.

- ✔ **Be flexible:** Remember, you're asking for *their* time. There may be restrictions in your schedule and theirs. Sometimes you can get an interview within 24 hours or you have to schedule it weeks or months in advance. You may have to take time off work from your regular job or re-arrange other plans.

Don't assume the person reading your interview request is going to know what a podcast is. You may have to explain your medium using alternative terms or a short explanation.

Preparing for Interviews

There's an approach that all interviewers, be they Barbara Walters or Stephen Colbert, should take in talking to guests — use a simple, basic plan to ask the questions that garner the best responses.

Asking really great questions

Chances are good that if you're new to podcasting, you've never held an interview quite like this — an interpersonal, casual chat that could get a bit thought-provoking or downright controversial, depending on your podcast's subject matter. The interview may be arranged by you, or it may be prearranged for you, but if you think what reporters do is easy, it isn't. There's a science to it, and here are just a few tips to take to heart so you can hold a good, engaging interview:

- ✔ **Know who you're talking to and what to talk about.** With interviewer Jana Oliver, former host of two shows on Leisure Talk Radio, the sheer number of guests she interviewed could cause a problem: trying to find the time to read all her guests' books. So she did a different kind of homework on her guests. "If my guest wrote a book about Charlemagne, I will go online and do my own research into the topic. This has two effects: (1) I sound like I have a clue what I'm talking about and (2) It allows me to ask better questions."

  It's also a good idea to visit guests' Web sites (provided they have 'em). You don't have to be an expert on their subject matter, but you should be familiar with it so you know in what direction to take the interview.

- ✔ **Have your questions follow a logical progression.** Say you're interviewing a filmmaker who is working on a horror movie. A good progression for your interview would be something like this:

  - What made you want to shoot a horror movie?

  - What makes a really good horror film?

  - Who inspired you in this genre?

  - In your opinion, what is the scariest film ever made?

  You'll notice these questions are all based around filmmaking, beginning with the director's choice and ending with a director's choice. The progression of this interview starts specific on the current work and then broadens to a wider perspective. Most interviews should follow a progression like this, or they can start on a very broad viewpoint and slowly become more specific to the guest's expertise.

- ✔ **Ask open-ended questions.** To understand open-ended questions, it's simpler to explain closed-ended questions. Close-ended questions are the kind that give you one word answers — for example, "How long have you been studying plate tectonics?" Don't count on your interviewee giving a dynamic answer to a question like that. Close-ended questions make the process harder than it needs to be. Instead, rephrase your question like "So what exactly got you interested in plate tectonics?"

✔ **Prepare twice the number of questions that you think you'll need.**
Some interviews you hear grind to a halt for no other reason than the
interviewer believed that the guest would talk his head off on the first
question. You're certainly in for a bumpy ride when you ask a guest,
"Tell the listener a little bit about your experience at WidgetCo" and the
guest replies, "It was a lot of hard work, but rewarding." (Yeah, this is
going to get painful.)

Write down a series of questions that could fill your podcast with brief,
one-or-two-word answers. This way, if you find yourself struggling, you
have a hidden stockpile of questions to call upon. After a few quick
answers, you can always fall back on the "Would you expand a bit on
that please?" question.

✔ **Never worry about asking a stupid question.** When asking questions
that may sound obvious or frequently asked, remember: Chances are
good that your audience has never heard them *answered* before. Okay,
maybe a writer has been asked time and again, "Where do your ideas
come from?" or a politician has heard, "So, when did you first start in
politics?" often. When you have a guest present for a podcast, there's
no such thing as a stupid question; what's really dumb is not to ask a
question that you think isn't worth the guest's time. He or she may be
champing at the bit in hopes you *will* ask it.

Avoiding really bad questions

Before you start percolating and dream up a few questions based on the
preceding tips, stop and think about the interviews you've listened to where
things suddenly headed south. Usually the interviewer ambushes the guest
or tries to dig into something that's either out of the guest's scope or none
of the interviewer's business. We've piled up the typical gaffes in a prime
example of a good interview gone bad.

Every podcaster should know how to turn a pleasant conversation sour (uh,
this *is* a satire and not a recipe, okay?); the following blunders should do it:

✔ **Ask inappropriate questions.** Keep in mind your podcast is not *60
Minutes, 20/20,* or even *Jerry Springer.* If you want to fire off hard-hitting-
tell-all-mudslinging questions, think about who your audience is, who
you're talking to, and whether the question is within the ability of the
guest to answer honestly and openly. If not, an awkward moment may be
the least of your worries.

Inappropriate can also mean irrelevant, wacky, off-the-wall, and far-too-
personal questions. For instance, author Neil Gaiman was once asked
completely out of the blue: "Mr. Gaiman, what is your best score in bowling?" Gaiman, somewhat baffled, replied awkwardly, "Well, um, I can't
really answer that question because I . . . don't . . . bowl. Never been
bowling. Don't know how. So . . . ummm . . . sorry."

Maybe silly questions work for shock jocks, but when you have an opportunity to interview people you respect in your field, do you really *want* to ask them something like, "Boxers, briefs, or none of the above?" Think about what you're going to ask before you actually do.

✔ **Continue to pursue answers to inappropriate questions.** If a question has been deemed inappropriate by a guest, don't continue to ask it. Move on to the next question and continue forward into the interview. Podcasts are by no means an arena for browbeating guests into submission till they break down in tears and cough up the ugly, sordid details of their lives. If this is the intent of your podcast, you've picked up the wrong book; you need *Psychotherapy For Dummies.*

Are there exceptions to this exception? We would say, yes, depending on the content of your podcast. Say after reading — and enjoying — *Podcasting For Dummies,* you decide to become the Tom Green of podcasting. Of course, if you're after irreverent material for your show and push that envelope as far as you can, your guests may not want to play along — especially if they don't get the joke. If that's the case, expect your guests to get up and walk away. Even in the most idyllic situations, guests can (and do) reserve the right to do that.

✔ **Turn the interview into the Me show.** Please remember that the spotlight belongs to your guest. Yes, it is your podcast, but when a guest is introduced into the mix, you're surrendering control of the show to him or her, and that isn't necessarily a bad thing. Let guests enjoy the spotlight; your audience will appreciate them for being there, which adds a new dimension to your feed. One way to avoid the "me factor" is to think of yourself as a liaison for the listener. Ask yourself, "As a listener, what questions would I ask or information would I be looking for from the guest?"

Feelin' the synergy

One final note on preparing for interviews: We've heard some guests say, "I'm doing these interviewers a favor by going on their show." And we've been told by other show hosts, "We're doing you a great favor with this chance to showcase your work on our show."

Both of these opinions are not just arrogant, they're just flat-out wrong.

The reality is that host and guest are working together to create a synergy. The interviewer has a chance to earn a wider audience and display mastery of journalistic techniques. The guest has a chance to get into the public eye, stay in the public eye, and talk about the next big thing he or she has coming in sight of said public eye. Working together, guest and host create a seamless promotional machine for one another.

If you decide to take on the art of the interview, keep these facts in mind; you and your guests will have your best chance to work together to create something special.

If your format allows it, ask your guest for an ID that you can drop in from time to time. You've probably heard these before on radio stations "Hi, this is Rex Cramer, danger seeker. You may remember me from such films as *Airplane* and *Kentucky Fried Movie,* and you're listening to The Shameless Self-promoting Podcast." If the interview guests want to be more creative, let them. These are a great self-promotion tool, a whole lot of fun, and a way to remind your listener of previous accomplishments. Remember to ask politely, and be aware that not everyone will (or can) comply.

Recording Interviews with Skype

Unless you're conducting in-person interviews, your podcast just got a bit more technically complicated. You need to have the appropriate software to record your interview over the phone.

The best option of recording your interviews is with Skype (www.skype.com). Skype is "free Internet telephony," which is akin to iChat's/AOL IM's Audio mode but is more stable and, in some instances, provides clearer reception. What makes Skype more appealing to Internet users than iChat/AOL is the expandability of the application. It's available for Windows, Mac, and Linux. Skype is the vehicle to make your calls, but it lacks the feature to record them. You can record Skype conversations with various methods and use downloadable software to monitor levels and volume as you record. You can also use Skype with a little more hardware for similar results. We discuss all your options — whether software or hardware — in the following sections.

As stated in Chapter 4, there are legal restrictions concerning the recording of telephone/Skype calls, and these restrictions vary from country to country, state to state, and region to region. Compliance with these laws is the responsibility of the podcaster. Always ask for permission (or better yet, get it in writing) before recording phone calls.

Recording using software

Recording using software or hardware — once again you're faced with choices. Software solutions are typically less complex to set up and use and cost less; however, they can put more load on the computer's CPU. If the CPU is too busy, it could impact the quality of the recording. The following sections cover some software options for recording Skype calls.

Call Recorder

Call Recorder for the Mac from eCamm Network (www.ecamm.com/mac/callrecorder) is a handy little piece of software with a simple interface that allows you to record Skype audio and video and save it to one of many formats for later editing. The only downside of Call Recorder is that the file is recorded as a robust MOV file. To reduce its size (for archiving purposes or to produce a smaller MP3 from), you need to run it through a media player like QuickTime Pro, producing a streamlined AIFF or WAV file. However, this step isn't necessary if you're using GarageBand or Soundtrack Pro. If you don't have the money for a mixer and second computer (or portable recording device), the $15 investment is a great deal.

SoundTap

For the Windows users, SoundTap, from NCH Swift Sound (www.nch.com.au/soundtap/index.html) lets you record just about any audio that plays through your Windows computer. Simply install the software and turn it on, and then all sound played on or through the PC, including Skype calls, will be recorded as WAV or MP3 files. All audio is "tapped" by a virtual driver, so the process is perfect digital quality. Current pricing for SoundTap is $19.40.

WireTap Studio Pro

As mentioned in Chapter 3, WireTap Studio from Ambrosia Software (www.ambrosiasw.com/utilities/wiretap) lets you record just about any audio that plays through your Mac and also allows you to record from a second source such as your mixer, iTunes, or another media player.

As for the steps involved in recording a Skype interview with WireTap Studio, it's a piece of cake:

1. **Launch WireTap Studio Pro and make sure the Controller window (shown in Figure 5-1) is visible. You can access it either by choosing Window➪Controller or by pressing ⌘+0.**

2. **From the top menu, select one incoming source of audio. From the menu underneath it, select your second input source.**

   The image on the right in Figure 5-1 shows you the input menus for the running applications that can serve as an audio input source.

3. **Choose File➪Preferences to access the Preferences of your WireTap Studio Pro application.**

   The Preferences window appears, as shown in Figure 5-2.

4. **Click the Source button at the top of the Preferences window. Have your interview subject (on Skype) talk as you check your own levels (on the mixer, USB microphone, and so on).**

Figure 5-1:
WireTap
Studio's
Controller
window (left)
allows you
to select two
separate
incoming
sources of
audio on
your Mac
(right) for
recording
and mixing.

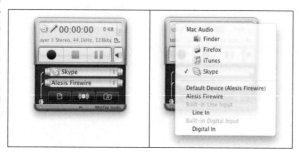

Figure 5-2:
The
Preferences
window in
WireTap
Studio Pro
gives you an
opportunity
to do a quick
sound check
before
recording.

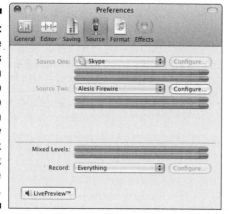

5. **Click the Format option to select an audio format.**

   You can record your audio as an AIFF, a WAV, or another uncompressed digital audio format or it can go directly to MP3 to the compression settings of your choosing.

6. **Close this window and then return to the Controller. The large, dark circle is the Record button. Single-click that to begin recording.**

7. **When the interview is concluded, end the recording by clicking the Stop button (the dark square).**

   Automatically WireTap Studio pulls up a window with the waveform of your newly recorded audio (see Figure 5-3). Here you have tools available for editing, creating loops, and creating basic audio effects. For more on the capabilities of these tools, review the online tutorials for WireTap Studio at `www.ambrosiasw.com/utilities/wiretap/videos.html`.

Figure 5-3:
After you make your recording, the final product is pulled up in a window, allowing you to review or edit what you've recorded.

8. **When your recording is ready, you can select it from WireTap's Library window and then click either the iTunes or the Local Disk button from the Send To options at the bottom of the window.**

   If the Library window isn't displayed, choose Window➪WireTap Studio Library to display it. Check out Figure 5-4.

   Your WireTap recording is then sent to your desired location either for ID3 tag editing (see Chapter 9) or for further editing.

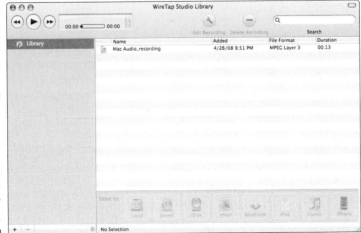

Figure 5-4:
WireTap Studio Library window allows you to manage your clips.

The Gizmo project: A recording option

Gizmo (`http://www.gizmoproject.com`) is an intuitive, multiplatform VoIP (Voice over Internet Protocol) application (much like Skype) offering additional features that Skype lacks. One of these additional features is the ability to record conversations and save them in WAV format. Gizmo also informs both parties in the call that the phone conversation is being recorded and when recording stops.

If you're looking for an easy way to record interviews, take a good look at Gizmo, the latest option offered by the Internet to make over-the-phone interviews cost effective for start-up podcasts.

WireTap Studio Pro is the more pricy of the software options at $69, but when you consider its capabilities of mixing in two separate audio sources, editing, ID3 tagging, and exporting options, it's an easy and reliable recording resource for those important Skype interviews.

SkypeOut

SkypeOut is a built-in feature that comes with Skype and gives you, the Skype user, the ability to dial a telephone number and use Skype to talk to people all over the world starting around 2 cents per minute. Rates to various destinations vary, so check the Skype Web site for details.

Follow these steps to start using SkypeOut:

1. **Go to the Skype Store Web site at www.skype.com/go/store, click the Account button, and log in using your Skype username and password.**

   You can also access this Web page by clicking the View Account button in Skype's startup window.

2. **Look for the SkypeOut link and click the Add Credit link.**

3. **Select the credit package you want (usually listed in Euros in increments of ten, but each package lists the details of what you're buying) and then purchase it by using PayPal or any major credit card.**

   Your SkypeOut account is activated.

   Your account can go inactive for two reasons. When your credit is at $0, or when it's been 180 days since your last SkypeOut call (credits have a shelf life of 180 days). So if you go three months between calls, you might find that your credit is gone and your SkypeOut feature is inactive. If your account goes inactive, simply purchase another block of credit to reactivate it.

4. **On the Skype Web site, click the Dial tab.**

   Skype opens a numeric keypad emulating a telephone, as shown in Figure 5-5.

5. **Enter a phone number and click the green Call button.**

6. **Record the phone call by using either WireTap Studio or Gizmo (both of which are described in this chapter).**

Recording using hardware

If recording using software has your head spinning, using hardware may simplify things a bit. The key to the operation is a device called a *mixer.* (You can find more details on mixers in Chapter 2.) You've probably seen mixers at music concerts or television studios — those are for the big boys and tend to be quite expensive. Fortunately for you, there are less expensive options that cost as little as $50.

The idea behind a mixer is to take multiple inputs and mix them to create an output. An input can be a microphone, a computer, a MP3 player, an electronic keyboard, or just about anything with an audio output to feed in to the mixer. For interviews, *your* input will come from the microphone, and your interviewee will be coming from a computer running Skype. The output needs to go to a recording device such as an MP3 player or a second computer. Why do you need a second device? Well, the output can't go to the machine running Skype, or your interviewee would hear his or her own voice (probably with annoying lag), and that would be bad.

Figure 5-5:
When
SkypeOut
is active,
you can
place phone
calls to
non-Skype
users.

Call button

Figure 5-6 shows an example setup that provides the ability to record Skype calls using a little more hardware.

For standard studio recording, the mixer is quite simple — microphones, computers, perhaps an MP3 player in the input port (or channels), and your main output going to a recording device. Of course, because we're talking about interviews, who wants simple?

Alright, it's not that complex. Whether you have a basic four-channel mixer or something the size of a cruise ship, most mixers have the same basic layout and features. Plugging in a microphone to a single audio channel is pretty straightforward. Adding the stereo output of a second computer is also pretty simple (given you have the right connecting cables). The real fun begins when you need to get your output back to the Skype machine and the recording device. This is where you need to take advantage of your mixer's *aux send* (sometimes called *effects send*) port. This is an output port that you will feed back to your Skype machine. So the question now becomes, how do you get your microphone input sent out the aux send?

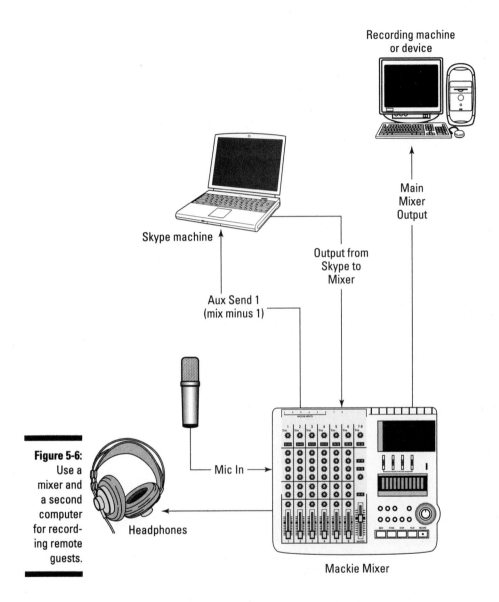

Recording machine
or device

Skype machine

Main
Mixer
Output

Output from
Skype to
Mixer

Aux Send 1
(mix minus 1)

Figure 5-6:
Use a
mixer and
a second
computer
for record-
ing remote
guests.

Mic In →

Headphones

Mackie Mixer

You see, most mixers have the ability to create multiple mixes. The *main mix* is what you typically record, but there are often hidden *mixers,* called *buses,* that let you create an alternative mix. How cool is that? You thought you were just buying one mixer, and you got yourself one (or more) for free! To make use of this additional output mix, locate the row of knobs on your mixer labeled Aux, which often are red in color. (If you have more than one row of Aux knobs on your mixer, each row corresponds to a separate aux send channel.) These are the volume controls for your aux send. If you turn up the volume on your microphone, whatever is connected to listen to the aux send output will hear it.

For example, if your Skype computer is connected to input channels 3 and 4, you want the red knobs on those channels turned all the way down so that input isn't fed back to the output on the aux send channel. This is called *mix minus 1* because you're taking the entire mix minus one input (the Skype machine). For a short video tutorial, watch the video at www.friendsintech.com/index.php/archives/23.

Prepping Your Green Room for Guests

A guest could be your dad, your mother-in-law, your best friend, or the man on the street. It could also be the friend of a friend who can get you on the phone with your favorite author, actor, or athlete. When you're interviewing, you have a second party to worry about.

Removing the "technical difficulties" element usually means either taking the show to the guests or bringing the guests to the show. This kind of interview not only is the most fun to do, but also gives you direct contact with the subject so you can observe body language, facial expressions, and reactions to questions and answers.

Welcoming in-studio guests

When you have guests visit your facilities — and because you're podcasting, this is probably your house — make them feel at home. Offer them something to drink. Offer to take them on a tour of your humble abode. Introduce them to your family. The point is to be polite. You don't have to cook dinner for them, but offering a hint of hospitality, be it a glass of water (or a beer, if you've ever worked closely with the *Draco Vista Studios* crew), is a nice touch.

If you're having in-studio interviews, it's also a good idea to get your home and yourself ready to receive guests. Sure, Tee has recorded quite a few podcasts in his pajamas, but because he's reading a book for his podcast, he's allowed. If fantasy and science fiction authors Terry Brooks and Catherine Asaro ever come over to his house for an interview, don't think he'd be greeting them in his Joe Boxer jammies and Guinness slippers.

Okay, maybe he *would* greet them wearing the Guinness slippers, but he would be bathed and dressed and have his teeth brushed and hair combed. The key word here is *guest*. Treat them as such. Be cool, be pleasant, be nice. And if you're a guest on someone else's podcast, the same rules apply. Don't prop your feet up on the furniture, don't demand hospitality, and don't be a jerk during the interview.

The in-studio visit is an audition for both guest and host. If the guest is abrasive, abusive, and just plain rude, chances are good that the guest will never be invited back, no matter how well the previous interview goes. If a host asks unapproved questions, continues to pry into personal matters that have nothing to do with the interview, or seems determined to take over the interview spotlight as if trying to impress the guest, said guest may never return, even if extended an invitation.

Meeting guests on their own turf

Be cool, be pleasant, be nice. These same rules apply when you take your podcast on the road. You may find yourself at a person's home, place of business, or some other neutral place. You're now practicing — for the lack of a better term — guerilla journalism, ambushing unsuspecting people with questions that may not strike you as hard and probing but could be to people who don't expect them. Make certain to show respect to your guests, wherever you are when the interview takes place.

A good approach for getting good interviews is to ask permission of your guests, be they passers-by or experts at their place of business, to interview them. Shoving a microphone in someone's face and blurting out a question is hardly a great way to introduce yourself and your podcast to the world. If the guest you want to interview has a handler or liaison, it's good protocol to follow the suggestions and advice of the guest's staff.

If you start out with a warm, welcoming smile and explain what you're doing and why, most people open up and are happy to talk.

When interviewing people on the street or in the moment, there are some easy ways to identify yourself. Michael Butler of *The Rock and Roll Geek Show* (http://rockandrollgeek.podshow.com) uses a *mic cube* around his microphone — these are sometimes called *mic flags*. The classic cube usually has a logo identifying a network, a show, or an organization affiliated with the interviewer. You can find mic cubes online (unprinted) starting around $25. There's also the simple greeting, "Hi, do I have your permission to record this for a podcast?"

Just as with the phone and Skype interviews, test your equipment. You're now out of the controlled environment of your home studio; you have to deal with surrounding ambient noise and how well your interview is recording in the midst of uncontrolled background variables. Set up your equipment; power up your laptop, mixing board, and mics; and record a few words. Then play back your tests and set your levels accordingly. When you have your setup running, you're ready to get your interviews.

Ensuring Trouble-Free Recordings

When it comes to recording conversations, here are a few points to keep in mind before asking the first question:

✔ **Get permission to record conversations, even if the interview is prearranged.** Laws (both federal and state) prohibit the recording of conversations without permission, and further restrictions limit broadcasting these conversations. If you plan to record *and* publish a conversation, get the subject's consent (for both) beforehand, both verbally and in written communication (even e-mail) to make sure your legal issues are covered.

✔ **Test the calling equipment.** If you have arranged a phone-in (or Skype-in) interview with someone for your podcast — say, a favorite musician or politician — prepare for the interview ahead of time. Skype (or phone) a friend to conduct a mock interview and make sure the recording setup not only works but also sounds good.

The bandwidth demand increases the more people you conference through your computer. Reception will be affected, so if you know more than one person will be involved in this interview, it's a good idea to test how many people you can effectively conference in one call.

✔ **Check your batteries.** If you're using a portable recorder (such as the Zoom H2), make sure your batteries are charged and you have spares. (Check the spares, too.) If you're really paranoid or live in an environment with periodic electrical problems, you can also pick up an uninterruptable power supply in case your main power cuts out.

✔ **Check your hard drive space.** Hard drives are getting bigger and cheaper, but that doesn't mean they're infinite. Audio files can be big — especially if you're recording to a raw format like WAV or AIFF! If you run out of space in the middle of recording a show or an interview, you lose time; lose pace; and in the case of interviews, lose face with your interviewee. If you're recording to a portable recording device, it's basically the same idea. Know how much storage you have, in megabytes or gigabytes, and how long you can record at your current bitrate. Don't worry; we talk more about bitrates in Chapter 9.

If you're doing an interview with multiple Skype participants (known as *conferencing*), it's often best to have the person with the highest-power CPU host the meeting. That person should initiate the call and invite the other attendees one at a time. The better the CPU, the better the conference will run and the better your recording will sound. Also, the conference host may or may not be the same as the person recording the call. Remember, your goal during an interview is to try and minimize the chances for problems.

And although this may sound a bit pessimistic, be ready for things to go wrong. Guests might not show up for interviews. Also, new high-tech toys, if not given a proper pre-interview shakedown, may not come through. Prepare to have plenty of topics to discuss on your own, and then your podcast can continue following a quick disclaimer. In podcasting, sticking to a regular schedule is reassuring to your listeners because they know you'll offer new feeds consistently and punctually.

Chapter 6

So What Are You Waiting For? Record, Already!

*O*kay, you've most likely gone through the hardware and software gadgets from Chapters 2 and 3. In this chapter, we make the bold assumption that you've made your purchasing selections, hooked up all the hardware according to the supplied documentation (you did read the documentation, right?), chosen your software, and gotten everything ready to record. This is it! You have a microphone pointing in the direction of your mouth, just waiting anxiously for you to begin podcasting.

So what's stopping you? Perhaps you have no clue how you sound to your recording equipment, or perhaps you're still trying to understand why your smooth and sultry voice sounds like you just finished a dozen espressos. The problem could be in your audio application's sound settings. Too much pep in the voice, and you sound like Rob Zombie crooning a goth's delight. Too little amplification, and you'd be better off if you just went out to your front porch and shouted your podcast's content.

So before the podcast itself comes *setting levels and parameters* — a fancy-schmancy way to say *fiddling with knobs and sliders* on your mixing board or your audio-editing software to ensure that the signal you're sending through the microphone is loud and clear. And once the technical side is running smoothly, give some thought to your voice — things like timing and enunciation. Because how you say your message directly impacts the listeners' interest in what you're saying.

Did Your Sound Check Clear the Bank?

If you show up early enough for a rock concert, you see those roadies setting up microphones, playfully waving to the crowd as they speak quickly into a microphone "Check one, check two, check-check-check!" It's a staple for rock 'n' rollers to do such a mic check because the fans expect a good performance — it needs to be done.

With podcasting, your own mic check should be more involved. In Chapter 4, we recommended you perform such an audio diagnostic just to assure yourself (and, if applicable, your guests) that the equipment is working and sound is, in fact, reaching your computer. The goal is not only to confirm that your mic is picking up sound, but also to check the volume of the voices — yours and that of whoever else is involved in this podcast.

Understanding dB levels

Setting levels is quite easy, provided you know where your *decibel (dB) input levels* are displayed on your software. The *decibel* unit is used to express the intensity of sound, beginning at zero for the least perceptible sound to approximately 130 for an intensely loud sound level. Your readout measures how *hot* you are (that's the power of your voice, not how good you look) on the microphone. Audio *signal strength* (measured in decibels) is the amount of power that goes into the signal, which affects how clearly it can be heard and how hard it hits the ears. "Loud and clear" is good; too much signal strength causes distortion, and that's a pain to listen to.

In vintage radio and audio equipment, this dB display was a VU (volume unit) meter — the little needle that bounced in response to your voice. Later, the needle was replaced by lights that reacted when you spoke into a microphone, going from green to yellow to orange to red. What the lights said was pretty easy to translate:

- ✔ **Green:** Well, I can hear you, but wow, are you quiet!
- ✔ **Yellow-Orange:** You're coming in loud and clear.
- ✔ **Red:** You're in danger of hitting the distortion level (clipping).
- ✔ **Red with double bars:** Your audio is going to sound distorted.

Across hardware and software, the volume meters appear different (Figure 6-1 shows the volume meter display for Audacity), but they all serve the same purpose: to make sure your content is heard clearly. Your aim, as you speak and watch the indicators speak back, is to keep your dB levels bouncing in the high level (low red) without lighting up those double bars. When you attain that average, your voice is rising and falling within a good balanced dynamic range. Try to keep things a little lower — in the red and orange range — with only the high points (when you raise your voice) going in to the red occasionally. You can always bring up the low spots with some simple post production tips (described later in this chapter).

Figure 6-1:
The input level meters for Audacity (shown in the upper-right corner) respond to your voice and allow you to monitor how loud you are when recording.

Input level meters

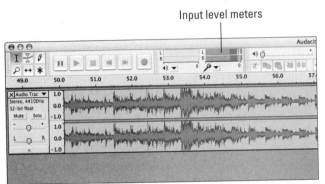

Because microphones, audio-capture cards, and mixing boards all work at different sensitivity levels, it's best to test your voice before you record. If your levels are in the green, it means you're loud enough to be heard by your equipment but still so soft that people will have to crank up the volume on their computers or portable MP3 players, consequently blowing out their eardrums on the next podcast or CD.

If your recording is too loud (or "hot"), it tends to cause problems for listeners. Listeners have their MP3 players set for a pleasant, comfortable volume . . . and suddenly your show begins with guns blazing and pipes blaring. As your levels reach deep into the red, listeners fumble for their players and try to turn down the sound so the program can be understandable through its own distortion. Sadly, the modulation is such a problem that your voice crackles and growls as it tramples the volume limits of your recording equipment, even at the lower volume.

You want try to avoid *clipping* to prevent that distorted sound. Clipping is when you're feeding too much signal to your equipment. It can come from many sources including incorrect settings on a microphone or other audio input, incorrect settings on a mixer, or the preferences in your software. Once audio is clipped, you can't get the original (or intended) quality back.

Calling in the crew

It'd be great to set your levels so "0 dB" is always where your lights remain, but recording is a real-world activity. Sometimes your meter may never reach yellow, and other times it might hit the double red bars. If your goal is to maintain perfect levels from the beginning to the end of a recording session, an audio crew can work with you in rehearsal and performance, adjusting levels when you go loud and when you go soft.

The downside of hiring a crew is an added expense to producing your podcast. Even if the crew is a collection of audio geek friends, it can still cost you sending for a *lot* of pizza every time you record.

In achieving a balance in your audio, you could spend the day setting and resetting those levels in quest of dB nirvana. That's time spent, but not *well* spent. It makes more sense to practice till you get a pretty good sense of what your best working level is and get comfortable speaking into a mic at that level. Time to go mano-a-mano with setting the levels.

Setting your levels

Your mission, should you decide to accept it, is to keep your levels in the neighborhood of 0 dB, dipping and spiking when necessary. For podcasting, consistency is key. You have your mixer turned on (if you have one), your mic is plugged in and turned on — check — and your software is running. Now follow these steps to check levels:

1. **Begin talking into the mic about your podcast topic or plans.**

   You can do a scripted test read or just talk off the top of your head, but be sure to speak in the manner and mood of your podcast.

   Instead of speaking to thin air in the vague direction of the mic (or the person next to you), speak in the exact direction of the mic, pointing your voice directly at the recording device (as shown in Figure 6-2). Even if the mic isn't omnidirectional (meaning it picks up sounds from all directions at once), it can pick up your voice better this way.

   If you speak directly into the microphone, you might hear some sounds — particularly *p*s and *b*s — causing an effect known as *popping*. An investment of less than $20 in a windscreen or pop filter can fix that. This device is a foam or nylon filter that stops the wind made by your mouth from hitting the microphones diaphragm and causing distortion.

2. **While you're talking (or if you're monitoring by playing back your test takes), keep an eye on your dB levels on the computer screen.**

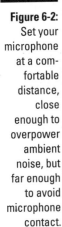

Figure 6-2:
Set your microphone at a comfortable distance, close enough to overpower ambient noise, but far enough to avoid microphone contact.

If the levels are spiking into the double-red/red area or remaining in the green, check your input volume settings on your mixing board or audio-editing software. This might require a bit of multitasking on your part, but continue to adjust the input levels while talking, as you watch the input meters.

3. **Re-record your voice at the new settings.**

   Try to speak in the same manner and inflection as you did on the first recording.

4. **As you review the second take, watch the dB input levels and adjust accordingly.**

   When in doubt, err on the side of caution on the input levels. Record your volume a little low. You can always correct it in post production. One way to increase the volume later, using Audacity, is to select your audio and use the Effects➪Amplify feature to bring it up. Another is to save your audio to WAV format and use a tool called The Levelator (http://gigavox.com) to fix the levels.

After you set your levels, make a note of the settings somewhere other than your computer (using, say, a PDA or its retro ancestor — a legal pad and pen), in case your preferences are lost or fiddled out of whack by somebody's child or best friend playing spaceship in your studio. (Yes, even adults enjoy playing spaceship with really super-cool-looking equipment!) That way, even if something awful happens to your application's preferences or your mixing board, you always have your last known settings to reference.

There's a right way and a wrong way . . .

Time for a confession.

When Tee got his MXL990, it was his first studio condenser microphone, and he was so excited about this microphone he failed to check the small slip of paper included that told him how to talk into it. Perhaps it was the excitement of venturing into new frontiers of creativity that made him hook up the equipment without reading the directions. Maybe it was a bold assumption that he knew what end to talk into with a mic as he had worked with (dynamic) microphones before. Whatever the reason, Tee was speaking into the microphone incorrectly (left image). His friends in the podosphere, on seeing Tee "in action," didn't really have the heart to tell him so — or didn't know any better themselves.

Fortunately, Evo Terra is a heartless evil mastermind. He told Tee he was doing it wrong, as any heartless evil mastermind would. On a podcast, naturally.

All microphones do not behave the same, and condenser microphones work best when speaking into them properly (right image), with the microphone pointed straight down. Tee, on hooking up his new AKG Perception-200, read the documentation included, reflected on Evo's "kind" advice, and then positioned the mic accordingly. When hooking up microphones, refer to the enclosed documentation for additional and essential information on getting the best sound out of your microphone.

You, too, can avoid the embarrassment (caught forever) that published photographs may deliver upon you . . . regardless of how good the content it generates for your podcast.

Noises Off: Capturing Ambient Noise

Part of the charm that is podcasting is just how varied the content is, as well as how spontaneous the shows tend to be when the record button is hit. Some podcasters believe that a "true" podcast (whatever *that* is!) must record everything in one take and deliver its content to listeners completely unedited. This supposed mark of authenticity includes any background noise (also called *ambient* noise) you happen to capture while recording — you know, rustling trees, birdcalls, pounding car stereos, jackhammers, the usual.

Hey, if that's the style of your show, that's great. However, if you're trying to take listeners to a place in their imagination, read on to find out how to reduce or eliminate ambient noise.

Identifying ambient noise

As we discuss in Chapter 7, how much you edit depends on what kind of content you're presenting. For example, if you're doing an off-the-cuff, off-the-wall podcast about your life and a typical day in it, you may just grab the iTalk, plug it into your iPod, and head out the door, recording every step along the way. This kind of podcast can be (note we said *can be*) easiest to record. You're podcasting a slice of Americana . . . or Britanniana, if you're in the United Kingdom . . . or Australiana if podcasting from Down Under. Especially if your goal is to capture the look and feel of your culture, ambient noise is not only welcomed, but desired. Up to a point.

Some podcasters cringe at the mere mention of ambient noise — ambient noise like . . . well, what was in Tee's very first podcast. When he podcasted *MOREVI: The Chronicles of Rafe & Askana,* he worked to create a magical setting with voice, story, music, special effects . . . a world that was completely shattered by real-world interference like school buses, kids at recess, UPS trucks, the Virginia Commuter Rail system, and air traffic from two nearby airports. (All this, and he's a dad.) Even if you love the *source* of the ambient noise, sometimes it just doesn't fit what the podcast is trying to do.

If your podcast could do without input from the outside world, scheduling recording sessions is the start of your production. The best noise reduction happens in pre-production. Try scheduling your recording at night or early morning. You'll find that traffic is lighter, the kids are in bed, workers aren't running those jackhammers, animals typically are less active — all adding up to less ambient noise, hence takes on the mic.

Minimizing ambient noise

To reduce the intrusion of the outside world and still maintain a budget, some creativity is in order.

Truth be told, there really isn't an easy solution to podcasting in a noisy world. One not-so-cost-effective answer is to rent a studio and record your podcast there. Unless you have a sponsor who bankrolls your costs, your "hobby" could easily max out credit cards and cast a hungry eye upon your nest egg. (Let's not even go there.)

A somewhat-less-expensive option is to soundproof your home-based recording room. That may sound simple, but it can involve a lot of home improvement before you have one room in which you can be sure the only sound is yours. But is it impossible or impractical? Not really. P.G. Holyfield of the podcast novel *Murder at Avedon Hill* (http://pgholyfield.com/maah) and the writing podcast *The NanoMonkeys* (www.teampodcasts.net/nanomonkeys) built his own studio for podcasting.

Holyfield's do-it-yourself adventure began with a house hunt, so a studio in a finished basement was on the list of what the house needed. The studio eventually came about from a large storeroom, a few new walls, and the addition of an air vent. The newly created 7 x 8 foot room was then soundproofed with foam tiles that cost around $500. Holyfield found the effort worthwhile. "The studio is working out great. It was amazing to hear the difference as the foam went up. Now I have a completely silent room, except when the A/C turns on (which I can turn off most times, since the basement is pretty cool)." Figure 6-3 shows the process he went through: the arrival of acoustical foam (left), measuring twice and cutting once (center), and the studio (right). The advantage of being in the basement is far less outside noise entering through the walls. The advantage of the acoustic foam is to reduce sound waves bouncing off the walls and creating unwanted effects.

Figure 6-3:
The Voices of Cairn Studios started as P.G. Holyfield's dream project.

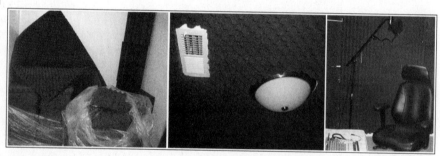

Renovation, especially if you're a fan of the DIY Network, makes this kind of home-built studio a possibility, but still may not be a practical solution for all homeowners. And this kind of aggressive home improvement is seriously frowned upon if you're renting an apartment.

You can keep this home renovation affordable and within the lease agreement terms:

✔ **Stuff towels under the door.** It decreases the amount of sound from inside your house filtering into your recording area.

✔ **Keep the microphone as far away from your computer as possible.** Its fan (if audible) simply becomes part of the natural ambiance for the podcasting room.

✔ **Turn off any ceiling fans, floor heaters, additional air conditioners, or room ionizers.** With fewer appliances running, you have less chance of additional ambient sound being created.

✔ **If you do encounter ambient noise that you don't want in your podcast, simply give it a few moments.** Wait until the noise subsides, pause, and then pick up your podcast a few lines *before* the interruption. That's for the sake of post-production: With a substantial gap in your podcast activity, you can easily narrow down where your edits are needed.

When noise interferes with your podcast, leaving gaps of silence so you know where to edit isn't exactly a foolproof method. Always set aside enough time to listen to your podcast — and *really* listen, not just play it back while you clean the office or call a friend. Make sure levels are even, no segments are repeated, and the final product is ready for uploading and posting.

Many podcasts rely on ambient noise to set a mood, but sometimes reality just doesn't cut it. If you want to put more craft into the setting for your podcast, the ideas in this section should help you keep the background down to a dull roar.

When holding podcasts on location, make sure the ambiance — be it a particularly busy crosswalk at a street corner, a frequented bar, or backstage at a concert — does not overwhelm your voice. Background noise belongs in (well, yeah) the background. Its intent is to set a tone for the aim of the podcast, not to become the podcast itself. It would also be a good idea, if possible, to do a few test recordings in the space to see how much volume you'll need and how close to the mic you have to be in order to be heard.

Now Take Your Time and Hurry Up: Pacing and Clock Management

Podcasts, whether short and sweet or epic and ambitious, all share something in common: the need for *pacing*. As a rule, you don't want to blurt out the aim or intent of your podcast in the opening five minutes and then pad the remaining ten or fifteen with fluff. Nor do you want to drone on and on (and on . . .) till suddenly you have to rush frantically into why you're podcasting on this particular day about this particular topic. Give yourself ample time to set the mood comfortably and competently and make it to the intent without dawdling. Enjoy your podcast but respect your listeners' time. Make certain you don't overstay your welcome. The trick in pacing is to understand how much time you have to get your message across.

So the big question is how to really grasp how much time you really have. Where to start?

It's a good idea to get a grasp of how much time you really have in one whole minute. To do this, find a clock, watch, or a stopwatch and for one minute (and *only* one minute) sit quietly and do nothing, say nothing, and remain perfectly still. That one minute will feel like a short eternity. Now imagine that one minute times 15. (No, no, no — do *not* repeat this exercise for 15 minutes. There's a fine line between an exercise and a complete waste of time.)

Fifteen minutes (for a start) is a good amount of time on your hands, so you should make certain that in your podcast you take your time to get to the message. The journey you take your listeners on doesn't necessarily have to occupy all of that time — be it 15, 20, or 30 minutes — but you have time to play. That's the most important thing to remember as you set your best podcasting pace.

Take the potato out of your mouth and enunciate

This section is dedicated to FarPoint Media's, Michael R. Mennenga. He's an easy guy to love; but, man, does he need to take a breath and give himself a moment before speaking. It's rough enough when your *Slice of SciFi* co-hosts are constantly riding you like a Triple Crown winner; but an intervention is in order when Bruce Campbell (Ash from the *Evil Dead* films, and Elvis from *Bubba Ho-tep*) puts you in your place — and on your show!

And sometimes, all you need to sharpen your speech and your vocabulary is to take a breath.

It isn't out of the ordinary to fire up the mic and launch into your podcast with enough energy and vitality to power a small shire in England. Nothing wrong with that — until you go back and listen to yourself. Your words, phrases, and thoughts are running together and forming one turbulent, muddy stream of thought. Yes, that is your voice, but even you're having a tough time understanding what the podcast is about and what the podcaster is saying . . . and you're the podcaster!

One way of getting a grip on pacing yourself through a podcast is *enunciation* — pronouncing your words distinctly, explaining your topic clearly — and there is no better way to do that than to slow your speech slightly and listen carefully to certain consonants (for example, the *t, s,* and *d* sounds). Proper enunciation can help you set a comfortable pace and keep you from rushing through your presentation. In fact, it isn't a bad idea to *over*-enunciate. In the excitement of recording, over-enunciation actually forces you to slow down, clean up your pronunciation, and make your voice easily understandable. That same excitement is likely to increase your pace of speaking. Again, if the rapid pace is part of your presentation, stick with it, but if you're doing anything like a narration for an audio book, slow down. If you think you're speaking just a little too slowly, you're probably going just the right speed.

Speaking a few tongue-twisters before going on mic helps your enunciation and also warms up your voice and prepares it for the podcast you're about to record. Here are some easy ones that emphasize the problem consonants lost when speaking too quickly:

- Toot the tin trumpet, Tommy, in time.
- Pop prickly pickles past the peck of parsley.
- See sand slip silently through the sunlit seals.
- The sixth sheik's sheep is sick.
- Will Wendy remember wrecking the white rocker?

If you perform a search online for tongue twisters, you can find a wide variety of classic and original warm-ups for the voice. You can also take the twisters you find and compose your own.

And now let's take a break for station identification

Ever notice that certain podcasts suddenly break in with a show ID or take some other marked break and then (if they're lucky enough to have sponsors) play their sponsors' spots? They're trying to emulate — and maybe make themselves easily syndicated by — conventional radio. You know — the broadcasting industry. *Clock management* is the careful, standardized interruption of a typical radio broadcast — usually every 15 minutes in a one-hour slot — for such necessities as station identification, show identification, public-service announcements (PSAs), and (of course) commercials.

Following this professional format has broadened podcasting's potential of becoming a commercial venue. Many shows such as NPR, *The Dragon Page: Cover to Cover*, and NBC's *The Today Show* are following clock management as they're syndicated for radio or television already. Tailoring a podcast for the broadcast airwaves, or even scheduling in quarterly breaks in the hour, can actually work in your favor. Some podcasts such as *Dancing with Elephants* (`http://dwithe.com`), and the audio novels of Scott Sigler (`http://scottsigler.net`) have found natural places in their episodes for ads. They may not be following strict clock management, but it's a step towards that model, making advertising and commercial gain in podcasting a possibility.

Another nice bonus of following clock management is you have several points in your show to give a quick "show ID" (something like "You're listening to Technorama with Chuck and Kreg . . .") that lets people know who you are. This show ID is great to catch the attention of people who may be walking into the middle of your podcast, and just as they ask the podcast listener "What are you listening to?" the show ID drops. Although "show IDs" are usually expected at the top of the hour and on the half-hour, you can drop in a show ID anytime you feel like it.

Clock management usually works in this fashion during an hour:

- :00 — programming break, station identification, show ID, PSAs, advertisements
- :15 — programming break, PSAs, advertisements
- :30 — programming break, station identification, show ID, PSAs, advertisements
- :45 — programming break, PSAs, advertisements

These breaks vary in length but can last anywhere from two minutes to five minutes. No surprise that this is where hardcore podcasters (anyone podcasting since before early 2005) get a bit restless. They find clock management and show ID redundant, if not frivolous. Why bother to break or even drop in a show ID? People have downloaded your feed specifically. They know what they're listening to, so what purpose does clock management serve?

It all comes back to what you see for your podcast's future. If you intend to remain in the *podosphere* (the community of podcasters and loyal listeners, a podcast version of the *blogosphere*), it really comes down to your format, your way. No constraints from the FCC. It's just you, the microphone, your listeners, and caution to the wind. However, if you set your sights for the broadcast airwaves — be it AM, FM, or satellite radio — you have to format your show to fit the standards. This may not sound like a challenge, but when Michael R. Mennenga and Evo Terra took the 2004 incarnation of *The Dragon Page* from a pre-recorded venue to a live call-in show on an Arizona radio station, their jump appeared no larger than a hop as the pace of the show was already tailored for clock management.

Podcasting goes pro

Broadcasting networks that present to the airwaves sensational commentators like Sean Hannity, Anderson Cooper, Bill Mahr, and Rush (no, not the kickin' rock group from Canada, but the big man of the Right Wing, Rush Limbaugh . . .) are now taking their shows to the podosphere as a way to market their shows and reach a worldwide audience.

Along with the talk-radio personalities, other major players in broadcasting turning to podcasting as an alternative include NPR, ESPN, Disney, the BBC, and ABC.

Think about the possibilities of your podcast and where you see yourself with it several months (or years) down the road. Maybe a bit of management and organization will aid your podcast in jumping to the airwaves.

Concerning Tangents and Their Val — Oh, Look, a Butterfly!

It's hardly surprising that broadcasters who have no experience in broadcasting tend to stray from their topic once the microphone goes hot, and then they lose themselves in the thickets and thorns of tangents. Defensive podcasters claim that's part of the charm of podcasting, but that charm fades as the topic gets closer to serious. If (for example) you launch a podcast intent on addressing the growing concern of television violence and wander into *American Idol* trivia, don't be surprised if your audience wanders away.

It's worth repeating: Stay focused on the intent of your podcast. Remaining true to your podcast's intent isn't just a matter of staying within your running time; it also makes clear to your listeners that, yes, you have a message and you *will* deliver it. You haven't promised something substantial only to let your mind and commentary wander aimlessly. When people listen, you want them to feel assured that what they will hear is exactly what you've offered.

Read on to find out how you can make tangents work and how to smoothly get back on topic after you've taken your side trip.

"Say, that reminds me of something . . ."

Tangents can be creative opportunities. You don't necessarily treat tangents as strictly *verboten* in podcasting. If your tangent is directly related to, or benefits/enhances, your topic, it can be effective and engaging.

Say your commentary begins with "Anyone notice how cell phones are no longer just cell phones but tiny PDAs that can be easily monitored and hacked into?" and covers that for a bit, and then you break off on a tangent about cell phone etiquette and the lack of manners it brings out of people, then this is a tangent that will *keep your listeners engaged* — and that can count as much as staying on topic.

What if your podcast isn't so structured, though? There's nothing wrong with hitting Record and forging ahead into the great unknown of the next 15 or 20 minutes, so long as you have an idea of where you want to go. Tangents are terrific in moderation, but put some reins on 'em and keep them at least (well, yeah) tangentially related to the subject matter of your podcast. If, say, your podcast is about movies but your review of *The Fantastic Four* suddenly goes into the decline of the comic book industry (regardless of the onslaught of comic-books-to-film productions), then you still have a sense of focus. However, if your review of *The Fantastic Four* wanders off into how your cat is throwing up hairballs every time you podcast or that your car's sunroof chose to stop working, blah, blah, what the heck is going on here? Your audience may grow frustrated enough to stop listening.

"But getting back to what I was saying earlier . . ."

When you're podcasting for 15 or 20 minutes (or longer . . .), it's okay to take the scenic route with your discussion, but make sure that you return to the point you wanted to make in this particular (weekly, bi-weekly, or monthly) installment. The listener's delight in podcasts is often the revelation that individuals who (in many cases) have never set foot in a recording studio can produce entertaining, and even informative, shows. Sometimes meandering back to the point is part of that delight.

For instance, a podcast might begin with something read in the headlines — say, a new marketing strategy launched by Apple for the iPhone to reach a wider client base. This can lead to a variety of topics in the discussion, such as the following:

- Multipurpose cell phones that play MP3s, video clips, text messages, and podcasts
- Costs for iPhone services from AT&T and other carriers
- Ways that carriers could bring down the costs of services
- Continued shortcomings and disappointments from the cell-phone industry

The name says it all

The ADD Cast (`http://addcast.net`) has a real charm about it in that its hosts Paul Fischer and Martha Holloway indulge in the many tangents that, on hitting the Record button, they explore with their numerous in-studio guests. What makes The ADD Cast so much fun to listen to is how they go completely off-topic and try to come back full circle at the end. Sometimes, it's the guests that bring Paul and Martha back to the starting point. Other times, it's the show hosts themselves. Many times, though, *The ADD Cast* lives up to its name and covers a lot of ground in less than an hour's time, ending with an offering from the Podsafe Music Network. Although most shows try to stay focused on the topic at hand, the cast of *The ADD Cast* creates engaging content with tangents. Have a listen and you'll soon understand what they mean by "If you can't control the stimulus, control the response."

But in the last five to ten minutes, a simple segue like "So, to recap our thoughts on this bold marketing strategy from Apple to offer the iPhone legally to other carriers. . ." can successfully steer you, or you and your co-hosts, back to the aim and intent of your podcast. If you return deliberately from a tangent, your listening audience arrives back at the point and knows the destination as well as the scenery they went through to get there.

Get your listeners there and back again. Not only will they appreciate it, but they'll tell others about your podcast, and your subscribers will grow in numbers.

We hit on the topic of using a script versus an outline in Chapter 4. When it comes to staying on track, clearly, a script has a distinct advantage over an outline. Regarding interviews (see Chapter 5), having a list of questions is important, but don't be afraid to ask impromptu questions — you can always go back to your prepared list.

Recording!

Whew — there certainly is a lot to think about before you get started. That's what makes a great podcast — someone did some planning. Now it's time to put that planning and practicing into action.

Getting started with GarageBand

When you first start GarageBand, you're presented with an array of choices. How you answer this first question has ramifications on what you can — and in some cases cannot — do in GarageBand: Should you create a new music project or a new podcast episode? Believe it or not, if your goal is to have an MP3 to distribute to the world, you want to create a new music project. Ah, the sweet ironies of podcasting. The reason is because so many of the defaults for a new podcast episode are set up to create an "enhanced" podcast, one that contains multiple images, discrete sections known as chapters, and a file format (m4a) that is playable only on an Apple-branded product like an iPod or iTunes. That isn't to say you can't create an MP3 by creating a podcast project in GarageBand, but it requires a few extra steps.

For simplicity's sake, choose to create a new music project. We also recommend changing a few settings that work better for music composition than they do for podcast recording:

- ✔ **Turn off the metronome.** The metronome is a device used to keep time in music. If you don't turn it off, you'll hear a click-click-click while you're speaking — annoying to say the least. The easiest way to turn it off is to press ⌘+U.

- ✔ **Turn off the snap-to-grid feature.** Again, this feature is beneficial to musicians but can be rather annoying to podcasters when it comes to editing. By turning this feature off, you can edit any arbitrary position rather than those based on measured spaces. To turn off snap-to-grid, press ⌘+G.

✔ **Delete the default track.** Not to sound like a broken record, but this too has a purpose for musicians. The first track doesn't really have a use for recording voice, so delete it by pressing ⌘+Del.

✔ **Turn off the keyboard display.** Unless you have a need to plink on the keyboard while recording your podcast, turn it off by pressing ⌘+K.

✔ **Show time in the LCD.** In the bottom of the GarageBand window is a display. Because you picked a music project, it shows measures. For your podcast, time is more appropriate so switch it by pressing Shift+⌘+F.

That may seem like a lot before you even hit the Record button, but it takes about a second to press all those key sequences. If you prefer, you can find most of these on the Control menu.

Now you have a clean slate to start with. There's just one more thing to check before you "throw the switch," and that's to make sure GarageBand knows where to get input from. Choose GarageBand⇨Preferences and click Audio/Midi at the top of the window that pops up. Check to make sure your Audio Input is selected correctly. The setting varies depending on your actual input (USB microphone, FireWire mixer, analog mixer to the built-in audio, and so on). After that's taken care of, close the window.

Go ahead and create a new track by choosing Track⇨New Track, click the big red Record button on the bottom, and begin speaking. When you're ready to stop, click the Play button. Note, clicking the Record button again stops recording, but GarageBand continues playing.

Congratulations, you've made your first recording in GarageBand!

Getting started with Audacity

Audacity was meant to be simple. To record a podcast in Audacity, follow these simple steps:

1. **Set your input.**

   At the top of the screen you can find a drop-down list with several choices — Line In, Microphone, CD Player, and so on. Your settings depend on your system setup. Audacity is pretty good at detecting what inputs it can use on your system. Go ahead and pick the proper one.

2. **Click the Record button.**

   Audacity creates a new track and begins recording. As you speak your words of wisdom to the world, you should see the meters moving and the waveform being created.

3. **Click the Stop button.**

   When you're done, just click Stop.

Congratulations, you've made your first recording using Audacity. Now you know why so many podcasters love it!

Chapter 7

Cleanup, Podcast Aisle 7!

Although a high-tech activity like podcasting doesn't exactly qualify as quaint, "the charm of podcasting" is (as Steve Jobs describes it) a Wayne's World approach to broadcasting. In Wayne's World (1992), two Illinois teenagers, Wayne and Garth, shoot a television show in Wayne's basement. They rock and roll their afternoons away for their local cable-access station, all on the budget that their allowance (and perhaps the odd sponsor or two) can swing.

Podcasts, much like *Wayne's World,* are often done on a shoestring budget and recorded in one take, with no editing. All the trip-ups and tangents are captured for posterity and sent to MP3 players everywhere. This is part of the homespun appeal that podcasting is not only known for, but prides itself on nurturing as new and innovative podcasters enter the podosphere.

Although podcasting purists may harbor animosity toward the editing process, sometimes it makes all the difference between a listenable podcast and an incoherent mess of senseless rambling. For example, you might want to eliminate the sound of a train going by or silence a cough that would otherwise distract your listeners from a brilliant riposte. This chapter shows you how to use editing to shape your podcast while retaining its natural atmosphere, adding depth to that atmosphere with music, and then give the final touch to your podcast's format with an introduction and exit.

A Few Reasons to Consider Editing

Take a serious look at the script and the mood you want to convey with your podcast. From there, you can judge how intense your editing workload will be. The following list explains some instances where editing is needed — and (trust us) your podcast will benefit from it:

✔ **Professional production quality:** You can't always get everything right on the first take — and sometimes not even on the second or third. Editing makes it sound like you got even hard-to-pronounce names and tricky tongue twisters right on the first try. What's more, you can drop in pre-produced clips with just the right amount of space before and after to give it that polished feel.

✔ **Removing boring material:** You've probably watched a live show or listened to live audio that doesn't go quite where it is intended. The content gets dull and uninteresting. As a listener, you can fast forward, change the channel, or just turn it off. As a podcaster, you can avoid this situation with editing. But even though it sounds easy to take out the boring bits, be careful that you maintain continuity. If edited improperly, the listeners may find themselves confused because the line of questions changed from space travel to herbs and spices in the matter of a few seconds.

✔ **Ambient noise:** As explained in Chapter 6, *ambient noise* is the natural and spontaneously occurring noise you may pick up when recording your podcast. In some productions, such as *podiobooks* (books podcast one chapter at a time, in a serialized format), moods and atmospheres must be maintained. In others — say, a radio drama like *The Radio Adventures of Doctor Floyd* (http://doctorfloyd.com) — continuity and clarity are established, requiring a certain amount of editing simply to control ambient noise. If you're conducting an in-studio interview and suddenly a passing siren or the rumble of a garbage truck makes it into your recording, the noise can disrupt the momentum of the interview and distract the audience.

✔ **Running times:** You just wrapped your latest podcast with a great interview, and you're confident that you have plenty of material for your 30-minute podcast. And then you check again and realize that you have recorded over *90* minutes' worth of interview. And you love all of it! Now here's where editing works in your favor. Your listeners expect 30 minutes, give or take a segment or two, from your podcast. You could run the whole thing, unedited, but that might test the patience of your audience members (not to mention their bandwidth and file storage). Or you could split it up into two 45-minute interviews — or even three 30-minute interviews — breaking up the airplay of the interviews with two smaller podcasts in-between the segments. In this approach to editing, everyone wins.

Editing can easily increase your productivity with podcasts. True, some podcasters define "editing" as cutting and deleting material, but there's more to it. Editing can actually help you rescue discussions and content that would otherwise be hard to shoehorn into one podcast.

✔ **Scripted material:** Some podcasters argue that the true podcast is done in one take, but as podcasting matures as a medium, audiences grow more and more demanding. Expectations for a podcast change when your podcast includes scripted material. Editing is a necessity in these situations. With dramatic readings and productions, moments of "ah" and "um" should be edited out to maintain the clarity of the story, as well as maintain the mood or atmosphere established in your reading.

With the rising popularity of audio literature in the podosphere, professionalism and performance are the keys to a good product — and usually that means (yep) editing. If you feel that editing would mar the spontaneity of your podcast — but still want to present literature or other scripted material — ask yourself how good you think *The Lord of the Rings* would had been if Ian McKellen or Viggo Mortensen did everything in one take. Imagine their dialogue sounding like this:

> *Gandalf:* Frodo . . . he, uuummm, grows closer to, you know, the end. I wonder if, um, he's, ahh . . . alive.

> *Aragorn:* Ummm . . . what *sneezes suddenly — sniffle sniffle* . . . what does your heart *ahem* tell you?

Not what we would call riveting drama. With scripted material, editing is a must.

The Art of Editing

Editing out breaks, stammers, and trip-ups may sound easy, but there's a science to it. If you cut off too much from a clip, one word comes right on top of another, and you sound unnatural. If you don't cut off enough, pauses last too long between thoughts.

When you're editing voice, the key is to review, review, review.

A lot of audio applications are out there, each with their own way to edit stumbles, bumbles, and moments of silence to honor a lost thought. The same principles apply to all of those applications:

1. Find the unwanted content.

2. Give your clip a little bit — perhaps a half a second — of silence as leader or "play area" between edits.

3. Review the edit, making sure it sounds smooth and natural; an effective edit doesn't sound like an edit.

But instead of talking about it, how about you do it? In the following sections, we go into basic editing using GarageBand (www.apple.com/ilife/garageband) and Audacity (http://audacity.sourceforge.net) as examples. These are two very common audio-editing software packages in podcasting, and both serve as our benchmarks for how to create podcasts. If you're using some other audio-editing software package, the steps are similar enough for you to apply to your own project.

Editing with GarageBand

You can use GarageBand to edit awkward gaps of silence or eliminate coughs and stammers from your podcast. We assume at this point you just finished recording or opened a GarageBand file with a recorded track already done (see Chapter 6 for instructions on recording with GarageBand). You can also import audio files (perhaps recorded on a portable device) by dragging them from the Finder into GarageBand.

To prepare for editing the silences and splutters, split your audio into smaller segments to isolate the audio that you want to remove. Then follow these steps:

1. **Determine where in the track you want to make the edit by clicking and dragging the playhead to the beginning point of your edit.**

   Use the Time Display readout to see exactly how long the gap of silence runs. The playhead tool is the triangle connected to a vertical red line. (See Figure 7-1 for details.) When creating segments, you want to place this line at the beginning and ending points of your edit.

   Silence is pretty easy to see when you're looking at a waveform of the audio. Coughs or other noise can be a little trickier to isolate. We suggest watching the waveform while you listen to the audio at the same time. You may want to use the slider in the bottom left to increase your time scale resolution and make it easier to work with smaller bits of information.

2. **Choose Edit⇨Split to make the first cut.**

   Figure 7-1 shows the first cut.

3. **Move your playhead to the location where you want the edit to end. Then choose Edit⇨Split to make your next cut.**

   As you edit, give yourself a second or two of silent "play area" at the beginning and end of your edits. It makes the editing of two segments sound like one continuous segment, and they'll be a little easier to mix together.

Playhead

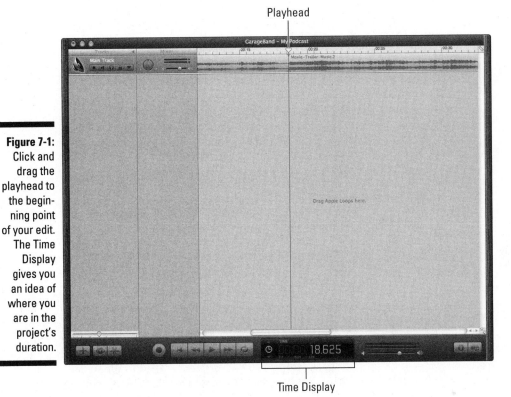

Figure 7-1:
Click and
drag the
playhead to
the begin-
ning point
of your edit.
The Time
Display
gives you
an idea of
where you
are in the
project's
duration.

Time Display

4. **Single-click the segment between your two cuts and then press the Delete key.**

   If you're working with GarageBand for the first time, note that the first track of audio is selected by default. To deselect the segment you're editing, single-click anywhere in the gray area underneath the track(s) you're working on.

5. **To join the two remaining audio segments, click and drag the right segment over the left segment, overlapping the two (as shown in Figure 7-2).**

   If the selected segment overlaps any part of the unselected segment, it takes priority over the unselected segment, effectively erasing any content there.

   You can combine the step of deleting a segment and closing the gap (delete and move) by using the GarageBand key sequence Ctrl+Backspace.

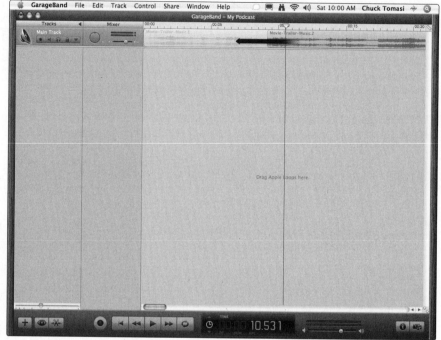

Figure 7-2:
To shorten
the silence,
move one
edit over
another.

6. **Click and drag the playhead to any point before the edit and click the Play button to review.**

7. **If the edit doesn't sound natural, undo the changes (by choosing Edit⇨Undo Change of Position Region) and try again.**

   Because you're allowed multiple undos in GarageBand, you can step back in your project to begin at the first Split command.

Hate editing? Get real . . .

Are there exceptions to the rule? Absolutely! Yes, a performance is at its best when your actors are stammer-free, but back in 1938 there was a radio drama that was chock-full of trip-ups, stutters, and "fluffs" as Paul Jenkins of *RevUp Review* (www.revupreview.co.uk) calls them. With all this going against its production, the Mercury Theatre terrified a nation with its adaptation of H.G. Wells' *War of*

the Worlds, arguably the first "reality-based" entertainment (well, a realistic *simulation* of reality, anyway) unleashed on America — the fluffs intensified the illusion of reality. If your podcast is primarily entertainment anchored in reality, you can probably avoid the arduous editing process. Again, it depends on the content you're podcasting.

As much as we would love to cover all the neat doo-dads in GarageBand — and there are a lot of them — we need to stick to the essentials you need to get started podcasting. For more in-depth information on mastering GarageBand, there are plenty of other resources available, including The Garage Door Web site at `http://thegaragedoor.com`.

Editing with Audacity

At this point, we assume you've just finished recording something awesome with Audacity (see Chapter 6 for instructions), or perhaps you've opened a saved project. If you have an audio file from another source, such as a portable recorder, you can import it using File⇨Import. Now you're ready to follow these steps to make a basic edit:

1. **Find the segment that you want to edit.**

   To view the entire timeline of your project, click the Fit Project in Window tool, shown here in the margin.

   You can easily navigate between the segments of your timelines selected and the project timeline as a whole with the Fit Project in Window and Fit Selection in Window tools, located in the top-right section of the project window.

2. **Click the Selection tool — in the upper left (Mac) and upper center (Windows) — and then click and drag across the unwanted segment.**

   The unwanted segment is highlighted, as shown in Figure 7-3.

   Right about here would be a good opportunity to use the Fit Selection in Window tool to double-check that the selection border doesn't go into the recorded content you want to keep.

3. **Single-click the segment between your two cuts and then press the Delete key (Mac) or the Backspace key (Windows).**

   You can also choose Edit⇨Cut or press ⌘+X (Mac)/Ctrl+X (Windows) to remove the unwanted segment.

   Do not use the Trim command. (HERE'S THE COMMAND NOT TO USE: Edit⇨Trim or ⌘+T for Mac/Ctrl+T for Windows.) You may think you are trimming away unwanted content, but this command works differently from the ⌘+T command in GarageBand: Just like when you crop an image, it trims off *unselected* material — leaving you with only the content you wanted to edit out. Ack!

4. **Review the clip.**

5. **If the edit doesn't sound natural to you, undo the changes by choosing Edit⇨Undo Change of Position Region or pressing ⌘+Z (Mac) or Ctrl+Z (Windows), and try again.**

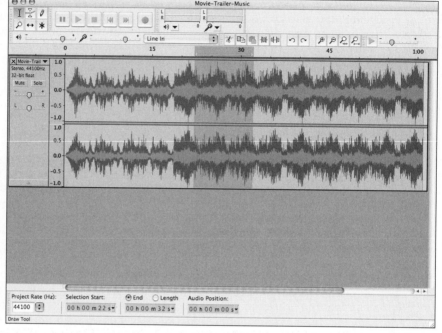

Figure 7-3:
With the
Selection
tool, click
and drag
across the
unwanted
content in
the timeline.

You're allowed multiple undos in Audacity, giving you the advantage to go back to the beginning point of your editing just in case you aren't happy with the sound of the edit.

Making Your Musical Bed and Lying in It: Background Music

On listening to podcasts of people in interview situations or in round table discussions, there can be a strange sense of isolation, especially if the conversation hits a pocket of *dead air* (when conversation or the signal stops), and only silence is recorded or broadcast.

A few podcasters like to add a little bit of atmosphere in their individual podcast with *bed music* — a background soundtrack that's usually two to three minutes long and is looped so it can play again and again throughout the podcast, if desired. Sometimes the bed music lasts only a minute or two into the podcast when the hosts return from the break, whereas other shows, like Chuck Tomasi's *Gmail Podcast*, keep it going from beginning to end, fading it out if they're bringing in any other sources of audio (voice mail, other podcast promos, ads, and so on).

Regardless of how long the loop is, you must obtain permission from the artists to use their music and give them audible credit — either at the beginning or end of your podcast. If you're using shareware music, such as from Podsafe Music Network (http://music.podshow.com), giving audible credit is one of the conditions you must agree to. Other options include using music loops found in GarageBand, Audition, or Soundtrack.

Finding the right balance

As you add music as a background bed, incorporate sound effects, and bring in pre-recorded audio from other sources (such as a Samsung H2 or a Skype call), the sound of your podcast gets more complex. Balance becomes not only harder, but even more essential. (Note, for example, the various volume levels of the multiple tracks in Figure 7-4.)

Bed music should add atmosphere to your podcast. That means finding a proper balance between the talking of the hosts and the soundtrack. The following sections explain why you want to avoid music that's too soft or too loud.

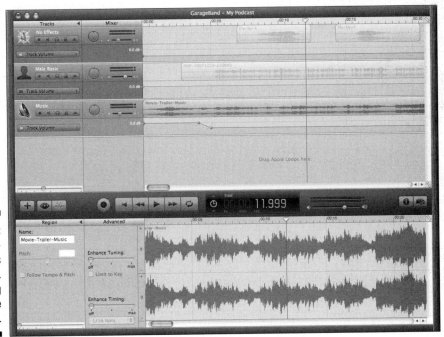

Figure 7-4: Adding multiple tracks is easy. Balancing them can be challenging.

What is that noise?

If your music is too soft, your looped music could be mistaken as unwanted ambient noise of someone listening to music in the next room. Or it could be regarded as some kind of technical difficulty such as a stray *signal bleeding* (another wireless audio signal accidentally being picked up by the same frequency as your own wireless audio device) into the podcaster's wireless microphone. Music too indistinct to hear can be a distraction, particularly in quiet moments or pauses in the conversation. Your audience might end up hammering out e-mail after e-mail (asking what's making that annoying noise) or trying to figure out what that faint music in the background is.

Could you speak up? I can't hear you for the music . . .

When bed music is too loud, your voice is lost in the melody. Music, especially classical music and selections that rise and fall in intensity (like any good Queen album) can be really tricky to mix into a conversation.

You do want to allow your audience to hear the music in the background, but the music, if you're using it as background music, probably isn't the point of the podcast. It shouldn't be so loud that you have to pump up your own voice track to be heard.

Never sacrifice audio clarity so bed music can be heard and identified clearly. If you want to showcase music, then showcase music properly. Otherwise, your bed music should remain in the background as a setting, not in the forefront of your podcast.

Applying bed music the right way

When you're setting audio levels, you want to find the best blend of music and voice, assuring one doesn't overpower the other. Both tracks should work together and not struggle for dominance.

Always listen to the podcast before uploading to the Internet — review, review, review, and find that balance.

To avoid music that's either too soft or too loud, keep the following points in mind as you apply the bed music:

- ✔ **Experiment with levels for the music *before* you record voice.** Watch your decibel level meter and set your music between –11 and 16 dB, depending on the music or sound effects you're using.

- ✔ **When you're comfortable with the bed's level, lay down a voice track and see how your project's overall levels look (as well as sound) on your decibel level meter.** Remember, your aim is to keep your voice in the "0" or red area without overmodulating. With the music bed now behind your voice, it's much easier to hit the red without effort.

✔ **Avoid "uneven" music, or music that suddenly dips low and then has moments of sudden intensity.** The best music-bed-friendly loops have an even sound (whether driving and dramatic or laid-back and relaxed) and an even level.

✔ **Experiment with putting your music at the beginning and at the ending of your podcast instead of throughout.** In these cases, music beds announce upcoming breaks and pauses in your podcast.

Setting volume levels for bed music

Each audio application has its own way to change volume dynamically — but the basic process is the same. In the sections that follow, you find out how to use GarageBand and Audacity to bring music into your podcast at full volume, and then balance it to be just audible enough in the background.

Setting volume levels manually with GarageBand

Follow these steps to set volume levels with GarageBand:

1. **Click to select the track icon (usually represented by a silhouette of a person) that *your voice* resides on.**

   All segments in this track only are selected.

2. **Click and drag the playhead to anywhere between five and ten seconds into the project.**

   If you look at the Time Display in GarageBand and see a music note in the left corner, single-click it. Doing so switches the display out of Beats and Measures mode and into Time mode.

3. **Click and drag the beginning of your vocal track (your voice) to the playhead.**

   You now have ten seconds of lead time between the beginning of the timeline and your podcast.

4. **In the Finder open a window and find the music file you want to use as your bed music. Click and drag the file into GarageBand, just underneath your podcast track, as shown in Figure 7-5.**

   When using sound effects or bed music, try to use AIFF or WAV files. An MP3 file is a *compressed* file. Compressed files (film, photo, audio, whatever) are usually far from ideal for editing because there's loss with every compression cycle — you lose a bit of quality. If you have audio bits you want to export for editing, perhaps in another program, we recommend to export them in a raw format such as AIFF or WAV so you don't lose any quality.

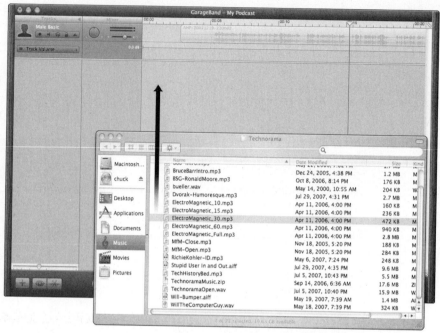

Figure 7-5:
A simple drag-and-drop from an open window to your Garage-Band window not only imports music but also adds a track to your podcast.

5. **Expand the new track of audio you just imported into the project by clicking the Expand Track (the upside-down triangle) tool located in the collection of tools grouped with the music track.**

   You should see a thin blue line against a simple grid. This is your *track volume control.* If your playhead isn't at the ten-second mark, be sure to put it there.

6. **Click at the point where the playhead line and the volume control line intersect.**

   You have now created a *control point* — a place you can click and drag to change volume levels at various times. (See Figure 7-6.)

7. **Move your playhead back two seconds to the eight-second mark. At the eight-second mark, click the volume control to create another control point.**

8. **Return to the first control point you created (in Step 6). Click, hold, and drag the control point halfway between the bottom of the track-volume partition and its current level.**

   You have just created a *volume curve.* Now the sound dips lower, allowing for a voiceover to be heard with music softly playing in the background.

9. **Move your playhead back to the ten-second mark, as shown in Figure 7-6.**

Doing so completes your *fade-down* (the automatic fading of the music to a subdued volume behind the voiceover).

10. **Select the podcast track and click and drag your podcast segments to where the content begins at the ten-second mark.**

    You now have a bed of music behind your podcast.

11. **Bring the playhead back to the beginning and review your podcast. Change the levels accordingly to set the music at a level you think works best.**

Setting volume levels automatically in GarageBand

Beginning in iLife '06, GarageBand includes a *ducking* feature to automatically lower (and raise) the volumes of your bed music. When enabled, ducking automatically senses audio from the other tracks and lowers any tracks. When there is silence or a gap in the other tracks, the ducking feature raises the volume.

Expand Track   Control points

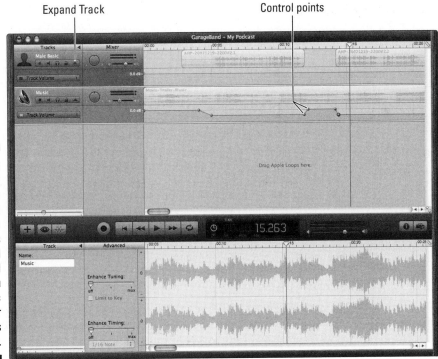

Figure 7-6:
Creating a volume curve for a fade-down requires two control points and gives you dynamic control over the track's output.

Follow these steps to have GarageBand automatically detect the volume levels in your podcast:

1. **Begin with the same four steps as the previous section, by dragging an audio file from the Finder to GarageBand.**

2. **Choose Control⇨Ducking from the menu.**

   A pair of arrows appears in the audio controls for each track.

3. **Click the top triangle for the lead tracks, where the volume should not be automatically adjusted, and click the bottom triangle to enable ducking on your bed music track. (See Figure 7-7.)**

   Now when your primary track(s) have audio on them, the bed music automatically fades down to roughly –14 dB and pops back up to 0 during gaps.

Ducking control

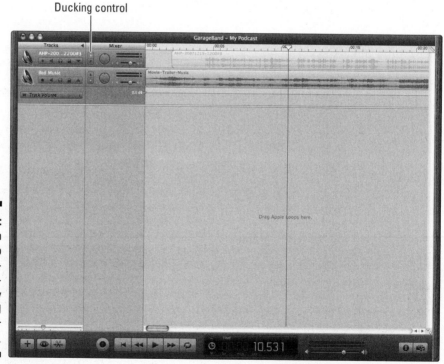

Figure 7-7:
Turn on ducking to let Garage-Band automatically raise and lower your bed music.

You may find that the ducker isn't responding rapidly enough. For example, you don't feel your bed music is coming back up quickly enough after you're done talking. If you have GarageBand '08, you can adjust the sensitivity of the ducker by following these steps:

1. **Choose Track⇨Show Track Info.**

2. **When the Track Info pane appears, click Master Track and then click the Details triangle at the bottom.**

3. **Choose a preset from its preset menu or click its Edit button (the little pencil) to fine-tune things with the sliders.**

 So the likely question in your mind right now is "Why would I want to set the volume levels manually instead of automatic ducking?" As with anything, manual control affords the ability to be in complete control of your volume levels — at the trade off of increased effort. If you plan on using bed music, our recommendation is to try the auto-ducking feature and see whether it meets your needs. If not, work with the manual audio controls.

Setting volume levels with Audacity

If you're using Audacity, you can set volume levels by following these steps:

 1. **Click the Selection tool to activate it and then click at the ten-second mark of your timeline, placing an edit line there.**

 2. **Click the Time Shift Tool button on the toolbar, shown in the margin.**

   The Time Shift tool takes an entire track of content and places it elsewhere along the project's timeline.

3. **Click and drag your audio to the edit line you created in Step 1.**

4. **Choose File⇨Import⇨Audio and browse for the music file that you want to use as bed music. Then select the file and click Open to begin the import process.**

 Although you can import MP3 files directly into Audacity when you're editing — be it film, photo, or audio — you shouldn't be working with compressed files. (It's just too easy to lose a bit too much quality along the way.) You can use them in Audacity, but do so at your own risk.

 5. **Click the Envelope Tool button on the toolbar.**

   The Envelope Tool allows you to dynamically control the audio levels over a timeline. Clicking at the beginning of the audio track establishes the first volume setting, and the second click (at the ten-second mark) establishes the new volume level.

6. **Select the track of recently imported music by clicking its name on the left side of the project window.**

7. **Click at the beginning of the music and then click at the point where your podcast begins (the ten-second mark).**

   Two sets of points appear in your track of music.

8. **Click and drag the second set of points to the 0.5 dB mark.**

   You now have a fade-down of the music that maintains its subdued volume behind the voiceover.

9. **Activate the Selection tool, click at the beginning of the timeline, and then click Play to review your podcast.**

   Now you can change the levels as needed to set the music at a level you think works best.

Making an Entrance: Intros

Now that your podcast has a solid lead-in and a cue to fade out — or you have a loop throughout your podcast that sets a tone — your podcast is beginning to solidify. It's establishing an identity for itself; be proud of the way this podcast of yours is maturing.

But when the microphone comes on, do you always know what those first words are going to be? For some listeners, you're about to make a first impression. What do you want that first impression to be? Are you looking for something spontaneous every time, or do you want to create a familiar greeting that makes listeners feel like old friends? Your chance to make a first impression with your listeners is with an *intro,* which is the first thing the listener hears, be it with a bit of theme music or a word or two about you and your show.

It's up to you, but think about how strong a first impression and a cool intro can make. Consider the ten simple words that became the signature introductions for George Lucas' *Star Wars* saga:

> *A long time ago in a galaxy far, far away . . .*

This intro leaves an unforgettable first impression. But even if you're not vying to be the next George Lucas, the first impression is always important. No matter who you are, this is a moment that can either establish you as a personality (and a podcast) that people will enjoy and anxiously await from episode to episode, or it will make winning over audiences a little harder. You want the first impression to be fascinating, lasting . . . and positive.

Consistent, iconic intros can serve as a polished touch of preparation or a subtle flair of professionalism. You're announcing to your audience that the show is on the launchpad, you're ready, and the journey is about to begin.

Theme music

How about a catchy theme? Just as television and motion picture themes establish a thumbprint for themselves in pop culture, an opening theme — be it a favorite song (used *with permission!*) or an original composition — can be just the right intro for your podcast. Perhaps you have a friend in the wide world of podcasting who can assist with audio production. Ask — you might be surprised how willing other podcasters are to assist. Earlier-mentioned software applications such as GarageBand, CakeWalk, Soundtrack, and Audition all offer royalty-free loops that can be easily edited into your own podcast intro. If you have a little cash in the coffers, check out Digital Juice (www.digitaljuice.com) for a large collection of royalty-free jingles and sound effects for around $50 per CD set.

Royalty free means you're free to use the audio clip over and over without paying a license fee. You may still need to purchase the audio clips such as Digital Juice. In the case of GarageBand, the loops and clips are included in the price of the package with additional add-on libraries, or JamPacks, available for $99 each.

Intro greeting

Some podcasters use quick, snappy intro greetings for their podcasts. For example, Adam Christianson opens every show with a heavy rock riff and the salutation "Hey, Mac Geeks, it's time for the MacCast, the show for Mac Geeks by Mac Geeks . . ." that kicks off his podcast, *The MacCast* (www.maccast. com). Others create an imaginative setting; for *Slice of SciFi* (http://sli ceofscifi.com), the crew has a more complex intro with music, sound effects, and other audio clips. Whether elaborately produced or just a simple welcome, a consistent greeting serves to bring listeners into your corner of the podosphere.

The elements you're looking for in a spoken introduction are

- ✔ The show's name.
- ✔ The name(s) of the host(s).
- ✔ Location of the podcast.

✔ A tagline that identifies your show. One of the more interesting tag lines, (and show titles), is Jimmy Jett's *Podcast About Nothing* (www.jimmyjett. com).

Sit down and brainstorm a few ideas on how to introduce your particular podcast. For example, try these approaches on for size:

✔ "Good morning, Planet Earth! You're listening to *My Corner: A Slice of Cyberspace*, and I'm your host, Tee Morris."

✔ "From Washington, D.C., welcome to *My Corner: A Slice of Cyberspace*."

✔ "With a perspective on politics, technology, and life in general, it's Tee Morris with the *My Corner* podcast."

As you see in these examples, you can mix and match the elements to drop into an intro. Come up with what feels right for you and your podcast, and stick with it. After you've put together your greeting, you can either keep it pre-recorded and use it as a *drop-in* (an isolated audio clip that you can use repeatedly, either from podcast to podcast, or within a podcast) at the intro-duction of your podcast, or you can script it and record it with each session. Whatever method you choose, a greeting is another way of bringing your audience into your 20 to 30 minutes (or five minutes to an hour and a half) of time on someone's MP3 player.

Exit, Stage Left: Outros

Now that you have reached the end of your message or the time limit you have set yourself for a podcast, what do you do? Do you just say "Thanks, everyone, see you next time . . ." or just a basic "Bye," and then it's over? Or do you want to go out with a bit of fanfare? Whatever you decide, an *outro* is much like an intro — as simple or elaborate as you want to make it. Your outro is your final word, closing statement, and grand finale (at least for this podcast).

In practical terms, putting together an outro is no different from putting together an intro — same approach, only you're doing it at the end. So review the earlier suggestions for intros and consider what seems a likely direction for an outro.

Some podcasters figure there's little more to think about for an outro than what to say and how to present it. Sure, you could keep it simple — say "Bye" and switch off, no fuss, no script, just do it, done, and then upload. But other podcasters see the outro as more of an art form. Before taking a shortcut to the end, check out the following sections for some ways to spiff up your outro.

Leave the audience wanting more

Continuing your podcast to its final moments is a gutsy, confident, and exciting outro, carrying your audience all the way to the final second. This is one of the toughest ways to end a podcast, but if it's done right, it can only make your podcast better.

For example, Jimmy Jett's *Podcast About Nothing* takes a cue dating back to "Smokey and the Bandit" movies with outtakes at the end of each show. While Jimmy's entire show has a clean, professional polish to it, he keeps you listening to the end to find out what really happened when he tried to produce those segments. Just when you think the show is over with his sign off *"Bye-bye, my friend,"* an announcer hits you saying *". . . and now, the outtakes,"* with all the bloopers Jimmy made along the way. The content continues right up to the end.

Catch phrase sign off

Your outro can be the final word from the host, and it should be your bow during the curtain call. A signature farewell is a classy way of saying "This podcast is a wrap. Thanks for listening."

For example, throughout the years that journalist Walter Cronkite reported the news to America, he always ended with the words, "And that's the way it is . . ." followed by the date. On *Technorama,* Chuck and Kreg have taken a similar approach with their signature sign off starting with Chuck saying "And until next time, a binary high five." To which Kreg always responds "1–0–1." It has become such a well known piece of the show that listeners writing or calling to leave feedback close their pieces with the same tag.

If you can't think of anything overly clever, a consistent exit such as "This has been my podcast. Thanks for listening . . ." works too.

Credits roll

Another possibility for your outro could be a scripted list of credits: Web sites where past shows can be downloaded, resources can be endorsed, and special thanks can be given to various supporters of your podcast.

When listing credits, take care that your list of thank-yous and acknowledgments doesn't ramble on for too long after every podcast. Some podcasters reserve a full list of end credits for special podcasts, such as an "end-of-the-season" or even "final" episode. By and large, a minute can serve as a good length for ending credits — plenty of time to mention relevant Web sites, tuck in the obligatory "Tune in next week . . ." statement, and ask for a vote of support on your favorite podcast directory.

Coming soon to an MP3 player near you

Just as television shows drops teasers of what will be coming up next week, podcasters can also give quick hints as to what is planned for future podcasts. Mark Jeffrey's *The Pocket and The Pendant* (http://pocketandpendant. com) and Scott Sigler's *EarthCore* (http://scottsigler.net) episodes had already been pre-recorded for the intent of podcasting. This gave both authors a terrific advantage to edit together montages of audio clips and even record a quick synopsis of what was to come in the next episode.

Previews for future podcasts tend to be difficult to plan — mainly because of the spontaneous nature of podcasting that the medium prides itself on. Many podcasters have no idea what will be on the agenda for their next show until the day or even a few hours before recording, and then there are other podcasts that start up the audio equipment and speak with no prep time for their latest installment. However, for those podcasts that can provide glimpses of things to come, this kind of outro serves as a commitment to the audience that there will be more content coming through the RSS feed and that programming is being planned for future installments.

As mentioned with intros, your outro can use one of these approaches or combine them. Find what best fits your podcast and stick with it. The more consistency your podcast can follow, the more professional it sounds — spontaneous but focused, right?

Chapter 8

Roll Camera: Video Podcasting

· ·

In This Chapter

▶ Making the jump from audio to video

▶ Finding out what you need to make a video podcast

▶ Creating a video podcast episode with iMovie

▶ Preparing your Windows Movie Maker video for podcasting

· ·

*I*n its first year, podcasting established itself as an exciting audio option. It was truly "The People's Radio" for your computer, promising a fresh alternative to cookie-cutter corporate radio. A few potential podcasters took a closer look at the way RSS 2.0 worked and thought, "Wait a second — if we can do this with audio, what about video?" So a few brave podcasters decided to put moving pictures to their podcasts; and while people still search for "just the right term" (vidcast, vodcast, vodblog, and so on) video podcasting came to be and continues to grow.

Once upon a time, professional-quality video production (such as editing, post-production effects, and DVD authoring) on a consumer market was either a pipe dream or a hobbyist's major investment. With the advancements in professional-grade cameras, advancements in home computing systems, and the ease of video-editing software, producing broadcast-quality video is not only affordable, it's expected. Add to this the popularity of services like YouTube (`http://youtube.com`) and LuluTV (`http://lulu.tv`), and creative minds both in the amateur and professional circles are now looking at video podcasting as an alternative to distribution.

We barely scratch the surface of video podcasting in this chapter. To go above and beyond, pick up your copy of *Expert Podcasting Practices For Dummies,* which goes into great detail on post-production with audio, post-production with video, and working with the professional applications like Final Cut and Premiere.

When to Go Video

While Evo and Chuck have only dipped their toes in working with video, Tee sports the longest track record with editing video, both in a *linear* (the traditional two video decks tied together to one central deck with a control board offering basic post production effects) and a *nonlinear* (all on a computer, in a digital format) method. Even in those early *Flintstones*-esque days of digital video, Tee thought this whole process very cool. Today, with terabyte drives, gigahertz processors, and 8-core computers, a lot of things have changed, and Tee's opinion has changed as well. He now finds editing video on his Mac very, *very* cool.

Video production is also *not* easy. Some of the downfalls to video podcasting are

- **A learning curve:** Despite what the commercials for Macs, Dells, and HP computers insinuate, editing video is not a push-button technology. A lot goes into video, even on the most basic of levels; with video podcasts like *Rocketboom* (www.rocketboom.com), *Calls for Cthulhu* (www.calls forcthulhu.com), and *The Onion News* (www.theonion.com), the bar to run with the big boys and girls of video podcasting is pretty high.

- **More production time:** With video, you have to contend with more than just ambient noise. Now you need to consider lighting, camera angles, wardrobe, make-up, and so on. Podcasting audio can prove daunting in its production needs, but video is a step up and demands a great deal of time and attention.

So with all these daunting challenges, why go video with your podcast? Here are some good reasons to step up to video podcasting:

- **Your message needs more than sound to get across to your audience.** If you're putting together a show for educational or training purposes, you may want to feature diagrams or procedures that require visual aids. With video, you now can appeal to listeners on a visual as well as an aural level.

- **You want a captive audience.** The ability or temptation to multitask is removed as your subscribers are now applying the visual senses, taking advantage of the video features in iTunes, iPhones, and iPods. They can't drive a vehicle, cook a meal, or walk Fluffykins at the same time that they watch your video podcast, so you gain greater audience focus.

- **You want to create your *definitive* vision.** In travel podcasts (also known as *sound-seeing tours*), where the sounds of a marketplace provide the host with a background, or beer tastings (also called *pubcasts, barcasts,* or *beercasts*) where the flavor of a local bar filters into the show, or podcast novels (also called *podiobooks*) where a few sound effects set the scene, the listener's imagination fills in the blanks on what is happening around the podcaster. Now, the subscriber can see and (virtually) experience walking through the marketplace in Athens, take in the sights and sounds of a Western Yorkshire pub, or see the characters as the author intended them to be seen, in the settings he or she imagined.

Enhanced podcasting: The happy medium

If you're an audio podcaster who's curious about going video but you aren't quite ready to make the jump, take a look at the rarely employed but extremely versatile format of *enhanced podcasting*. Enhanced podcasting gives producers the ability to drop *into* their podcasts chapter markers, images, and even URLs. On iTunes, the Album Artwork window provides visual aids for what the show hosts are talking about. Although not as visually demanding as video (you can still listen to the audio without following the images), enhanced podcasts are a terrific way to grab the attention of your audience: Keynote and PowerPoint presentations can now be podcast as they are presented, podcasters can now give you direct access to resources cited, and chapter markers can now help listeners navigate to their topic of choice. With enhanced podcasting, the experience becomes more interactive.

So what's the catch? Enhanced podcasts use the AAC format. These M4A files play back only in iTunes and QuickTime and can go portable only on iPods. This can limit your audience, so many enhanced podcasters produce two feeds, essentially doubling their workloads. Also, at the time of writing this edition, the best applications for creating enhanced podcasts are GarageBand and Soundtrack Pro 2 (both from Apple) and also Lemonz Dream's Podcast Factory. These applications run only on Mac OS.

Still, with a bit of thought, planning, and panache, an enhanced podcast can bring a lot to your audience. *Podcasting For Dummies: Season Two,* the companion podcast for this book, is an enhanced podcast. The enhanced version of *MacCast* (www.maccast.com) gives links and images of various product reviews and new items, providing an interaction with tech hungry audiences. *Stephen Fry's Podgrams* (www.stephenfry.com/podcasts) gives you maps, images, and even a potential look at "branding" in a podcast about the British actor Stephen Fry's travels across England and various points of the world. To find out more about enhanced podcasting and what it offers, check out *Expert Podcasting Practices For Dummies.*

Earl Newton is the creator and executive producer of the award-nominated podcast, *Stranger Things* (`http://strangerthings.tv`), the world's first speculative fiction podcast offered to its viewers in *high-definition* video. When you see what he produces, it's obvious that Earl is truly a professional, and he brings that skill and expertise to the enhanced feed of *Podcasting For Dummies: Season Two*. If you're looking for additional tips, tricks, and techniques in creating a top-notch video podcast, subscribe (for free) to the Enhanced Podcast Feed on *Podcasting For Dummies: The Companion Podcast*, available from iTunes and Dummies.com.

The Price of Pretty Pictures

You can create video podcasts with any video-editing application running on either Mac or Windows. You can use Apple iMovie, Windows Movie Maker, Apple Final Cut Pro, or Adobe Premiere Pro to create your episode. When it's time to export your movie out of your video-editing software, many of these applications use a format optimized for podcasting. If you're using older video editors, you can invest into QuickTime Pro (a $30 upgrade available from `www.quicktime.com`), which can export a video file to a format specific for the iPod (which also includes iTunes).

Of course, you could do the compression by hand, but the question here is *"Why?"* Take advantage of the shortcuts because in this section, we take a closer look at other considerations concerning video podcasting.

Sorry, we don't do windows (Media Player)

So if video is so cool, so easy, and (while demanding) so powerful, why isn't everyone doing video podcasts? For one thing, the most common video podcast format (`.m4v`) plays only on iTunes or QuickTime for the desktop computer and in iPod portable players (iPod, iPod Touch, iPhone, and so on). You could release your podcast in a variety of multiple formats such as MPEG, MOV, and AVI. MOV and AVI files, though, are huge in comparison to the M4V counterpart. As far as MPEG compression, the format come in various versions (MPEG1, MPEG2, and so on). You can export to multiple formats, but now comes the added responsibility of managing numerous feeds, tracking which feed people are subscribing to, and exporting for playback in specific devices. M4V (which uses the H.264 codec in podcasting) performs best in QuickTime and iTunes and is the simplest format to export in (as illustrated later in this chapter). M4V doesn't perform at all in Windows Media Player.

That file is how big?!

Provided you follow our Cheat Sheet's compression specs, the standard audio podcast of roughly 80MB will cover anywhere from 90 minutes to two hours — *of audio.* When compared with other podcasts that are far more economical in their running times, 80MB is huge.

To video, this is chump change.

80MB might earn you *15 minutes* of video time, and that depends on whether you go with the M4V format or a flavor of MPEG. When video podcasting first came to the hearts and minds of audio podcasters, it was a bit of a shock when they tried to make their 20-to-30 minute audio into a video equivalent. "How do I get my file size smaller?" podcasters asked on various discussion boards. Although the reply might have come across as snarky, it was the only available answer: "Make a shorter podcast." If you have a two-hour podcast and are planning to compress your video down to the same size (or thereabouts) as that 80MB MP3, well . . . that just won't happen.

For standard 720 ¥ 480 digital-video resolution that you will probably import into iMovie or Windows Movie Maker, the iPod compression setting takes one minute of video and squeezes it down to 5MB. Take your epsiode's running time and multiply it by five to get an approximate size before compression.

Burn, bandwidth, burn!

Bandwidth is the factor most new podcasters tend to gloss over. That can prove to be costly, especially if your podcast is 50MB or higher per download. If you garner 1,000 listeners, for example, you've gone through 5GB simply for that file transfer. If these 1,000 listeners are going through your archives, your bandwidth needs to increase exponentially.

Now, suppose you decide to produce a video podcast with some length — and even dare to explore the possibilities of high-definition video podcasting. What happens? Your first episode is 100MB — a very hefty download.

It's even heftier if your podcast is a runaway success. If you have 2,000 subscribers in your first week, you have burned through 200GB of your monthly bandwidth. What about the weeks — and the listeners — to come? What does your webhost offer, and can it handle this kind of traffic for your podcast? When you're looking at video podcasting, consider the running time and file size of your episodes, and then look at your Web host's bandwidth.

Lock and Load (Your Camera): Planning Your Shooting Schedule

Nonlinear (that is, digital) video applications like iMovie and Movie Maker have dramatically simplified the process of editing video. However, the commercials aren't quite accurate when describing the ability to make a movie as quick and easy. It's still far from a push-button technology. We've been talking about the various demands for your video podcast, but perhaps the greatest demand of them all is *time*.

Here's how the process works:

1. Set up the camera, rehearse your podcast (if applicable), and then make time to shoot *from that angle*.

2. Reset for the same shot but from a different angle. Shoot your footage from the new angle.

3. Review your video footage and *capture* (get the video off the miniDV cassette or your DVD and into the video editor) it onto your computer.

4. Edit your footage together, remove your mistakes, continuity errors, and small trips and tumbles, and make the whole project appear seamless and fluid.

5. After all the editing, post-production, and reviewing is done, you must *render* the video, outputting this production in the desired format — be it podcasting, full-screen video, or DVD.

Depending on the power of your computer's processors, the length of your video, and what format you're outputting it to, this could take anywhere from a few minutes to a few hours to a full eight-to-nine-hour work day.

The allure of video is intense — and don't mistake us for a moment, we love it! — but make sure you give yourself *time:* time to shoot, time to edit, time to review, and time to render.

Make that first episode and then give a second episode a shot. Go for three, if you can. Once you have those episodes edited and ready to go, you can decide on what kind of posting schedule you want your podcast to follow.

iTarantino: Creating with iMovie

If you've just purchased a new Macintosh computer or picked up the most recent incarnation of iLife, you have *iMovie* (www.apple.com/ilife/imovie) within reach. This unassuming application grants you the ability to edit video by dragging and dropping clips where you want them on your project's timeline.

Capturing video with iMovie

You need to get the video off the camera or media it is currently recorded on (DVD, cassette, and so on) and into your computer. This process is called *capturing*. The video is played back and then captured into the video-editing application in a format that the program can understand.

We're going to make the bold assumption that you have a miniDV camera or some other DV playback device that has your video footage ready for capturing. Here's how you get your video off the camera and into your computer for editing:

1. **Launch iMovie.**

2. **From the intro window, select Create a New Project from the offered menu options.**

3. **From the introduction window, change the default title to whatever you want to name your project.**

   By default, your selected video format will be DV, which is a basic video format common with many consumer miniDV cameras. Stick with the default.

4. **Connect your video camera to your computer and set it to playback mode.**

   iMovie detects the camera automatically. If it doesn't, you won't have any options available for capturing footage. If iMovie doesn't detect your camera, check your camera to make certain it's in playback mode, has power, and is plugged into your computer.

5. **Click the Import button, and iMovie automatically captures what's on your miniDV tape or miniDV tape deck.**

   Your clip is imported into the Clips Pane, the area on the right in iMovie, as shown in Figure 8-1.

   If you have an older version of iMovie, your clips are imported by segments. If you have iMovie HD, choose iMovie HD⇨Preferences and select whether to import clips either by scene breaks (where the camera turns on and off) or by segments with running time designated by you.

   The version of iMovie Tee is using on his Mac is iMovie HD. There is a more recent version available now — iMovie '08, part of iLife '08. Some of the interface may have changed between versions, but the steps should be easily applied to either version.

Clips Pane

Figure 8-1:
Your video
is brought
into the
Clips Pane
in the order
of capture.

6. **After capturing the clips on your camera, in the Clips Pane, double-click the name of the first clip labeled Clip 01.**

   The Clip Info dialog box opens, as shown in Figure 8-2.

7. **Name the clip something easier to identify it by.**

   For example, Wide Angle A or Close-Up: Guest Name.

   Custom-naming clips allows you to organize your clips, which helps you put your podcast together.

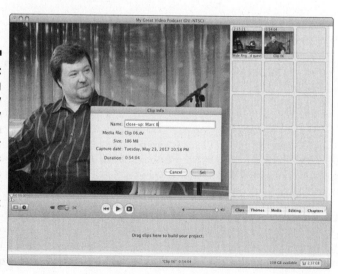

Figure 8-2:
Labeling
clips by
what they
are, camera
angles, or
keywords
makes
for more
efficient
workflow in
video
editing.

8. **Repeat Steps 6 and 7 for all the remaining clips in the iMovie Clips Pane.**

9. **When your tape is concluded, move the switch currently on Edit (Scissors) back to Capture (Camera) mode. Then repeat Steps 4 through 8 for any remaining miniDV tapes you need to capture.**

If your video is on your computer as a data file (MOV, M4V, MPEG, and so on), choose File⇨Import (or press Shift+⌘+I) to import your clips into the Clips Pane.

A walk in the park on a clear Spring day, don't you think? This process is known as *logging,* where you go through your video (be it one cassette or many) and organize your clips as needed.

Creating your episode with iMovie

When you have your video imported and organized in iMovie, you're ready to edit it into a video podcast. Follow these steps:

1. **Switch iMovie from Capture to Edit mode by moving the switch to the right (to the scissors icon).**

   Or simply select a clip in the Clips Pane. iMovie automatically switches from Camera to Edit mode.

2. **Click and drag your opening clip from the Clips Pane into the Timeline along the bottom of the iMovie interface.**

   The *Timeline* in your iMovie interface is where you assemble and edit your clips. Simply drag and drop clips in the order you want them to appear. By default, you're viewing video in the Timeline as clips (View Clip mode).

3. **Repeat Step 2 for the remaining clips in your Clips Pane until you have your clips in the order you want. See Figure 8-3.**

   What you have now is commonly referred to as a *rough cut.* This is your video podcast without transitions, set volume level, or any detailed editing. It gives you an idea of what the video will look like when it's done.

The amount of editing your video podcast needs depends on the amount of footage you shoot and how detailed you want your production to be. When you have a rough cut, here are some editing tricks to try:

✔ **View your video by running time.** Click the icon of the clock in the iMovie interface. This switches your Timeline mode from viewing video as individual clips to viewing video by running time. When you edit video in this mode (View Duration mode), you can adjust the timing and duration of individual clips accordingly.

✔ **Navigate throughout your video.** A scroll bar across the bottom of the Timeline will allow you to move from the beginning to the end of clips, going back and forth as needed.

✔ **Zoom in and out.** Underneath the scroll bar is a Zoom slider that allows you to view the project from beginning to end, or zoom in on specific edit points.

✔ **Scrub through video.** With your playhead, you can *scrub* through the video. *Scrubbing* is the process of viewing audio at a user-designated speed. You scan through segments, find what you're looking for, and make edits. With the left and right arrows, you can also advance through a clip frame by frame.

✔ **Make a cut.** Move your playhead in the Timeline to where you want to make an edit. Choose Edit⇨Split Video Clip at Playhead (or press ⌘+T).

✔ **Delete a segment.** Click the segment you want to remove and press Delete to remove the unwanted video.

✔ **Create a cutaway.** Sometimes, you want video that breaks the monotony of a single shot, more commonly known as a *cutaway*.

✔ **Assemble you episode.** Using either View Clip or View Duration mode, assemble your episode.

✔ **Drop in a transition.** Click the Editing tab and then the Transitions tab. A *transition* is a cool way to get from one clip to the next (a crossfade, wipe, or some interesting bridge), unlike a *cutaway* or *jump cut* where one video source switches to another. Click and drag the desired transition between two clips to apply it.

To see a preview of a transition, simply click it.

Figure 8-3:
After you move your clips from the Clips Pane to the Timeline, you have completed your rough cut.

Timeline

TIP

✔ **Place a title at the beginning of your podcast.** Click the opening clip, click the Editing tab, and then click the Titles tab in the iMovie interface. With the iMovie Title Interface, design your opening title and then click the Add button (see Figure 8-4). The *Titles Pane* is the feature of iMovie where you can place animated or static text at the beginning, middle, or end of your movie, giving your podcast a polished Hollywood touch.

Click an offered title template, and iMovie renders a preview of that title.

You can either have the title appear over one of your video clips or over black video by selecting or deselecting the Over Black feature.

iMovie renders the title and then incorporates it into the project. If your title needs to change, return to the clip marked with the Title icon (a small T icon next to its duration), edit the title, and click the Update button.

Figure 8-4:
With the iMovie Titles Pane, you can come up with sharp titles for your video podcast.

When you have your video how you want it, follow these steps to finish your podcast:

1. **Choose File⇨Save Project or press ⌘+S to save your video.**

2. **To export your video, choose Share⇨iPod.**

   A dialog box opens, giving you the *codec settings* (the particular video compression format you've selected) that your movie will be saved as. The dialog box also lets you know what you can do with the video and what device(s) it can be best played back on. You select iPod as it is using the codec optimized for podcasting purposes.

3. After reviewing the dialog box, click the Share button.

Your video opens in iTunes.

4. Select your video and then choose File⇨Get Info or press ⌘+I. Click the Info tab to add in your ID3 Tags (see Figure 8-5). When your tags are completed, click OK.

For more on ID3 Tags and why these are important to your podcast, take a look at Chapter 9.

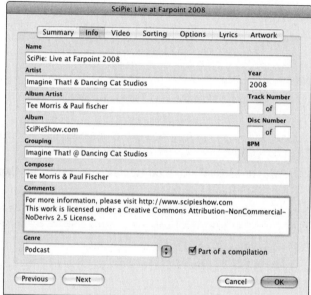

Figure 8-5: ID3 tags are just as easy (and as important) with video podcasts as with audio podcasts.

Congratulations, you have just edited and output your first video podcast.

It's just that easy! With upgrades to Leopard and various incarnations of iMovie, your interface and your results may vary. You may also find iMovie has a lot of features we haven't even touched. That's because we're keeping it quick and easy, fast and furious, and above all, to the basics. If you want to find out more about editing with iMovie, there are many books on the market that will take you deeper into the power of this application. You may also pick up a few cool tips from *Videoblogging For Dummies, Digital Video For Dummies,* 4th Edition, or Earl Newton's video episodes on the *Podcasting For Dummies: Season Two* enhanced feed.

DV on the PC: Podcasting with Windows Movie Maker

Attempting to keep up with iMovie is its Microsoft equivalent, Windows Movie Maker (www.microsoft.com/windowsxp/using/moviemaker). This application comes with your Windows OS and offers nonlinear editing goodness similar to what iMovie offers its Mac users.

Capturing video with Movie Maker

Getting your footage from your camera or hard drive to Windows Movie Maker differs slightly from what you have to do with iMovie. You need to go through a setup process so Movie Maker knows what kind of video you want to make:

1. **Make sure your video camera or DV playback device is connected to your PC. Then launch Windows Movie Maker.**

2. **Under the Movie Task window on the left side, click the Capture from Video Device option.**

3. **Give a name for your *Collection* — your video — and a destination folder for your captured footage. Then click the Next button.**

   The Video Settings page of the wizard appears.

4. **Select one of the three offered codecs from Windows Movie Maker, as shown in Figure 8-6.**

   Windows Movie Maker gives you an approximation of how much data is needed to capture and save your video in the desired format.

5. **Click the Next button.**

   Under Other Settings, a variety of optional formats are offered. We recommend sticking with one of the first two offered:

   - *Best Quality for Playback on My Computer:* Your video is captured at 320 x 240 pixels, which is less than half of full-screen video (720 x 480). This will limit the output options for your project.

   - *DV-AVI for Full Screen:* Choose this option if you want to be able to output to DVD or show off your video podcasts to people who aren't quite up to speed with podcasting.

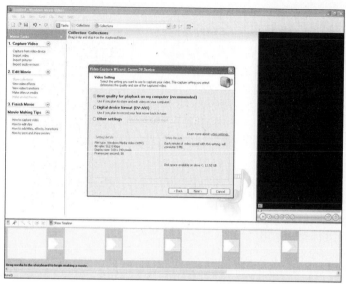

Figure 8-6:
Before capturing video, Windows Movie Maker needs to know what kind of project it'll be creating.

Because you're video podcasting, it would seem common sense to select the recommended Best Quality for Playback on My Computer option, but before jumping to that option, consider the DV-AVI option.

6. **Decide on how you want to capture your clips and make sure you have the Preview Clips while Capturing option selected.**

7. **In the final window for capturing video, click the Play button underneath the Preview window to play the video in your camera or DV device.**

8. **Use the Fast Forward and Rewind buttons to visually search (also called *jog*) through the footage to find what you want. Click Start Capture to begin capturing a clip. (See Figure 8-7.)**

9. **Click Stop Capture when the clip is captured.**

10. **Repeat Steps 7 through 9 for all clips on this DV cassette (also referred to as a *reel*) and then eject the reel. Insert any additional reels and capture your footage.**

    This is known as *logging* in the video-editing industry. You go through your footage (be it one reel or numerous ones) and capture what is needed for your podcast.

11. **When your footage is logged and captured, click the Finish button.**

12. **Go through your clips and custom name them something easier to identify (such as Wide Angle A or Close-Up: Guest Name) by double-clicking the clip's default names.**

    Custom-naming makes it easier to organize your clips when you're ready to edit your podcast together.

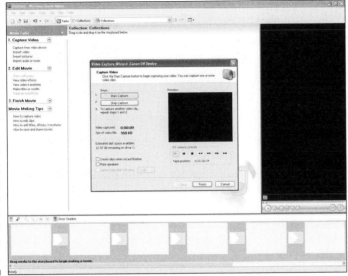

Figure 8-7:
The Windows Movie Maker video capture interface.

Windows Movie Maker stores your video in Collections and when you repeat Steps 2 through 10, you create a new collection that can be accessed for a single project. The actual editing process in Windows Movie Maker is similar to iMovie, and if you want to find out more about how this PC option works (and maybe solve a few odd obstacles it might throw your way), refer to the Windows Movie Maker Web site on Microsoft.com or pick up a copy of *Digital Video For Dummies,* 4th Edition.

Creating a video podcast with Movie Maker and QuickTime Pro

When you work your way through the Windows Movie Maker video-editing process, you have an AVI or MPEG file ready to go for playback on your computer. Not for podcasting. Although Microsoft is doing its best to keep up with the medium, it still has yet to include a one-click option in Windows Movie Maker for podcasting.

Fortunately, Apple has an option that plays on Windows, and it costs approximately $30. It's QuickTime Pro (www.quicktime.com), and unlike the free player you can download, QuickTime Pro comes with a handy Export feature that makes the final steps for your video podcast on a PC a piece of cake.

1. **After reviewing your movie in Movie Maker, go under the Movie Task window on the left side and click the Save to My Computer option under Finish Movie.**

Make sure you know where on your computer Windows Movie Maker is saving the final file.

2. **In the offered pane, select from the list of formats DV-AVI and then click the Next button. Then in the final window, click the Finish button.**

   Exporting your movie may take some time, so walk away from the computer and give yourself a well-earned break.

3. **Close Windows Movie Maker and then launch QuickTime Pro.**

4. **Choose File⇨Open File or Ctrl+O to open your newly produced AVI file.**

5. **Choose File⇨Export or Ctrl+E and from the Export drop-down menu, select the Movie to iPod option.**

   Although you may think the Export for Web would be the option to choose, Export provides you everything you need for podcasting. By selecting Movie to iPod, everything (the codec, screen resolution, audio compression) is set.

6. **Click Save.**

   Again, this may take a few minutes as you're processing the video a second time. When the processing is done, you have a M4V file, ready for ID3 tagging.

7. **Open your video in iTunes. Choose File⇨Get Info or Ctrl+I.**

8. **Click the Info tab to add in your ID3 Tags (refer to Figure 8-5). When your tags are completed, click OK.**

This method takes a few more steps than iMovie, but it's still very easy, provided you're willing to make the investment for QuickTime Pro. When you consider the mistakes, the hassles, and the time in reprocessing a file if the codecs aren't exactly right, the simplicity and ability to select a format optimized for iPod makes video podcasting stress-free.

Although programs like iMovie and Movie Maker have simplified video editing dramatically, as mentioned before, this isn't a quick-and-easy process. When the video is done, it must be processed, and that can take anywhere from a few minutes to a few hours. You want to give yourself that time to edit and time to process the video you're creating. Before announcing your video podcast, try to find out how those first few episodes will progress in production and finally what the processing time will be for a single episode. You may find that a missed mistake can cost you hours. Always preview and then preview again before processing.

Screencasting: What's on your desktop?

Taking both enhanced and video podcasting to new applications, *screencasting* is emerging as a new delivery method of an established teaching tool: recording actions of your desktop.

In a screencast, a podcaster is usually showing off features of a computer application (like InDesign, Final Cut Pro, Word, and so on); but instead of using screen captures that show drop-down menus already deployed or attempting to film your monitor and sacrificing clarity of image, a third-party application like Ambrosia Software's SnapzProX (www.ambrosiasw.com/utilities/snapzprox) captures all actions taken on your desktop in a live recording and then saves them as video footage. Now, you can edit your various desktop actions in your video editor of choice. Subscribers can follow along with the video, cursor, menus, and actions all happening clearly and vividly on your media player.

The Digital Media Dude podcast (www.pixelheadsnetwork.com) takes full advantage of programs like SnapzProX and Final Cut Pro and produces *Digital Media Quick Tips,* an impressive, user-friendly, and downright slick screencast that can easily teach you something new in your favorite application, be it Mac or Windows software. So, if you're learning an application for the first time, are interested in learning a new trick on an old favorite, or if you have a question about software, check out *Digital Media Quick Tips* and see just what you can do with screencasting.

Part III

So You've Got This Great Recording of Your Voice. Now What?

The 5th Wave   By Rich Tennant

INSTEAD OF AN RSS AGGREGATER, GLEN SUBSCRIBES TO AN RSS AGGRAVATER SERVICE.

©RICHTENNANT

Okay, that was "Swarming Mosquito". For the next half hour we'll be listening to "Whining Dental Drill".

In this part . . .

For every would-be podcaster who salivates at the thought of creating a recording, ten more faint at the thought of the technical hurdles involved in getting their work online. This part shows you how easy the technology really is and how to make it work for you, and it guides you through the (elementary) process of launching your show into the *podosphere*.

Chapter 9

Shrink That Puppy and Slap a Label on It

You've finished your final edit (and if you think we're skirting blasphemy whenever we use the E word, trust us — creativity sometimes demands a sacrifice). At last you're ready to compress your mondo-super-sized AIFF or WAV file down to the format that inspires terror and indigestion in RIAA representatives everywhere: MP3.

The MP3 format was designed to reduce the amount of data (via compression) required for digitized audio while still retaining the quality of the original recording. MP3 files are the best way to keep the audio small enough in size to make it a quick-and-easy download, and it's this format that podcasting uses to get content efficiently from podcaster to podcatching client. Although creating MP3s is a simple enough process, you do need to make some tradeoffs between quality and compression.

A Kilobit of Me, and a Whole Lot of You: Understanding Kbps

The compression process begins with proper *bitrate* settings, measured in Kbps (kilobits per second). Bitrate is a method of measuring data transmission from one point to the next. The higher the Kbps value, the more data being transferred between two points. The more data being transferred per second, the better the quality of information. With each rate of data transfer offered by recording applications, you can digitally reproduce the various qualities of audio:

- ✔ **8 Kbps,** matching the vocal quality of a telephone conversation

- ✔ **32 Kbps,** yielding audio quality similar to AM radio

- ✔ **96 Kbps,** yielding audio quality similar to FM radio

- ✔ **128 Kbps,** matching audio CD quality, and the most common Kbps used for MP3 compression of music

- ✔ **192 Kbps,** a "Higher Quality" setting Kbps used for MP3 compression of music; better audio sound, but higher data files

You aren't married to this listing of Kbps by any stretch of imagination. Figure 9-1 shows that Audacity offers in its Preferences plenty of variations from the five common settings. Tweak till you find the Kbps best suited for your podcast.

Figure 9-1: You find a wide variety of bitrates for compressing your podcast to MP3 with Audacity.

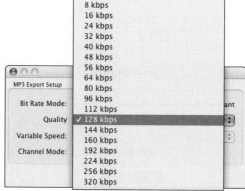

It's a tradeoff: The higher the bitrate, the larger your file size is — but the smaller your bitrate, the lower your audio quality is. A good idea is to experiment: Compress your podcast using one bitrate, save it that way, and then change your bitrate to something higher (or lower), save it, and play back each clip to compare how they load and how they sound. Note any changes in sound quality and file size. When you find that happy medium between quality and compression, stick with that number for your current and future podcasts. If you want to skip experimentation, refer to the suggested compression settings we have outlined on the included Cheat Sheet at the front of this book.

In the following sections, you find out how to change bitrates using Audacity and iTunes. If you're using applications like Audition or Soundtrack, you can find out more about what they offer in *Expert Podcasting Practices For Dummies*.

Setting bitrates in Audacity

Changing bitrates in Audacity (version 1.3.3 featured here) is a multistep process. The first step is to get your editor all set for creating MP3 files:

1. **Choose Audacity⇨Preferences (Mac OS X) or choose Edit⇨Preferences (Windows).**

   The Preferences window opens.

2. **Choose the File Formats option in the left column (see Figure 9-2).**

3. **Click the Download Free Copy of LAME button in the MP3 Export Setup section or point your browser directly to** `http://audacity.sourceforge.net/download/lame`.

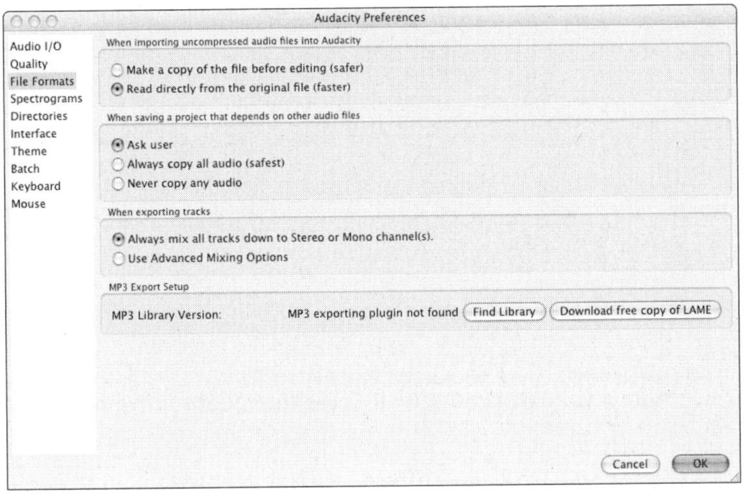

Figure 9-2: Before setting bitrates in Audacity, you need to download a LAME file.

4. **Follow the steps for your OS as outlined on the Web page to download the proper files.**

5. **Open the archive file (no need to worry — it's a safe download) and drop it into your Audacity folder.**

6. **Return to Audacity and click the Find Library button.**

7. **Choose Applications⇨Audacity (Mac) or My Computer⇨(Main Drive)⇨Program Files⇨Audacity (Windows) to navigate to the libmp3lame file.**

8. **Select the libmp3lame file and click Open.**

This step in setting up the LAME Library is a one-time thing. You won't have to repeat this process again unless you move the library to another location.

Now you've come to the point where you set the bitrate. When you have a file, follow these steps to export it as an MP3 file:

1. **Choose File⇨Export.**

2. **From the Format menu, select MP3 Files.**

3. **Next to the Format: MP3 Files menu, click Options.**

   The Specify MP3 Options dialog box opens, as shown in Figure 9-3.

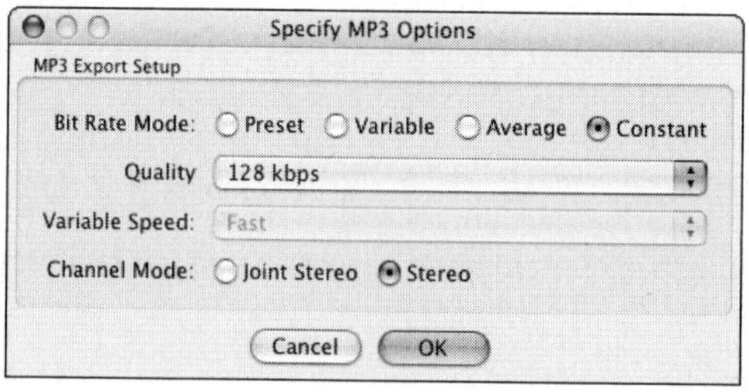

Figure 9-3:
Under the MP3 options, you can set bitrates and other variables for your compressed audio.

Specify MP3 Options
MP3 Export Setup
Bit Rate Mode: ○ Preset ○ Variable ○ Average ● Constant
Quality [128 kbps]
Variable Speed: [Fast]
Channel Mode: ○ Joint Stereo ● Stereo
Cancel   OK

4. **Choose your desired bitrate from the Quality drop-down menu.**

   If you're following our recommendation from the Cheat Sheet at the front of this book, you would set the bitrate to 128.

You can also set up your Bit Rate Mode (Constant) and your Channel Mode (Joint Stereo). Constant bitrate ensures the bits are output at a steady (constant) rate despite the audio that is being used (including silence). Variable bitrate attempts to do a bit of compression — for example, the bitrate of a complex music sample would take more space than that of the same length of time in a spoken piece with several pauses. Although variable length audio sounds good on the surface, it can present problems to the listener — actual playback times may not be correct, causing problems when people pause a long podcast. Joint Stereo refers to a technique that saves some space when your recording includes mono channels or tracks. Rather than using the space of a stereo track (left and right) to save that information, joint stereo techniques recognize it and save space by only using half the space.

5. **Click OK to return to the Export window.**

6. **Name your file and then click OK.**

After you set the bitrate for this one file, your settings are automatically applied to other MP3 files created from this point. Only when you go into the Options for MP3 files will you change bitrates.

Changing bitrates in iTunes

It doesn't matter how your audio files get in to iTunes, be it from Audacity, GarageBand, or anywhere else. When you get the files in to iTunes, you can easily convert them to a different bitrate, change the file format, or make any number of other changes to the file.

You can't get better quality out of a file by changing it from a lower bitrate to a higher bitrate. For example, once a file has been saved at 32 Kbps, converting it to 128 Kbps won't make it sound any better.

To set the bitrate in iTunes, follow these steps:

1. **Choose iTunes⇨Preferences (Mac OS) or choose Edit⇨Preferences (Windows).**

   The Preferences window opens.

2. **In the Preferences window, choose Advanced⇨Importing.**

3. **Choose Custom from the Setting drop-down menu.**

   The MP3 Encoder dialog box opens.

4. **Select your desired bitrate from the Stereo Bit Rate drop-down menu (shown in Figure 9-4).**

   You can also choose to make your channels mono, stereo, or Joint Stereo and what your sampling rate is. (See the following section for more about sampling rates.)

5. **Click OK.**

   You return to the Importing tab. The default settings for your MP3 compressions are now in the Details area.

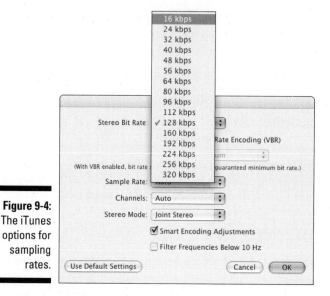

Figure 9-4:
The iTunes options for sampling rates.

Care for a Sample, Sir? (Audio Sample Rates)

When you have a grasp of bitrates, you're ready to move on to *sample rates*. This may strike you as a tad redundant, particularly when you see the list of common audio-sample rates. A strange *déjà vu* makes you wonder whether you're in the real world or exist merely as part of The Matrix. No biggie — sometimes technology *is* redundant.

As we discuss in the previous section, bitrate is a measurement of how much audio data is transferred between two points, such as the computer and your headset. The *sampling rate* is a measurement of audio samples taken from a *continuous signal* (a signal of a varying quantity, defined over a period of time) in order to create a *discrete signal* (a signal made up of samples from a continuous signal).

Very simply, the sample rate determines the maximum sound frequency that can be reproduced — the value you set is twice the frequency value. For example, a 44.1 kHz sample rate can reproduce sounds up to 22.05 kHz, which is slightly above the range of human hearing.

The most common audio sampling rates found in MP3 encoders are

✔ 8,000 Hz / 8 kHz, telephone-quality recording or lo-fi

✔ 22,050 Hz / 22 kHz, equal to AM radio transmission

✔ 32,000 Hz / 32 kHz, equal to FM radio transmission, minimum sound quality on miniDV digital video camcorder

✔ 44,100 Hz / 44 kHz, audio-CD quality

✔ 48,000 Hz / 48 kHz, digital TV, DVD, films, maximum sound quality on miniDV digital video camcorder, and professional-grade audio recording

As with your audio-recording applications, you have a range of bitrates available — and you can type in your own custom sampling rates.

Using different sample rates in compressed audio files does not affect the file size — only the bitrate and duration affect file size. A high sample rate at a low bitrate can result in poor signal representation and thus poor quality, but if you're using at least 64 Kbps (bitrate), there's no good reason to ever use anything except 44.1 kHz as the sample rate.

Setting the standard for a new kind of book, a new kind of podcast

When Evo Terra, Chris Miller, and Tee Morris launched Podiobooks.com in October 2005, they knew setting an audio standard for current and future podcasters would be important. The challenge was in establishing standards that podcasters could easily follow, but that listeners would find comfortable. In the end, they looked to *The Dragon Page* (now known as *Cover-to-Cover*) and its podcast (that, at the time, was syndicated on XM Satellite Radio and AM/FM radio stations) as a benchmark. Now, Podiobooks.com asks for the following parameters:

✔ 64 (voice only), 96 (voice with intro/outro music), or 128 (voice, music, SFX) Kbps

✔ 44.100 kHz / 44,100 Hz

✔ Joint Stereo

We haven't discussed the difference between stereo and joint stereo output in this chapter, for one reason: It all depends on the method you use for recording — and on how you're listening:

✔ **Stereo:** By default, many applications that export to MP3 also export as Stereo. Stereo encoding takes the left and right audio separately and divides the selected bitrate for each. The drawback to (plain) stereo is that the channels are equal width, so a 128 Kbps encoding of a mono signal is really two identical 64 Kbps channels, resulting in a 50 percent inefficiency.

✔ **Joint Stereo:** With this option, one channel carries sound that is identical in both the left and right stereo tracks, and the other channel carries the difference. Both channels are only as big as they need to be, so if your podcast is mostly mono — with just one microphone — you'll get more out of your bitrate than you would with a plain stereo file, but without the reliability issues of a mono file.

With these parameters in place, Podiobooks.com ensures consistency between the numerous titles featured. Something to consider when setting standards for yourself and your podcasts.

Be careful when using a sample rate other than a multiple of 11. Many Web sites use Flash players that don't work well with other sample rates. Choosing a sample rate other than 11.025 kHz, 22.5 kHz, or 44.1 kHz can produce an effect similar to the voices of Alvin and the Chipmunks. It might be funny at first, but most listeners won't stick around to hear your entire message.

Changing sample rates in Audacity

Sample rates are located in the Preferences window and extremely simple to either change or customize to your podcast's personal needs. Follow these steps to customize sample rates in Audacity:

1. **Choose Audacity⇨Preferences (Mac OS) or File⇨Preferences (Windows).**

   The Preferences window appears.

2. **Click the Quality option in the left column.**

3. **Select your desired bitrate from the Default Sample Rate drop-down menu (as shown in Figure 9-5), or enter your own custom sampling rate by selecting the Other option and entering a number.**

   If you're entering a custom sampling rate, make sure you enter the rate in *hertz* (Hz) and not *kilohertz* (kHz). For example, if you decide your sampling rate is 44.1 kHz, you have to enter **44100**, not 44.

4. **Click OK.**

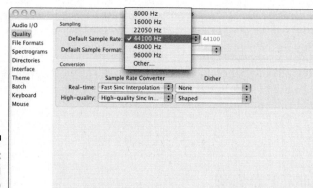

Figure 9-5:
Changing
your audio
sampling
rate in
Audacity.

Changing sample rates in iTunes

iTunes makes the process of changing the sample rate easy — what else would you expect from Apple?

To get an idea of what a good sampling rate is, take a look at the podcasts your aggregator is pulling down and check the settings. Press ⌘+I (Mac) or Ctrl+I (Windows) to see the MP3 Summaries. Settings may vary from file to file. As you work out the final technical details of your podcast, make sure that one of them is the setting that best suits your needs and (of course) your ear.

Follow these steps to change the sample rate in iTunes:

1. **Choose iTunes⇨Preferences (Mac OS X) or Edit⇨Preferences (Windows).**

   The Preferences window appears.

2. **Choose Advanced⇨Importing.**

3. **Select the Custom option from the Settings drop-down menu.**

   The iTunes MP3 Encoder dialog box opens.

4. **Select your desired sampling rate from the Sample Rate menu.**

   Apple loves to make things easy for its users, and we love that. However, Apple sometimes takes out the *"I did it MY WAY!"* alternative and does not allow for custom settings. Here, iTunes keeps this sampling to the common settings, so you're given no leeway.

   Note that iTunes offers your sampling rates at kilohertz (kHz), a more common, recognizable presentation of a sampling rate. Again, this is Apple looking out for you, keeping it to the basics.

5. **Click OK.**

   You return to the Importing tab. The default settings for your MP3 compressions are now visible in the Details area.

ID3 Tags: They're Not Just for Music Anymore

Is it soup yet? Not quite yet. Adding ID3 tags is the final step before you can upload the podcast to your Web site. This is the final detail (okay, batch of details) that not only tells other podcasters who you are, but also tells listeners what your podcast is all about, and which episode they're listening to.

Because this is a final detail, we find that some podcasters either skip it or just don't care how they tag their podcasts. And there goes any hope for their listeners to effectively organize podcasts in a computer's MP3 player. Maybe some podcasters are unaware of where or how to identify their podcasts — or want to get their content out to the fans ASAP without taking the time to implement these tags.

Whatever the case, we entreat you: Stop the madness, stop the insanity, and stop the monkeys. Proclaim your true self for the sake of MP3 players everywhere — implement your ID3 tags!

Tell me about yourself: All about ID3 tags

First created in 1996, *ID3 tags* were designed to be added to audio files in order to have the artist, album, and track title displayed in a computer's MP3 player when the file is played back. The current ID3 tags now include composer, bitrate, and even genre.

Of course, another question that comes to mind is *why* would a podcaster want to even bother with ID3 tags?

Take a look at a podcast you're listening to, regardless of whether it's on your portable MP3 player or the player on your desktop. Your podcatching client probably organizes your various feeds by the date downloaded, either with the most recent show at the bottom or at the top of your playlist, depending on the player's preferences. Each individual podcast has an episode title, an artist, and a podcast title. If your MP3 player and the podcaster working with the ID3 tags are particularly savvy, artwork associated with your show is also displayed.

Now hop from podcast to podcast in your MP3 player, and you can tell which people care — or don't — about identifying their shows. Some podcasts simply use obscure numbers that could be a date, but when you hear two episodes of the podcast back to back, you find out the number and the date read at the intro of the show (provided there is one) don't match up (confusing). With ID3 tags in place, you can now look at your portable MP3 player or your desktop player to get an idea of what you're listening to.

When you add ID3 tags to your podcast, you set apart individual podcasts from one another, making each one unique but keeping it grouped with your podcast show.

IDentity crisis: Making ID3 tags work for podcasting

Some ID3 tags really don't work for podcasting. Album? Track number? Composer? You're podcasting, not producing music. Your responsibility (as a podcaster) is to redefine the following tags we have found useful for the podcasting medium:

- **Name:** This should be the name or number of your podcasting episode. Examples are Show #19, Episode 3: One of Those Faces, BOOK THREE: Chapters 39 & 40.

- **Artist:** This one is pretty self-explanatory. You're the artist behind this podcast, so let people know who you and your group are. Put in your name (or at least the pseudonym you're using as a podcaster) or the name of your podcasting team. For example, Philippa Ballantine, Earl Newton, and J.C. Hutchins.

- **Album Artist:** Many times left blank, this tag can be a bit tricky for users. The Album Artist usually refers to the Artist, but you can also use it to refer to the artwork artist, the production studio, or the creator of the podcast. Examples are Philippa Ballantine, Stranger RSS LLC, and Carrie Seidman (artist for Tee's *MOREVI: Remastered* artwork, used for the podcast).

- **Album:** In most instances it is the name of your show or your show's Web site. Good examples are Whispers at the Edge, Stranger Things - iPod (640 x 480), and 7th Son Podcast Novel Trilogy.

- **Track Number:** Purely optional, this ID3 tag allows you to make sure your podcasts remain in some kind of sequential order. For podcast novelists, the track numbers coincide with the chapter numbers. If podcasts follow a season of multiple episodes, the Track Number coincides with the episode in that season.

- **Year:** The year this podcast episode was produced.

- **BPM:** If you are into staying fit and are listening to or producing a workout podcast, you want to fill in this ID3 tag as BPM is for Beats Per Minute. BPM is also good if your podcast is a house music-dance mix podcast. A good example of a podcast showing off BPM is any one mixed by D.J. Steveboy (Podrunner).

- **Grouping:** This tag may remain blank until you're affiliated with a network or distribution hub of some kind. Good examples are Podiobooks.com and Farpoint Media.

- ✔ **Composer:** If Album Artist already sports the name of your cover artist, this tag can be used to host the name of your producer. You can enter your engineer's name, or the studio where the show is produced. For example, *MOREVI's* artist is listed as `Tee Morris` but the composers are `Tee Morris & Lisa Lee` as the original work was co-written.

- ✔ **Genre:** The genre "Podcast" wasn't offered in drop-down menus of MP3 creators, but with the growing popularity of the medium, it's becoming more and more common.

  If you're using iTunes and don't see the **Podcast** genre, you can manually type **Podcast** into the field.

- ✔ **Comments:** Similar to comments you leave in XML, you can give a quick two or three lines of show notes for your podcasts. It's also a great place to put in any Creative Commons notices, Web sites for more information of the show and its hosts, and special dedications.

- ✔ **Album art:** Don't forget, a big piece of successful podcasting is marketing — and a big part of marketing is branding. Your podcast logo (or album art) is very important to help set you apart. Although not all MP3 players have this feature, don't discount its importance. A large percentage of podcast listeners use iTunes and listen at their computers — where the album art may be prominently displayed.

Reminiscent of John Cleese's aside in a *Monty Python* robbery sketch ("Adapt, and improve. That's the motto of the Round Table"), we podcasters must adapt these ID3 tags to our podcasts to improve how they appear in our players. On playback, the ID3 tags appear on the listeners' interfaces, offering a quick glance at the content of the podcast (as shown in Figure 9-6).

If you're using iTunes as your podcatching software, be aware that it doesn't use most of the information supplied in ID3 tags. iTunes picks up much of the information from the RSS feed and retags your files. We cover more RSS details in Chapter 12.

A peril in working with ID3 Tags is spelling errors. There is no spell check in Audacity, iTunes, or any other tag editor. Because many directories, search engines, and players rely on the ID3 tags to organize and properly display your show, make sure to double-check the spelling of your show title, names of people involved, and any other text you're putting in place. Also, some editors like iTunes create "quick fill" databases that help you fill in your File Info quickly. This database also includes the misspellings. So when filling in your ID3 tags, take your time and check your spelling.

Figure 9-7:
The Edit
ID3 Tags
(for MP3
Exporting)
window in
Audacity.

4. **Give a brief description of your podcast in the Comments field.**

Don't make your comments a long, detailed description of your podcast's content. Keep it simple and brief. For example, if the creators of *The Dragon Page: Cover-to-Cover* were to write comments for Show #174, it wouldn't say "On this show we interview Brandon Sanderson about his debut novel *Elantris* and then turn our attention to Steve Alten's latest novel, *The Loch*." Instead, the creators would boil down this description to "Show 174 — Interviews with Brandon Sanderson and Steve Alten."

5. **Click Done.**

And that's it! When Audacity generates your MP3, your show is tagged and ready for uploading.

Audacity's ID3 tagger does have its limitations. It cannot, in the version covered in this edition, embed artwork into your audio metadata. For that extra touch, use an ID3 Tag editor such as ID3X (`www.three-2-one.com/321apps/main/global/index1.htm`) or iTunes.

Creating and editing ID3 tags in iTunes

Using iTunes to tag your files offers more flexibility in customizing genres and even incorporating artwork than Audacity does. Apple's MP3 player, encoder, and podcatcher also make adding and editing ID3 tags extremely easy. Follow these steps:

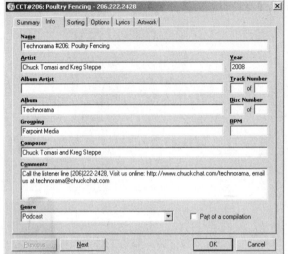

Figure 9-6:
How a properly tagged podcast appears in iTunes.

Creating and editing ID3 tags in Audacity

Unlike iTunes where you tag individual files after they are created, Audacity lets you set up a template for the ID3 tags that gets applied when MP3 files are created. To create this template, open Audacity and follow these steps:

1. **Choose File⇨Open Metadata Editor.**

   The Edit ID3 Tags (for MP3 Exporting) window opens (shown in Figure 9-7). The ID3v2 option is already selected by default.

2. **Fill in these fields:**

   - *Title:* The episode name or number

   - *Artist:* The podcaster or name of the podcasting crew

   - *Album:* The show's name or Web site

   - *Track Number:* The field is optional, unless numerical order is a priority in your podcast

   - *Year:* The podcast publication's year

3. **From the Genres drop-down menu, select the option best suited to your podcast.**

   Audacity on version 1.3.3 doesn't offer "Podcast" as an option. You can always select Speech to indicate this is a non-musical podcast.

   Click the More button to add a customized tag (refer to Figure 9-7). You can also add additional ID3 tags and save your tags as a template.

IDentity crisis: Making ID3 tags work for podcasting

Some ID3 tags really don't work for podcasting. Album? Track number? Composer? You're podcasting, not producing music. Your responsibility (as a podcaster) is to redefine the following tags we have found useful for the podcasting medium:

- **Name:** This should be the name or number of your podcasting episode. Examples are Show #19, Episode 3: One of Those Faces, BOOK THREE: Chapters 39 & 40.

- **Artist:** This one is pretty self-explanatory. You're the artist behind this podcast, so let people know who you and your group are. Put in your name (or at least the pseudonym you're using as a podcaster) or the name of your podcasting team. For example, Philippa Ballantine, Earl Newton, and J.C. Hutchins.

- **Album Artist:** Many times left blank, this tag can be a bit tricky for users. The Album Artist usually refers to the Artist, but you can also use it to refer to the artwork artist, the production studio, or the creator of the podcast. Examples are Philippa Ballantine, Stranger RSS LLC, and Carrie Seidman (artist for Tee's *MOREVI: Remastered* artwork, used for the podcast).

- **Album:** In most instances it is the name of your show or your show's Web site. Good examples are Whispers at the Edge, Stranger Things - iPod (640 x 480), and 7th Son Podcast Novel Trilogy.

- **Track Number:** Purely optional, this ID3 tag allows you to make sure your podcasts remain in some kind of sequential order. For podcast novelists, the track numbers coincide with the chapter numbers. If podcasts follow a season of multiple episodes, the Track Number coincides with the episode in that season.

- **Year:** The year this podcast episode was produced.

- **BPM:** If you are into staying fit and are listening to or producing a workout podcast, you want to fill in this ID3 tag as BPM is for Beats Per Minute. BPM is also good if your podcast is a house music-dance mix podcast. A good example of a podcast showing off BPM is any one mixed by D.J. Steveboy (Podrunner).

- **Grouping:** This tag may remain blank until you're affiliated with a network or distribution hub of some kind. Good examples are Podiobooks.com and Farpoint Media.

✔ **Composer:** If Album Artist already sports the name of your cover artist, this tag can be used to host the name of your producer. You can enter your engineer's name, or the studio where the show is produced. For example, *MOREVI's* artist is listed as `Tee Morris` but the composers are `Tee Morris & Lisa Lee` as the original work was co-written.

✔ **Genre:** The genre "Podcast" wasn't offered in drop-down menus of MP3 creators, but with the growing popularity of the medium, it's becoming more and more common.

If you're using iTunes and don't see the **Podcast** genre, you can manually type **Podcast** into the field.

✔ **Comments:** Similar to comments you leave in XML, you can give a quick two or three lines of show notes for your podcasts. It's also a great place to put in any Creative Commons notices, Web sites for more information of the show and its hosts, and special dedications.

✔ **Album art:** Don't forget, a big piece of successful podcasting is marketing — and a big part of marketing is branding. Your podcast logo (or album art) is very important to help set you apart. Although not all MP3 players have this feature, don't discount its importance. A large percentage of podcast listeners use iTunes and listen at their computers — where the album art may be prominently displayed.

Reminiscent of John Cleese's aside in a *Monty Python* robbery sketch ("Adapt, and improve. That's the motto of the Round Table"), we podcasters must adapt these ID3 tags to our podcasts to improve how they appear in our players. On playback, the ID3 tags appear on the listeners' interfaces, offering a quick glance at the content of the podcast (as shown in Figure 9-6).

If you're using iTunes as your podcatching software, be aware that it doesn't use most of the information supplied in ID3 tags. iTunes picks up much of the information from the RSS feed and retags your files. We cover more RSS details in Chapter 12.

A peril in working with ID3 Tags is spelling errors. There is no spell check in Audacity, iTunes, or any other tag editor. Because many directories, search engines, and players rely on the ID3 tags to organize and properly display your show, make sure to double-check the spelling of your show title, names of people involved, and any other text you're putting in place. Also, some editors like iTunes create "quick fill" databases that help you fill in your File Info quickly. This database also includes the misspellings. So when filling in your ID3 tags, take your time and check your spelling.

1. **Single click your newly created MP3 in iTunes. Choose File⇨Get Info or press ⌘+I (Mac) or Ctrl+I (Windows).**

   The Info window appears, which gives you a summary of your MP3 file.

2. **Fill in the following fields:**

   - *Title:* The episode name or number.

   - *Artist:* The name of the podcaster or podcasting crew.

   - *Album Artist:* This would be a good spot to give credit to the artwork artist or show producer.

   - *Album:* The show's name or Web site.

   - *Track Number:* This is optional, unless numerical order is a priority in your podcast.

   - *Year:* The podcast publication's year.

   - *BPM:* If you're doing an exercise show or a music podcast featuring original house mixes, give your Beats Per Minute here. Listeners will dig that.

   - *Grouping:* If you're part of a group or network like Farpoint Media, or FriendsInTech, give credit here.

   - *Composer:* Fill in this field if you have a separate sound engineer, a tech guru handling the editing, or if you're doing the work yourself.

   - *Genre:* Select one of the offered genres from the drop-down menu, or you can select the genre in the field and type **Podcast** (or whatever genre you want to use to classify your work).

   One of the cool bonuses of iTunes is how you can create custom genres. Choose File⇨Get Info⇨Info and enter your own genre here. Or go to the song in your iTunes Library and click in the Genre column and edit the genre name. When you return to the Info window later, you can see your custom genre offered as an option on the Genre drop-down menu.

   - *Comments:* A brief version of show notes.

3. **Take a last look at your ID3 tags to make sure everything is spelled properly and listed the way you want it, and then click the Artwork tab.**

4. **Drag and drop a desired piece of artwork into the Artwork field or click the Add button and, using the window that appears, navigate to the artwork you want to have associated with your podcast.**

   If your logo is in a format that iTunes recognizes, it appears in the Artwork field, as shown in Figure 9-8. See the sidebar "Art for art's sake" to make sure your logo has the appropriate format.

5. **Click OK.**

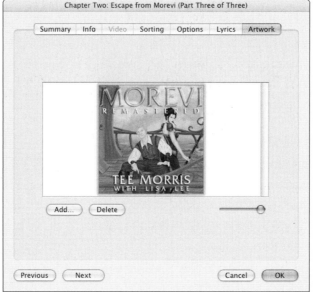

Figure 9-8:
iTunes
offers an
ID3 tag
option for
podcast-
ers to
incorporate
artwork,
giving your
episode a
slick final
touch.

Artwork by Carrie Seidman

Art for art's sake

Album artwork, commonly seen in many desktop MP3 players and now in iPods that display photos, is a nice option for podcasters who want to brand a podcast with a logo. Mur Lafferty's Parsec-winning *I Should Be Writing* logo is a classic broadcast microphone with a sticky note slapped on it and a pencil, sharpened and ready for use. Then you have *The Onion Radio News*'s trademark onion with a globe ghosted behind it, the stamp of quality journalism at its funniest. These are icons associated with their shows, and this kind of branding is becoming more and more common in podcasting, especially with the iTunes Store becoming podcast friendly.

But what is the best way to make sure iTunes (and for that matter, the iTunes Store's Podcast Catalog) recognizes your artwork? Just make sure that your logo fits the following parameters:

- ✔ 300 x 300 pixels, both in width and height, or 600 x 600 if you anticipate listeners/viewers on Apple TV. This isn't required, just an Apple recommendation that has become a de facto standard.

- ✔ JPEG (`.jpg`) format

Keep in mind that when you compress your artwork, overcompression can distort and deteriorate its visual quality. Some JPEG settings work in numbers 1–10 or 0–100. As a rule, if you compress your logos no more than "50", your artwork should retain visual quality.

Chapter 10

Move It on Up (To Your Web Server)

*Y*ou've managed to figure out what it is you want to say (or show), you've gone through the trials and tribulations of the editing process (or not), and you've faithfully employed correct ID3 tagging (nonnegotiable). That's great, but no one is going to hear your contribution to the podcasting world until you put your files up on the World Wide Web.

In Chapter 1, we cover the hosting provider selection process. In this chapter, we take an extensive look at the mechanics of the process, including how to appropriately name and organize your files.

Podcasters have a variety of options when it comes to moving files. Many people employ specialized software, and some podcast-specific hosting companies make moving your files to the Web as simple as point and click. And for the "old school" folks, text-based applications baked right in to the operating system might be the preferred method.

Although the methods for uploading files are all different, they all help you accomplish the same job: moving files from your personal computer to their new home on the World Wide Web.

Adopting an Effective Filenaming Convention

In Chapter 9, we talk about the importance of "the little things," such as ID3 tags. Equally important is how you decide to name your podcast media files.

In this section, we illustrate the importance, not only to you as a podcaster, but also to your listening audience. Although no hard and fast rules for naming files exist, following some common conventions allows everyone to easily find your podcasts.

A good naming convention of a podcast accomplishes the following:

- **Easy sequential ordering:** Files should not appear at random in your directory. They should line up — first, second, third, and so on.

- **"At a glance" recognition for your listeners:** Calling a podcast media file `my media file` doesn't help very much. Calling it `Bob's Fencing Podcast` certainly does.

Here's an example of a well-named podcast media file, if we do say so ourselves:

```
Tech_Ep200_080102.mp3
```

Although the structure may not be obvious, this filename adheres to both rules and even adds one more:

- **Tech:** This abbreviation stands for *Technorama,* one of the many podcasts Chuck produces each week. Starting the filename with these four letters organizes the files together in the media folder. For listeners who can see only the filename on their MP3 players, they can quickly recognize that files starting with these four letters belong to his show.

- **Ep200:** This is Episode 200 of the show. Referring to each show with a sequential number is a good idea, giving you and your fans a common reference point that is easier than "remember when you did that one show with that one guy who said that funny thing? Man that was great!" Having the episode number right after the name also ensures that the files "stack up" right in the media folder, as well as in your listeners' MP3 players. You may want to consider adding some leading zeroes to the number so episode 3 (003) comes before 200. Add more zeroes if you plan on doing more than 999 shows.

- **080102:** The date Chuck posted the live file. The order he uses here is year-month-day. He uses `08` instead of `8` so that dates from October (10), November (11), and December (12) don't intermingle with January (which would happen if he used `1` instead of `01`). True, in this case the files were already sorted by episode number, but you may choose to go with the date first.

Between each element, he adds an underscore (_) simply to provide a clear distinction of each part for his eye, or anyone else's eye looking at the filename.

Don't use any spaces or special characters in your filenames. Stick with A–Z, 0–9, dashes, and underscores. Slashes (/, \), octothorpes (#), ampersands (&), and others can and do cause problems when creating RSS 2.0 files or when clients are handling the file. Also, leaving a space in the filename might mess up a URL, so if you want to space things out, use underscores or dashes (for example, use `My_Podcast.mp3` instead of `My Podcast.mp3`).

The following examples are from well-respected podcasters who all follow the guidelines we set forth earlier:

- ✔ `JimmyJett-2007-12-17.mp3`
- ✔ `Gmail-063-Security.mp3`
- ✔ `VF_Ep060_paidinfull-120407.mp3`
- ✔ `DSC-704-2007-12-27.mp3`

Note how each of them identifies the name of the podcast and provides a sequential way of ordering the files. If you leave out the episode number, as in the case of the JimmyJett file, the year of the podcast ahead of month and day also ensures that 2007 files are always grouped together. If the podcaster had used the month first, as people traditionally think of dates in the United States, files would be mixed based on the month they were released, regardless of the year.

If thinking about the date that way seems a little too strange for you, do what Chuck does — stick a sequential episode number in front of your date, and don't worry about it.

Understanding How FTP Works •

FTP (File Transfer Protocol) is the method by which you can transfer files from one destination to another over the Internet. You likely transfer files every day, from your desktop to your documents folder, from an e-mail to your desktop, or even MP3 files from your podcatching client to your MP3 player.

Transferring files to and from the Internet isn't much different, at least on the surface and even at any depth necessary for podcasters to ply their trade. Lucky for you, specialty software exists to make this process even more simple. FTPing files has become as simple as dragging and dropping.

Some podcast hosting services, such as Liberated Syndication (`http://libsyn.com`) make this simple process even simpler by providing a Web form to handle the uploading of podcast files, as described later in the chapter in the "Uploading to a Podcast-Specific Host" section. Browser-based systems certainly remove the complexity for many, but it doesn't hurt to understand the processes outlined in this chapter. Many experienced podcasters need more flexibility than the limited functionality a browser-based upload process allows.

Regardless of what software, forms, or other assistance you use to move files around, the concept of FTP is the same.

FTP has been around for quite a while now. As such, archaic and seemingly nonintuitive names abound from the start — such as the following two computer systems involved:

- ✔ **Local host:** The local host is the computer you are sitting in front of and initiating the file transfer from. If you're using a laptop to connect to your Web server, your laptop is the local host. If you're at work and logged in from a workstation, your office computer is the local host.

   The *local directory* or *local path* is the folder on your local host that contains the files you want to transfer. You can change local directories at will, but most FTP programs have a default starting place. Feel free to move around after that.

- ✔ **Remote host:** The remote host is the computer or Web server to which you've connected. It's likely the spot where you're trying to get your MP3 files to go so you can start podcasting.

   Not surprisingly, the remote host has its own *remote directory* (the folder on the remote system where you drop your files). Again, you can change or navigate through remote directories just as you can change the file folders on your computer.

Making Your Connection with an FTP Application

You need three pieces of information to initiate an FTP connection:

- ✔ The IP address or hostname of your Web server
- ✔ Login name
- ✔ Password

Your hosting company should have provided this information to you. If you don't have it handy, find it. You're not going any farther without it.

All FTP programs do the same job but have slightly different methods of going about it. After you grasp the concept, using just about any FTP client is a simple process. Here are the general steps you follow to set up a connection in any FTP client:

1. **Launch your FTP client and create a new connection.**

   Because this step is what FTP clients are designed to do, they usually make this process very simple.

2. **Enter the hostname of your Web server, username, and password.**

   This step identifies the remote system and shows you have access to the files and folders it contains.

3. **Connect using either a button or a menu option.**

   Depending on the speed of your connection, the connection is established in a matter of seconds.

The following sections show you how to use Cyberduck (`http://cyberduck.ch`), a free and handy FTP program for the Macintosh system, and FileZilla (`http://filezilla-project.org`), a similar program for the PC. You can find many FTP programs as freeware, shareware, and shrink-wrapped software, for every brand of modern day operating system. We picked these two for their ease of use and streamlined approach to getting the job done, but you can use the FTP program of your choice.

Step by step (or quack by quack) setup for Cyberduck

After you download the Cyberduck program from `http://cyberduck.ch` onto your Mac, you can follow these steps to set up an FTP connection in Cyberduck:

1. **Click the New Connection button in the upper-left corner.**

   The Connect dialog box appears, as shown in Figure 10-1.

2. **In the Server text box, enter the name of your server.**

   Depending on the requirements of your ISP, this name can be in the format of `ftp.`*mydomainname.com* or perhaps simply *my_domain_name.com*. And of course, you need to be sure and use the name of your Web server. Chances are good that you don't really own the domain *my_domain_name.com*, right?

3. **Leave the Path text box blank.**

   Every Web server is configured differently, and most ISPs have things configured to put you in the appropriate place. Later, you may want to add something to this line so you don't have to move around file folders each time you connect.

4. **Enter your Username and Password in the text boxes.**

   The hosting company should have provided this information. If your hosting company is the same company that is supplying your connection to the Internet, it might be the same information you use to check your e-mail. But if you toss some additional money each week at a hosting provider, it's likely something completely different.

Select the Add to Keychain option to store your username and password for the next time you connect.

5. **Click the Connect button in the lower-right corner.**

   If you entered things properly, you now see the file folders on your remote Web server. If you didn't, you get an error message or a login failed dialog box. Correct what's wrong and try it again.

When your connection is established, choose Bookmarks⇨New Bookmark. Give your newly created connection a catchy name and simply double-click the given name the next time you need to connect.

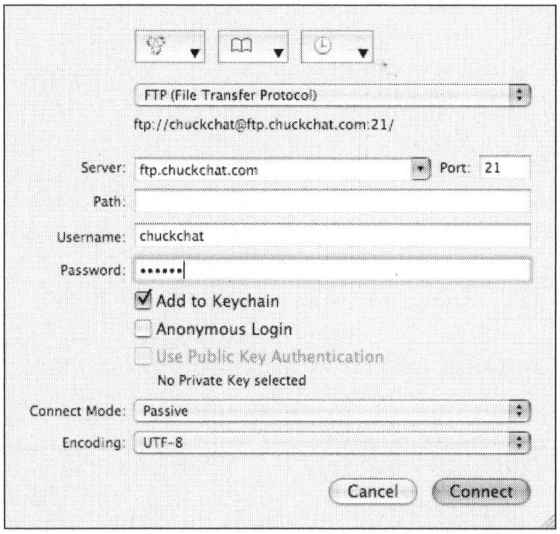

Figure 10-1: A properly configured Cyberduck FTP connection.

Step by step setup for FileZilla

FileZilla (`http://filezilla-project.org`) operates much the same as Windows Explorer, allowing you to drag and drop files between your PC and your FTP server. When you've downloaded the FileZilla program, follow these steps:

1. **On the Login toolbar (shown in Figure 10-2), enter your server name, username, and password.**

   Leave the port blank. (It defaults to 21.)

2. Press the Quickconnect button.

> If you did things right, you see a lot of text scroll by in the upper-most window and content from your Web server appears in the right windows, labeled Remote Site.
>
> Congratulations; you're now connected to your Web server. If you entered something wrong, you get an error message in red text in the upper window. Correct your mistakes and try it again.

From here, you can navigate through the folders on your Web server much as you do on your computer's hard drive. You can move up or down the file system, finding the spot where you want to drop your podcast files.

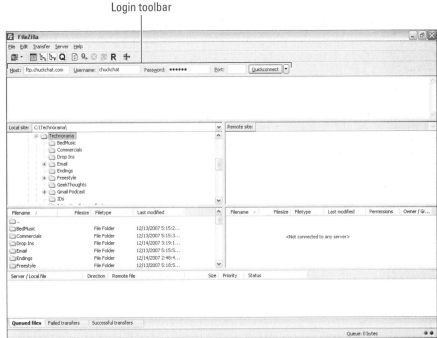

Figure 10-2: A properly configured FileZilla connection.

A place on your Web server for your stuff

Logging in to your Web server for the first time can be an intimidating process. In this section, we show you how to place your files in a location so you can easily create links to your podcast files.

Don't be intimidated by the odd directory names on your Web server. The only one you really need to know is Public_html. Other hosts may call it www or simply html. If you don't have one of those three, poke around until you find one that has a bunch of files in it that end in .html.

Unmetered and unlimited explained

Okay, we can't throw out terms like that without saying something about them:

✔ **Unmetered bandwidth** refers to the policies of certain hosting companies, like Liberated Syndication (`http://libsyn.com`), that don't base their monthly charges on the amount of files transferred (podcasts downloaded) each month.

✔ **Unlimited server space** means you can host 1 or 1,000 different podcast media files on the Web server and be charged the same flat fee. We don't know of any hosting company offering unlimited server space currently, but you can get close. Many hosts offer gigabytes for a cheap price — sometimes even hundreds of gigabytes — which is effectively unlimited.

Look, but don't touch. Going into folders doesn't hurt anything, but doing silly things such as deleting, renaming, and moving files you know nothing about is a bad idea. All those strangely named folders do something, and they're likely necessary to make your Web site work right. Remember the proverb "'Tis best to leave functioning Web servers lie. . . ."

You may see lots of different files and a few folders. We show you how to add even more files to this system, so now is a good time to think about organizing and housekeeping.

Start by creating a special place to keep your podcast files. Making a new folder exclusively for your podcast media files not only separates your podcasts from your other critical Web server files, but it also allows you to quickly see what is currently live and what needs to be cleaned up.

In your root directory (the top level folder usually denoted with a forward slash), create a new folder called `media`. With Cyberduck, choose File↵New Folder, followed by entering the name in the resulting dialog box. On FileZilla, right-click the window with the details (date, size, permissions) on the remote file server and choose Create Directory.

After you create the new media folder, double-click the name of the folder to open it. You're now inside your totally empty media folder, and ready to load it with your podcast media files.

Uploading your files

After you set up a folder for your podcast media files and decide on a filenaming convention, you're ready to move your freshly named files to the Web server.

Using your blogging software to upload

Many popular blogging tools allow podcasters to upload files without the need for special FTP software, much like the HTTP process.

However, podcast media files often exceed the file size requirements for these services. For this reason, we recommend not using your conventional blogging software to handle your podcast media file uploads.

Consider that blogs are primarily used to communicate text. Although you can easily extend the functionality of a blog to support a podcast, the site management tools are designed for text and images.

WordPress (http://wordpress.org) does allow file uploads, but the file size depends on system parameters that are often set by the Web host and can't be changed by the individual. You can upload, but it does take a significant amount of work that exceeds the scope of this book.

Instead, we recommend using blogging software to manage the posting of your content after your file is uploaded to the server. In WordPress, this is easily done with a plug-in called PodPress. For more detailed information about PodPress, be sure to pick up a copy of *Expert Podcasting Practices For Dummies,* by Tee Morris, Evo Terra, and Ryan Williams.

Both Cyberduck and FileZilla support *drag-and-drop* file transfers. If you're new to FTP, the FTP program interface may be easier for you to use.

For Cyberduck, follow these steps:

1. **Choose File⇨Upload.**

2. **Browse your system to find the podcast media file you want to upload.**

3. **Click the Upload button.**

For FileZilla, here's what you do:

1. **Navigate to the desired folder using the Local Site window on the left.**

2. **Select one or more files and/or folders from the window directly below.**

3. **Drag the selected files to the Remote Site window on the left.**

Depending on the size of your file and the speed of your Internet connection, the file may transfer in a matter of seconds or a matter of minutes. When completed, the file appears in your FTP client and is ready to be linked in your show notes and RSS 2.0 feed, as we discuss in Chapters 11 and 12.

Uploading with Command-Line FTP (Speaking of Old School . . .)

Earlier in this chapter, we talk about FTP clients that handle the uploading process for your podcast media files. Each option requires you to either download some specialty software or make a selection of a hosting company that offers HTTP transfers. But there's another way. . . .

Each PC and Mac has a built-in FTP program, but the programs are neither elegant nor pretty, and they're the antithesis of simplicity at first glance. But these built-in tools are handy to know about, especially if you can't install new programs (library or shared-school computers may have this restriction) and/or your hosting provider doesn't provide a Web-based HTTP transfer option.

We talk about command-line FTP in this section, and it comes with none of the conveniences and assurances of the other options we covered earlier in this chapter. But it's a sure-fire way to get your files uploaded no matter where you are. (Almost.)

Before you get into the program itself, you need to move the podcast media file to a staging area on your desktop. Follow these steps:

1. **Create a new folder on your desktop.**

   We recommend naming your folder something like *media* or *media staging.*

2. **Move your podcast media files to this folder.**

   Drag and drop the files from a new Finder window, My Documents, or wherever you may have them stored.

Accessing Terminal on a Mac

If you're a Mac user, follow these steps to use Terminal to access the podcast files you want to upload:

1. **From Applications, open the Utilities folder and activate Terminal.**

   A small window appears, reminiscent of old-time computers where unstyled black text appeared on a white background, or vice versa. Your graphical interface is gone, and you might as well move the mouse out of your way for a bit; you won't be using it.

2. **Type** cd Desktop/media **at the flashing cursor prompt.**

   Your local directory changes to the media file staging area that contains the podcast files you're about to upload.

   Be sure to substitute the name of your folder if you've named it something else beside *media.*

Jump ahead to the section "Uploading your files" to find out how to finish the uploading process.

Accessing the command prompt on a PC

If you're a PC user, follow these steps to use the command prompt to access your podcast files:

1. **Choose Start⇨Run, type** cmd, **and click OK.**

   A small window appears, reminiscent of old-time computers where unstyled white text appeared on a black background, or vice versa. Your graphical interface is gone, and you might as well get your hand off the mouse for a bit; you won't be using it.

2. **Type** cd Desktop\media **at the flashing cursor prompt.**

   Your local directory changes to the media file staging area that contains the podcast files you're about to upload.

   Be sure to substitute the name of your folder if you've named it something else beside *media.*

   Be sure to use the backwards slash (\) located above the Enter key on most keyboards. Using a forward slash (/) doesn't work on a PC.

Now you're ready to upload your files as described in the following section.

Uploading your files

After you access the podcast files you want to load (see the two preceding sections), the uploading process is the same on a Mac or a PC. (Bet you never thought you'd see that happen, huh?)

Follow these steps to upload your files:

1. **Type** ftp *my_domain_name* **and press Enter.**

   For example, we typed **ftp ftp.chuckchat.com** and then pressed Enter.

   A variety of text appears in this window, followed by a prompt to enter your name.

2. **Type your username and press Enter.**

   If your username is accepted, you get some positively reaffirming text followed by another prompt.

3. **Type your password and press Enter.**

   If you've typed your password correctly, several more lines of text describing the server appears, followed by a new prompt. You're now connected to (and controlling) the remote server.

4. **Type** cd www **and press Enter.**

   That step takes you to the root directory where your files are accessible to Web browsers and podcatching clients. Depending on your server configuration, it may be public_html or simply html. If you try changing to a directory that doesn't exist, you get an error message indicating as much. You may need to check with your ISP if neither of these works for your situation.

5. **Create a media folder for your podcast media files. Type** mkdir media **at the prompt, press Enter, and then type** cd media **and press Enter to move to that folder.**

   You've just created a connection between your local media folder and your remote media folder.

6. **Type** bin **to ensure the files are transferred accurately as binary files.**

   This is a safety step. To the FTP protocol, there are two types of files: ASCII (or text) and binary. Some command-line FTP programs default to ASCII, which does a translation on certain characters. Because your MP3 file is not a text file, you want to ensure the contents are transferred exactly byte-for-byte.

7. **Type** put *my_podcast_file*.mp3 **at the prompt.**

   Replace *my_podcast_file* with the name of your file.

   Type the name exactly as it appears, with proper capitalization, because case is important. If you want feedback that your file is transferring, type **hash** (before the put command) to see hash marks (#) print as the file copies. For large files, it can be a bit discomforting to just see a blinking cursor for several minutes. When the file is done transferring, you see a status message stating "File Successfully Transferred" and some statistics about how much data and how long it took, and you are pleasantly returned to the FTP command prompt.

That's it! If you've done things properly, you've now placed your podcast media files on the server and are ready to create your show notes and/or create your RSS 2.0 file. You can exit the command line by typing **quit**, **exit**, or **close**, depending on the application.

Uploading to a Podcast-Specific Host

Podcast-specific hosting companies significantly simplify the uploading process; many include Web-based forms that take the place of additional computer programs to handle the uploading process. They also take care of archiving, RSS 2.0 creation, and even ID3 tagging.

Although this Web-based uploading process is simple, we prefer the flexibility of using an FTP client — or better yet a command line interface. Or maybe we're old school. . . .

For the purposes of illustration, we use an account with Liberated Syndication (`http://libsyn.com`) in this section. If you haven't already, you need to sign up with LibSyn and create your own account. Then follow these steps:

1. **Begin at LibSyn's home page. Enter your username and password and press the Login button.**

2. **Click the Settings tab to access your blog and podcast settings.**

3. **Enter the information for your blog and/or podcast. When you finish, click the Save Changes button.**

   The blog settings are very simple; things like the name of your blog, your e-mail address, and what category you want it placed in. Nothing here is mission critical, so fill it out however you want to see it listed. You can always come back and change it later.

4. **Click the Media Files tab.**

   If you've never uploaded any media files, no media files are listed.

5. **Click the bright green button labeled Upload a File.**

   You're taken to the upload page, as shown in Figure 10-3.

6. **Click the Browse button.**

   The File Upload dialog box opens.

   Note: *HTTP upload* is another name for form-based transfers.

7. **Find the podcast media file you want to upload and either double-click the file or select it and click Open.**

8. **Click the Load File button.**

   Depending on the size of your file and the speed of your Internet connection, the page may refresh in a matter of seconds or a few minutes. After completion, the screen refreshes, and your podcast media file displays. Note also that the text box under Advanced Users contains a string of RSS 2.0 code. Remember this Web page and text box because we revisit it in Chapters 11 and 12.

Figure 10-3:
Adding
media files
to a LibSyn
account
doesn't
require an
FTP client.

LibSyn offers an FTP interface if you prefer to use an FTP client or command line interface. Your login and password are the same as through the Web interface.

If you like to try it before you buy it, LibSyn lets you log in to a demo account, move files around, and generally get a feel for how it works before you sign up. Not that the very inexpensive monthly fees will break you or anything, but it's nice to know how your future home might work.

Chapter 11

Providing Show Notes

Show notes are brief summaries of each podcast episode. Show notes can take the form of an outline, a bulleted list, or just a few sentences of text. In this chapter, we show you how to effectively use show notes to enhance the listener experience of your show and bring in additional traffic to your podcast through search engines.

And where do you find these show notes? Simply enough, on the podcast's Web site.

Getting additional traffic means additional bandwidth consumption, which can cause issues. Flip to Chapter 10 for tips on ways to reduce the load on your servers and for info about optional hosting plans that don't charge for additional bandwidth.

Show Note Etiquette

Several schools of thought exist on how to approach show notes. Some say you should be very brief, using notes only to hold URLs and other pieces of important offline data that your listeners may not have had time to write down as the show was playing. Others suggest show notes should be filled with information on each and every concept touched upon in the show. We prefer a more moderate approach, and your personal tastes and style go a long way in determining what is right for you.

Regardless of the length of your prose and the level of detail you want to explain, you need to follow some basic rules of etiquette:

- ✔ **Use intriguing and informative titles.** In general, and to keep things simple, the title of your show notes should match your episode title. Your title is your pitch; you're a huckster competing for the attention of listeners. Some listeners may know all about you; others could be seeing something from you for the first time. Include keywords in your title that accurately and specifically represent the contents of this episode. Your keywords should also generate some excitement and make the episode sound interesting and intriguing to potential listeners.

- ✔ **Include links to all the locations mentioned in the podcast.** If you're talking about a trip to the local museum, provide a link to the museum's Web site in your show notes. If you mention another podcast, link to it. Good linking brings good karma, and it may provide some interesting and potentially helpful "Hey, you linked to me!" comments (and back-links) from others.

- ✔ **Concise or complete?** Show notes can be as simple as a bullet list of topics or as detailed as a word-for-word transcript of your show. It's up to you. The advantage to the bullet list is that it's quicker to put together, obviously. If you're already scripting your podcast, it's no extra trouble to post the script, but be aware of the length. A transcript for a 3-minute show is pretty easy for someone to read from their browser; however a 45-minute transcript — yes, there are 45-minute shows that are completely scripted — may be something you don't want the reader to go through.

Figure 11-1 displays how Phil Clark and Mike (Lingo) Lingafelter of *The Brit and Yankee Pubcast* (`http://thebritandyankee.com`) use show notes. The notes include plenty of backlinks, time marks, and a brief discussion about the topics covered. A thing of beauty, to be sure.

When we think of show note etiquette, we're reminded of a commercial that aired years ago for a small car company. The premise was "if everyone drove one of our tiny cars, traffic congestion would vanish, the demand for fossil fuels would drop, and the world would be a generally nicer place." We're convinced that if every podcaster followed the preceding three simple show note guidelines, the podcasting world would be a better place. The impact on traffic jams and oil consumption remains questionable, but one can dream. . . .

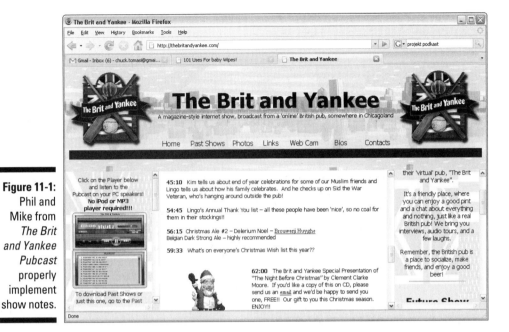

Figure 11-1:
Phil and
Mike from
*The Brit
and Yankee
Pubcast*
properly
implement
show notes.

Planning the Post

The amount of time you spend planning your show notes is inversely proportional to the amount of time you spend during your show prep (see Chapter 4). If you forgot everything from your high school Algebra II class, allow us to paraphrase: The more you prepare for your show, the less time you spend working on the show notes — and vice versa.

Examine the notes you used when you recorded your podcast. Did you talk about any Web sites? Find the URLs and make sure you spell them right. We highly recommend the copy-and-paste technique for URLs, rather than relying on your typing skills, especially for lengthy URLs.

If you recorded and/or edited your show hours or days before you started this notation process, replaying the media file with pen and paper at the ready is a good idea. Look for need-to-know moments and jot them down as the show plays. After it finishes, use a search engine to find additional, relevant URLs you may want to provide to your listeners.

The following sections help you create powerful show notes that benefit you, the listener, and potential listeners.

It's all in the details

Now is a good time to figure out what level of detail you're going to employ in your show notes. Several factors can influence your decision, and audience expectation and personal choice are among the more important.

Here's a good rule: The deeper you dive in to a single topic, the less detailed your notes need to be. That may sound counterintuitive, and please keep in mind this is only a general rule and not a law. For example, if your podcast episode features a 20-minute interview with Theoretical Physicist Dr. Michio Kaku on his book *Physics of the Impossible* and how applicable those ideas are to the Star Wars Universe, you likely won't have much more than a link to buy the book and/or rent the movie.

Show note details serve several primary purposes:

✔ To act as a table of contents for the episode

✔ To allow listeners to skip ahead if they so choose

As the podcaster, you can decide how much or how little you embrace these purposes. Here are some approaches that other podcasters have adopted:

✔ **Add a time stamp.** Some podcasters put the exact time stamp of when they change topics, which is quite frequently. Time stamps can be quite helpful to your listeners if you cover a wide range of topics in a given episode and want to assist possible listeners in jumping around.

✔ **Write in complete sentences and paragraphs.** Taking cues from the world of blogging, many podcasters follow a similar approach to Kris Smith of *The Croncast* (http://croncast.com). Kris writes his show notes in prose, using complete sentences and paragraphs in place of bullet points and time stamps. This approach feels better to potential readers, giving them a flavor of the show without having to listen. However, we've also heard listeners complain that key elements are difficult to find in this format.

✔ **Create more than a one-line summary.** Some podcasters, such as Dave Winer (http://morningcoffeenotes.com) take the opposite approach and post a simple one-liner that isn't much more than a title. We suggest new podcasters not follow his lead because it doesn't do much for helping attract new listeners. Dave is a seminal figure in the world of podcasting and gets most of his listeners because he's Dave Winer, not because he posts great show notes.

Detailed show notes are also useful for attracting new listeners. Show notes improve your search engine rankings, and they enable Web surfers to determine the value of an episode before listening. For his *Gmail Podcast*, Chuck started with a synopsis of each show (for example, "Learn how to be more effective using labels"). After seeing little increase in listenership for 18 months, he started including the full transcript to the 5 minute show, and listenership doubled — that's how powerful show notes can be.

A picture is worth a thousand words

Some podcasters include a representative image or two in their show notes. Although random graphics serve only to increase your bandwidth consumption and clutter your page, well-selected images can add flavor and dimension to your show notes. In some cases, these are the same images used as album art in the episode files.

Before you add an image to your post, keep in mind these three considerations:

- ✔ **Is the image protected by copyright?** Posting someone else's creative work without first securing permission (which may include royalties and fees) is stealing, pure and simple, and can land even the most well-meaning podcaster in a heap of legal trouble.

- ✔ **Can you link directly to the image, or do you need to copy it to your server?** Some sites, such as Amazon.com, allow you to link directly to images as they sit on the Web site. These sites have a huge technology infrastructure and can handle remote hosting images that appear on other sites. But many smaller and personal sites can't handle the load a popular podcast can put on their systems if they allowed direct linking to their stored images. In these cases, copy the image to your own server before adding it to your page. If you're going to do this, it's good karma to provide an "image courtesy of . . ." link to the original site. Again, this assumes you've received the appropriate permissions to copy the file. When in doubt, don't.

- ✔ **Does the image fit on your page?** Images too small or too large aren't doing your listeners any favors. Make sure the image you select is the right size. You can add `width="x" height="x"` declarations to your image tags to control the size, but keep in mind that this distorts the image. Previewing your post with resized images is a must. If your HTML is a little rusty, check out *HTML 4 For Dummies,* by Ed Tittel and Mary Burmeister (Wiley Publishing, Inc.), for additional help.

We can't stress enough how important it is that you not take, post, modify, or use any image without the express permission of the copyright owners. The act of someone posting an image to a Web site does not give you carte blanche to use it as you see fit. When in doubt, leave it out.

Posting Your Show Notes

If you've planned and prepared, posting your show notes is easy. And if you've decided for the minimalist approach or don't really care to use show notes, this process can go quickly as well because there's nothing to do.

In this section, we show you how to enter your show notes by using WordPress and Libsyn as examples. If you use another tool to make your posts, or if you create your notes by hand, you still get value out of these examples as we show you things to consider along the way.

Posting in WordPress

WordPress is free, easy-to-use blogging software that also works well for podcasters. Follow these steps to post show notes in WordPress (`www.wordpress.org`):

1. **Log in to your Web site's site administration page.**

   By default, you typically can find a Login link on WordPress pages. If you've already provided credentials, the link may say Site Admin. In most instances, the URL looks something like: `www.your_domain_here.com/wp-admin`

2. **Click Write from the menu along the top to start a new posting.**

   A new posting page opens. Here's where you fill in the details of your new posting. Although this screen displays a lot of items, you don't need to use them all to get started.

3. **Select the appropriate category for your podcast from the Categories section.**

   Though not critical, categories help keep things more organized. It's not uncommon to have one category for text/blog entries and another for podcasts.

4. **Enter the title of your podcast in the Title text box.**

   Label your show with a short descriptive tag, *Classic Car Auction,* for example. For more titling help, see the "Loading up your titles" section, later in this chapter. To make the reader's life easier, we recommend using the same title on your show and your show notes.

5. In the large text area below, type your show notes.

Follow a chronological order and list the various topics covered in your show, one on each line.

6. Be sure to add URLs to any Web sites you mention.

To create a link, highlight the text you want to link and then click the Link button. Copy and paste the full URL — including the `http://` part — you want to link to in the pop-up box (see Figure 11-2). Click OK.

Figure 11-2:
Enter a URL to create a hyperlink to a podcast media file.

7. Create a link to your podcast file.

Enter text like **Listen Now** or **Download MP3**. Just as you create a link to a URL in Step 6, you can add a link to your podcast file. If the file is on your server, use the pathname on your server. If your file in on another server, use the entire URL — for example, `http://servername/path_to_myfile.mp3`.

8. When you're done entering your show notes, click the Save button.

You can see a preview of your posting by clicking the Preview button — it's not a bad idea to verify the format and ensure links will work before releasing it to the public.

9. Scroll down to preview your post.

Make sure the links work properly — including your podcast file. Few things are more embarrassing than releasing that long-awaited podcast only to find that a link in your show notes doesn't work. When you're just starting out, you likely won't have a lot of people letting you know of technical issues. It's up to you to test as much as you can before releasing a new podcast.

10. Make any adjustments necessary.

If you notice links that don't work or typos, you still have an opportunity to fix them by scrolling back up, making the edits, saving your work, and repeating Step 9 until you're satisfied.

11. When you're satisfied with your show notes, click Publish.

The system takes care of generating the RSS 2.0 feed. We discuss RSS in more detail in Chapter 12.

12. Click View Site link at the top of the page to see how your entry looks.

Visiting your Web page is a good idea to make sure everything looks as you expected it to. If it doesn't, simply edit the post and resave your changes.

We've only scratched the surface of what WordPress can do. If you really want to take advantage of the software, we suggest *WordPress For Dummies,* by Lisa Sabin-Wilson. You can also listen to *The WordPress Podcast* with Charles Stricklin to keep up on plug-ins, software changes, and security updates.

Many podcasters with detailed show notes use the `<More>` tag in their WordPress postings, as shown in Figure 11-3. Any text above the More link is displayed on the main page. Those with interest to view the detailed content can click the link. If you have lots of show notes to include in your post, this is a good way to keep your front page tidy with a few bullet items for each show, and then you can "hide" the longer list.

In the next chapter, you find out about creating the RSS 2.0 feed so that people can subscribe to your podcast. Assuming you've installed the PodPress plug-in, WordPress makes RSS feeds easy. Don't worry about it for now because we cover it in detail in Chapter 12.

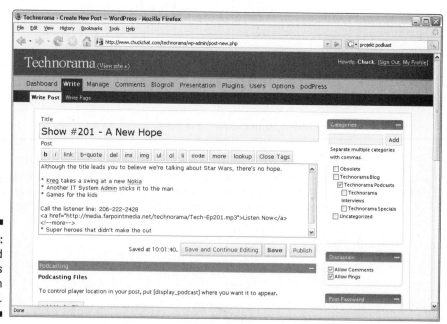

Figure 11-3:
A completed WordPress screen with show notes.

Posting on LibSyn

Because LibSyn (`www.libsyn.com`) is a dedicated podcast hosting provider, the steps are quite intuitive and a bit different than those used by folks who work with blogging software.

Follow these steps to post your show notes on LibSyn:

1. **To create a new post, click the Publish tab or the link of the same name from the main page.**

2. **Click the New Post option button.**

   LibSyn also allows text-only posts to the site, which is great for times when you want to post some text without a media file, such as to say "I'm on vacation for the next two weeks."

3. **Enter a title for this episode.**

   We cover some titling tips later in this section. For now, simply enter a basic description of what this episode is about — "Classic Car Auction" for example.

4. **Choose a category for your podcast from the Category drop-down list.**

   Categories on LibSyn work like they do with most blogging applications. To keep this simple, choose Podcast from the list.

5. **Skip the Post Image drop-down list for now.**

   Yes, you can put something in there if you must. But it's not required. See our earlier comments on using images in this chapter if you decide you can't live without one (but you probably could).

6. **Enter the detailed show notes in the Show Notes text box.**

   This is the appropriate place for your detailed show notes. Follow a chronological order and list the various topics covered in your show, one on each line. Be sure to add URLs to any Web sites you mention.

Typing the URL in this section isn't quite as effective as providing a true hyperlink. Making a hyperlink isn't difficult, though it may look that way if you aren't familiar with the mysteries of HTML.

Hyperlinks follow this convention:

```
<a href="link/to/website/or/web/page">Name of link</a>
```

Basically, you fill out what's between the quotes, replace the name of the link, and you're done. Here are a few real-world examples:

```
<a href="http://www.chuckchat.com/gmail">Gmail Podcast</a>
<a href="http://morevi.net">Morevi podcast</a>
<a href="http://marsrovers.nasa.gov/gallery/images.html">Pictures from
        Mars</a>
```

7. Chose your podcast media file from the drop-down list.

If you haven't uploaded the show yet, LibSyn makes it easy. Simply click the Browse button and navigate to the appropriate file in your media folder (which we show how to set up in Chapter 10).

Because LibSyn doesn't allow you to preview your post first, we highly recommend checking your spelling and double-checking your links before you proceed. An ounce of prevention and all that.

Figure 11-4 shows how your post looks on LibSyn before it is posted.

8. Click the Publish button.

LibSyn makes it hard to screw up, requiring you to fill out the appropriate fields before allowing you to continue. If you're successful, you see a green check box next to your new post.

9. Check your page.

Click the link to your show name and see how it looks in the real world. Check your links, spelling, and layout. If it's not the way you want, close the window and click the name of your post to edit it.

It never hurts to mention that you have show notes. You can do so as part of the running dialog — for example, ". . . We found a great deal on those at Frobozco. We'll have a link in the show notes on our Web site . . ." or mention it at the end of the show with contact information, as in "Don't forget to stop by our Web site, where you'll find links to everything we mentioned in the show notes, information on how to contact us, and much more at www. . . ."

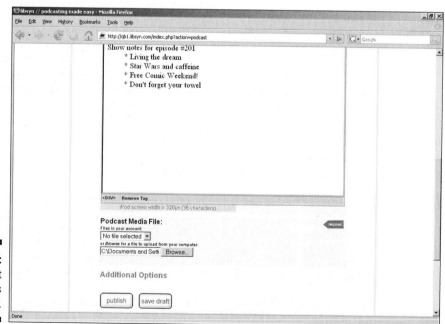

Figure 11-4:
Filling out show notes on LibSyn.

Using a wiki for your show notes

A *wiki* is a Web site that allows your listeners to contribute to your show notes. This may sound rather scary — "let others modify MY Web site? Are you crazy?" Before you dismiss the idea, consider sites like Wikipedia (`www.wikipedia.org`), one of the foremost reference sites built entirely by volunteer public efforts. Now imagine the power of your listener community helping you build and maintain your show notes.

One method of using the wiki is to post a framework, or bullet list for your show notes, and let the users contribute. Another way is to just start writing and let the user community come along and do the clean up.

Note that wikis won't work for every podcast. It takes a certain level of listener loyalty — something the podosphere has no shortage of.

You can employ a wiki in two basic ways: Build one yourself or use a wiki someone else has built. We discuss each way in this section.

Using MediaWiki

MediaWiki (`www.mediawiki.org`) is the software that runs the popular Wikipedia. The software is freely available to anyone who wants to set up a wiki. It does require you to maintain a database with your Web hosting provider. Check the Web site to install the software.

Installing MediaWiki is similar to installing WordPress in that it requires you to have a Web host that allows you to upload and install software and access to a MySQL database.

When it's installed, you can create pages specifically for show notes. MediaWiki does use special formatting characters to create links, bulleted lists, numbered lists, and more; however, using the wiki formatting characters is simpler than trying to teach yourself HTML. An example of your show notes in a MediaWiki page might look something like this:

```
=Show 15: HP Laptops and me=
* Introduction
* The week in review
* [http://www.microsoft.com Software troubles]
```

In this example, the line flanked with one or more equal signs (=) indicates a section heading. The more equal signs, the further the indent. The lines starting with asterisks (*) are a bulleted list. The last line enclosed with the single square brackets ([ ]) is a link to another site, everything after the site is the text displayed. In this example, the Web browser displays a link that says Software troubles, which takes users to the Microsoft home page.

The following steps show you how to create a new page of show notes. We assume the top level page is at `http://www.mysite.com/wiki`.

1. **Click the Log In/Create Account link in the upper-right corner.**

2. **Log in to your wiki with your username and password.**

   Assuming you set up the wiki, you already have an account. New visitors have to use the link Create an Account.

3. **Click the Edit tab.**

   The page will change to "edit mode" allowing you to enter text in a large text area.

4. **Create a page link.**

   Enter the formatting code [[*Some Text*]], where *Some Text* is the name of your page. For example, [[**April 30, 2008**]].

5. **Click the Save Page button.**

   MediaWiki goes back to browse mode. You now see a link with the text of your new page link. Note that the link is in red, which means there's no actual page for this link — yet.

6. **Click the newly created link.**

   You're taken to the same page editor as before, but there's no content. This is where you enter your show notes using the formatting codes for headers, bullet lists, and so on.

7. **Click the Save Page button.**

   Congratulations! You've created your first set of show notes using MediaWiki.

In very little time, you can create fairly extensive show notes and then link to them from your blog post. Other listeners can them come along (and set up accounts if necessary) and make changes.

You can use the wiki for more than show notes. You can create almost any Web content to support your show from listener show suggestions to results to a contest — there's practically no limit to the ideas.

Most wikis feature revision control — meaning you can roll-back changes in the event something goes wrong. With multiple people editing the same information, it happens from time to time.

Using Wetpaint

If you don't have the ability to install software on your hosting server (which MediaWiki requires), or setting up your own wiki just isn't your thing, you can still take advantage of a wiki's features with a site like Wetpaint (www. wetpaint.com).

Wetpaint is a free site to manage wikis. Begin by going to the site and creating a login ID. You can create a personalized wiki and give it your own hostname — for example, http://technorama.wetpaint.com.

Spend the time to watch the video that takes you on a demo to get a tutorial of the system.

Updating your wiki is as simple as running a word processor. Just click the Easy Edit button at the top of any page. The graphical toolbar makes it easy to create headings, bulleted lists, and even insert widgets like an RSS feed so visitors to your wiki know your recent postings to your Web page. And the best part for you is that no HTML is required!

Figure 11-5 shows what your show notes look like in Wetpaint.

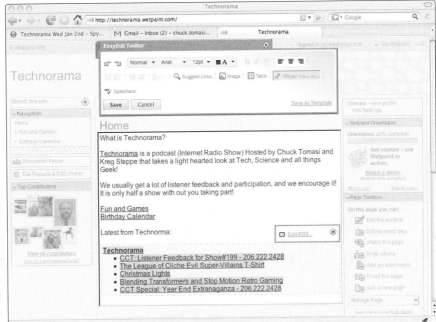

Figure 11-5:
Wetpaint makes maintaining a wiki for your show notes very simple.

Boosting Search Engine Rankings with Good Show Notes

One tangible benefit of quality show notes is the impact they can have on your listings within search engines. Traditional search engines cannot (yet) scan and index the contents of your podcast media files. As such, you need to provide text for the search engine spiders and bots to examine and evaluate for index inclusion.

We go into more detail about spiders and bots in Chapter 13. For now, you just need to know that they are tools that search engines use to find interesting information when people search for a particular topic.

Podcasters can pick up a lot of tips and tricks from bloggers and other Web site owners on how to boost search engine rankings. Many include page-level changes to positioning of elements, correct usage of headings, meta and image tags, and back-linking techniques. All of that conversation is far beyond the scope of this book. Grab a copy of *Search Engine Optimization For Dummies* by Peter Kent (published by Wiley) and break out your code editor if you want to make a bigger splash.

In the following sections, we show you some best practices you can implement right away that can make your notes (and podcast) more accessible to search engines — and ultimately search engine users.

Loading up your titles

Search engines (and searchers) pay close attention to titles. You should consider the title of your individual podcast episodes every bit as important as the title of a given Web page.

Important as they are, most podcasters struggle with effective titles. The biggest problem comes from confusing titles with descriptions. If your title starts with "In this episode," stop right there. You're writing the description, not the title. A title is a string of well-chosen and crafted words that has no room for superfluous baggage.

We find that the best titles come from a re-examination of your show notes. If you haven't made your notes yet, you may find coming up with a solid title quite tough. Here's the process we suggest:

1. **Read your show notes and pull out the key elements, thoughts, or themes covered on the show.**

   For example, for the Classic Car Auction we've been using throughout this chapter, we've come up with the following completely made-up topics and themes from an imaginary show:

   - Sleeping in the Seattle airport while the flight was delayed

   - Interesting discussion during the flight with an 80-year-old man who is a car restorer

   - Under the hood of the 1965 Ford Mustang

   - Custom headers and exhaust systems

   - A short interview with the owner of a 1972 Chevy Nova

- Taking a 1957 Chevy Belair for a cruise
- Listener feedback request: What's your favorite classic car

2. **Boil down each element to a single word or phrase, if possible.**

Think about the people who might be interested in the contents of your show and pick common words they're likely to search for.

For example, if you're a comedian, the airport delay and the old man on the plane might be good places to start. If this is a more serious car show, the experience with the '65 Mustang and the Belair might be a good place to start.

If your show is a relatively serious collector/restoration show, you're trying to entertain and attract like-minded listeners. Getting rid of the fluff is a good idea. You can select the key points and condense them to the following:

"Experienced restorer, a peek at a Mustang, and driving a true classic."

That's a solid title, giving searchers a good tease about what they can expect.

Notice how the title doesn't cover everything, and it shouldn't try. That's the job of the description where you can go into even greater detail on those three elements, plus the many other things you talk about on the show.

The title also carries good keywords likely to be of interest to car buffs or admirers considering a purchase, looking to get in to restoration, and those who may already own a classic.

Chances are good that you know your audience much better than we do. Think about how people are likely to search and write your titles for that. Keep them short, don't try to cover everything, and employ more detailed descriptions to carry the rest of your story.

Soliciting backlinks

Backlinks are the Holy Grail of search engine optimization. A *backlink* is simply a link from someone else's Web site to yours — whereas a regular link is from your site to another. Sites that have a lot of backlinks pointing to them are considered "more important" to the computers that control where your site shows up on a search engine. To get backlinks from others, you have to create links to their Web sites in your show notes.

When you're soliciting backlinks from sources, make each e-mail personal, provide the exact link you want them to use, and tell them why you think it's important for them to link it.

In the highly suspect classic car auction we've been using as an example, you could link to several things, and you really should link to a few things. For example, you could provide a link to the airline that messed up the flight, but what's the point? On the other hand, you most certainly want to create a link to a place to buy or read more about sources of parts, and you likely would want to link to the auction site.

Before you post the show, it may be a good idea to contact other podcasters, bloggers, and perhaps notable Web sites to see whether they're interested in linking to you (and you to them) to generate interest in your podcast, rather than a specific show. Many sites have a section somewhere for related sites. This can be a very effective tool for drawing people to your site and your podcast. Then you can also find folks who might want to backlink to particular episodes.

So, you've posted your show and got your show notes online. It's time to start soliciting backlinks to individual episodes:

- **Company backlinks:** Write to the company who manufactures the custom headers to tell them you're posting a review of one of their products. Getting big companies to link to you doesn't always happen, but sometimes it does. And getting backlinks from big popular sites is very beneficial to your rankings.

- **Courtesy backlinks:** If someone helped you with a part of your podcast and you mention it in your episode, let that source know. Send an e-mail to the agency you booked the trip with and maybe even the hotel.

- **Backlinks from fellow podcasters:** If other podcasters cover topics related to your episode, let them know about it because they might be willing to spare you a backlink. Notify various car bloggers and podcasters about the new episode. It takes only a few moments of your time and is information they would or should welcome.

A fine line exists between asking for backlinks and spamming someone. If you can't think of a good reason why that site should link to you, then you don't ask for it; otherwise, just mention what your show is and what you've covered that might be of interest and let them decide whether they want to provide a backlink.

Chapter 12

Geeking Out on RSS

- -

In This Chapter

▶ Understanding RSS

▶ Creating good introductions

▶ Handling multi-format podcasts

- -

*Y*ou've entered the dark and murky waters of the RSS generation — a region of the podcasting sea that strikes fear into the hearts of the uninitiated, causes mild-mannered podcasting preachers to break out into curse words that would make a sailor blush, and has soured more than one would be independent media producer on the whole prospect of podcasting.

Relax. For the most part, the trials and tribulations you might have heard others had to go through are overblown. If it were as hard as some have made it out to be, there wouldn't be as many podcasts as there are available today. The RSS step wasn't designed to be complicated; it's just quirky, and it's been tainted by the experiences of a few who jumped in a little too fast, without a trusty guide to show them the path.

This chapter shines a big bright spotlight on RSS elements, showing you that they aren't as mean and scary as they've been made out to be. After reading this chapter, you'll have a solid strategy for generating your podcast's RSS 2.0 file, some options for dealing with multiple media files, and the confidence to tweak your RSS file as you see fit.

You're probably asking yourself: "Do I need to know all that"? Well, yes and no. Granted, you'll likely be using blogging software or some podcast-hosting company that takes care of the RSS 2.0 feed for you. It's still a good idea to know what goes on under the hood, in our opinion.

Elements That Make the RSS Go 'Round

The main function of your RSS 2.0 file is to distribute your media files to people who have subscribed to your podcast. RSS is nothing more than

Getting a handle on TLAs (three-letter acronyms)

XML stands for eXtensible Markup Language. "Markup" is a lot like what your teacher used to do to your homework, only more useful: "marking up" a text file with some special tags that control how the text is used by various applications, like a podcatching client. This is good news if you're without an advanced degree in computer science: It's text (in this case, English or something a lot like it) that tells other text how to present itself.

"Extensible" means developers can add other tags beyond the original "set" that was designed for XML. In other words, a developer can add to the *code base* of XML, adapting it to individual needs. Okay, feel free to forget that if you want — you won't have to worry about creating new tags, thanks to RSS 2.0.

RSS is a *flavor* (modified version) of XML, and it stands for *Really Simple Syndication*. (*Syndication* is the process of getting the goods — whether a Web site update, news bulletin, or podcast — to the intended audience.) Lucky for us podcasters, XML was extended to RSS, which was further extended to create RSS 2.0. And inside RSS 2.0 is where you find the appropriate tags and elements that make podcasts work.

You'll hear podcasters use the terms *XML* and *RSS* interchangeably. Sometimes people say the version number (2.0) out loud and in print, other times it's simply implied. There's at least one other version of XML that works with podcasting: Atom. No, it's not a TLA, because it has four letters and it doesn't stand for anything, but it is a version of XML. The differences between Atom and RSS 2.0 are beyond the scope of this book. The good news is that most podcatching clients read either Atom or RSS 2.0 files. In fact, advanced RSS 2.0 feeds often incorporate Atom elements, further blurring the differences between the two formats. To minimize headaches, this chapter focuses on RSS 2.0 as the preferred method of syndicating your podcast to podcatching clients. And yes, iTunes fans, we do cover the extra tags your podcatcher of choice has made us all deal with.

If you want an even deeper dive into the world of RSS syndication — because you can do some *really* cool stuff with it — we highly recommend Ellen Finkelstein's *Syndicating Web Sites with RSS Feeds For Dummies* (Wiley Publishing, Inc.).

"marked up" text with special tags. (For more about the technical aspects of RSS, check out the nearby sidebar.) Here's a sample RSS 2.0 feed:

```
<?xml version="1.0"?>
<rss xmlns:content="http://purl.org/rss/1.0/modules/content/"
            xmlns:itunes="http://www.itunes.com/DTDs/Podcast-1.0.dtd"
            version="2.0">
<channel>
  <title>The Car Collector Podcast</title>
  <link>http://www.mypodcast.com/</link>
  <description>The best podcast on the planet. Period. With your host, me!</
            description>
  <webMaster>chuck@mypodcast.com</webMaster>
```

```
<managingEditor>chuck@mypodcast.com (Chuck Tomasi)</managingEditor>
<pubDate>Sat, 31 May 2008 12:02:28 -0800</pubDate>
<category>Automotive</category>
  <image>
    <url>http://mypodcast.com/images/logos/ccp100x86.jpg</url>
    <width>100</width>
    <height>86</height>
    <title>The Car Collector Podcast</title>
    <link>http://mypodcast.com</link>
  </image>
  <copyright>Creative Commons Attribution 2.5 License</copyright>
<language>en-us</language>
<docs>http://blogs.law.harvard.edu/tech/rss</docs>


<!-- iTunes specific namespace channel elements -->
<itunes:subtitle>The best podcast on the planet. Period. With your host, me!</
            itunes:subtitle>
<itunes:summary>This podcast blows the doors off all other automotive
            podcasts. Listen to this and leave the others in the dust.</
            itunes:summary>
<itunes:owner>
  <itunes:email>chuck@mypodcast.com</itunes:email>
  <itunes:name>Chuck Tomasi </itunes:name>
</itunes:owner>
<itunes:author>Chuck Tomasi</itunes:author>
<itunes:category text="Games & Hobbies:Automotive">
    <itunes:category text="Automotive" />
</itunes:category>
<itunes:category text="Society & Culture:History" />
<itunes:link rel="image" type="video/jpeg" href="http://mypodcast.com/images/
            logos/tDPWI300x300.jpg">The Car Collector Podcast</itunes:link>
<itunes:explicit>no</itunes:explicit>

  <item>
  <title>TCCP 013 - Experienced restorer, a peek at a Mustang, and driving a
            true classic.</title>
  <link>http://www.mypodcast.com/tccp.html</link>
  <comments>http://www.mypodcast.com/tgop13.html#comments</comments>
  <description>Synopsis: Steel Headers are the people who made this trip
            possible. I appreciate it and can't recommend them enough. Take
            off with me to LA California for the fifth annual Classic Car
            Auction. A little trouble with the travel, a great discussion
            on the flight with a man who has been restoring classic cars
            for decades, a look under the hood of a 65 Mustang, and you
            get to join me for the experience of a lifetime - driving a 57
            Chevy Belair. Download The Car Collector Podcast Episode #13</
            description>
  <guid isPermaLink="false">1808@http://www.mypodcast.com/</guid>
  <pubDate>Sat, 31 May 2008 12:02:28 -0800</pubDate>
  <category>Outdoors</category>
  <author>editor@mypodcast.com</author>
```

```
<enclosure url=" http://mypodcast.com/media/TCCP013_20080531.mp3"
        length="24849394" type="audio/mpeg" />

<!-- RDF 1.0 specific namespace item attribute -->
<content:encoded><![CDATA[<p><strong>Show Notes</strong></p>

<p><a href="http://www.steelheaders.com/">Steel Headers</a> is the company
        that made this trip possible. Can't recommend them highly enough!

<p>Thanks to <a href=http://davewishfieldcars.com> Dave Wishfield</a> from
        San Jose, CA for talking to me about his 1965 Ford Mustang. Listen
        and find out how much he got at the auction! Special thanks to
        Aiden Somerset from Sun Prairie, WI for allowing me the privilege
        to drive the 1957 Chevy Belair. What a ride!</p>

<p>Download <a href="http://mypodcast.com/media/TCCP013_20080531.mp3">The
        Car Collector Podcast Episode #13</a></p>]]></content:encoded>

<!-- iTunes specific namespace item attributes -->
<itunes:author>Chuck Tomasi</itunes:author>
<itunes:subtitle>My recent trip to LA's antique car auction, plus my
        adventures.</itunes:subtitle>
<itunes:summary>Synopsis: Steel Headers is the company that made this trip
        possible. Can't recommend them highly enough. Thanks to Dave
        Wishfield from San Jose, CA for talking to me about his 1965
        Ford Mustang. Listen and find out how much he got at the auction!
        Special thanks to Aiden Somerset from Sun Prairie, WI for allowing
        me the privilege to drive the 1957 Chevy Belair. What a ride!
        Download The Car Collector Podcast Episode #13</itunes:summary>
<itunes:category text="Games & Hobbies:Automotive">
    <itunes:category text="Automotive" />
</itunes:category>
<itunes:category text="Society & Culture:History" />
  <itunes:duration>00:45:00</itunes:duration>
  <itunes:explicit>no</itunes:explicit>
  <itunes:keywords>tomassi,thomasi</itunes:keywords>
  </item>
</channel>
</rss>
```

Okay, that's a lot to digest in a single sitting. The next sections of the book break it down into individual parts to show you how un-scary it really is.

If you're currently using (or planning to use) blog software or your dedicated podcast host to generate your RSS 2.0 feed, it'll take care of just about all this brouhaha for you. It's still a good idea, however, to have a solid grasp of this section in the event you want to make some modifications to your RSS 2.0 feed in the future. (Most podcasters do, sooner or later.)

Well, your software may not be of much help with the iTunes-specific stuff. iTunes burst on the podcasting scene without much (read: ANY) advanced notice. And when it did, it came up with unique tags to extend what RSS 2.0 already provided. Take a good hard look at the tool you're using to generate your RSS feed and see whether there are any iTunes-specific tags. If not, you may have to break out the manual and see how you can add them yourself. In some cases, it's easy — for example, adding the PodPress plug-in to WordPress — and in other cases, it's a bit daunting.

Do you have anything to declare?

All RSS 2.0 documents start with a *declaration statement.* Think of this declaration as working with a "Hello, my name is . . ." badge. This statement identifies the contents of the file, allowing podcatching clients and other XML parsers or readers to know what to expect and how to handle the contents. Some declarations wear their hearts on their sleeves, some are terse, but all RSS 2.0 documents do the initial honors with these first two lines of text:

```
<?xml version="1.0"?>
<rss version="2.0" xmlns:content="http://purl.org/rss/1.0/modules/content/"
          xmlns:itunes="http://www.itunes.com/DTDs/Podcast-1.0.dtd">
```

With those two lines of text, you've declared that the document is written in XML version 1.0 and is of the special flavor RSS 2.0. Additionally, it calls out two specialized *namespaces,* which we get into in a bit. You might want to write those two lines on your forehead backward (metaphorically speaking, of course) so you'll always see 'em in the mirror as a reminder: They are what you use to start every RSS 2.0 file you create as a podcaster.

A *namespace* is denoted by the `xmlns:` statement, followed by the URL of the "home" of the namespace. In the preceding instance, we call the namespaces for the *encoded content* module as well as iTunes tags. Purists will argue that *encoded* content isn't necessary and that even the iTunes tags are optional. But they both go a long way to getting your podcast listened to by the most people.

What's on this <channel>?

An RSS 2.0 document contains a single `<channel>` statement, complete with lots of other information to help describe the channel. A channel can contain multiple `<item>` statements, and each `<item>` can have lots of other information to describe the individual item.

Okay, here's a real-world example to clarify the issue: NBC is a "channel" on your television. Depending on the day of the week and the time of the day, various "items" are made available for viewing. It's not an accident that podcasting works the same way.

In the following sections, we examine the contents of the `<channel>` declaration from the example at the beginning of the chapter. (We cover `<item>` tags in the later section "Loading up on <items>s.")

XML tags are case-sensitive. For example, `<description>` has a different meaning than `<Description>` or `<DESCRIPTION>`. Additionally, the case of the *opening* tag (the one that starts a section) must match the case of the *closing* tag (the one that ends the same section). `<webMaster>` and `</webMaster>` are okay, but `<webmaster>` and `<Webmaster>` are not.

<title> tag

You use the `<title>` tag to hold the title of your channel, that is to say the title of your overall podcast. Here's the title from the example just given:

```
<title>The Car Collector Podcast</title>
```

This line of text says, "Here's what's inside me." It never changes, unless you decide to change the name of your podcast. Don't abbreviate or shorten the name unless you have a very good reason for doing that.

Almost every markup language uses this format of beginning and ending tags encapsulated in angle brackets, < and >. The ending tag uses the same name, but it's preceded by a / character to tell the software that the tag is now closed. In the example just given, you can think of the code as talking to the podcatching client, along these lines: "(The next thing you'll read is the title.) The Car Collector Podcast (That was the end of the title.)"

<link> tag

Here's a good place to put a link that leads back to your Web site or blog. The beauty of RSS and podcasting is that the listeners don't have to be looking at your Web page to listen to your show. This link allows them (through their podcatching clients) an easy way to find your Web site if they so desire:

```
<link>http://www.mypodcast.com/</link>
```

<description> tag

Your description, much like your title, will rarely (if ever) change. Find a good description for what your shows are about. The following example is pretty poor (just kidding, okay?), so try to put in some words that truly identify what your podcast is about:

```
<description>The best podcast on the planet. Period. With your host, me!</
            description>
```

Technically, the RSS 2.0 specifications allow you to place images, links, and even text formatting inside the <description> tag. However, there's some question as to how many of the podcatcher developers have allowed for that. Be safe. Keep straight text in your <description> tag and use the new <content:encoded> tag to pass HTML. See the section later in this chapter, "<content:encoded> tag," to find out how to use this tag.

<webMaster> and <managingEditor> tags

The webmaster is the person responsible for the technical accuracy of the information contained in the feed. The managing editor is the person responsible for the messaging and content contained within the tags. For most podcasters, these both reflect the same e-mail address. Note that the <managingEditor> tag requires a name in parentheses to follow the e-mail address:

```
<webMaster>chuck@mypodcast.com</webMaster>
<managingEditor>chuck@mypodcast.com (Chuck Tomasi)</managingEditor>
```

Okay, maybe the words webMaster and managingEditor aren't a perfect fit with podcasting, but including an e-mail address for the person responsible for this feed as well as the content is an excellent idea. We've e-mailed the keepers of various feeds to report problems we've encountered with their feeds — and each one has been very appreciative. Although having that information can help improve the podcasting experience for everyone, there have been (and likely will be) many feeds that don't provide contact information. If you make it easy for people to help you, you're ahead of the game. Include a valid e-mail address in your feed.

<pubDate> tag

At the <channel> level, the <pubDate> tag indicates the last time the feed was updated. It's very important that you follow the correct convention when adding this element — you can't just put any old date in here.

Getting the <pubDate> (publication date) correct is terribly important, but it's often overlooked by podcasters in a hurry. Don't fall into this trap. The publication date is used by listing sites and directories as a way to show fresh content. Don't be stale; use the publication date, and make sure you do it right:

```
<pubDate>Sat, 31 May 2008 12:02:28 -0800</pubDate>
```

The <pubDate> element must follow the RFC #822 guidelines (asg.web. cmu.edu/rfc/rfc822.html), which are simply

```
[day of week], [day of month] [month] [year] [24 hour time] [time zone (GMT)]
```

Simple as that may be, you have to follow the correct naming convention for each of those elements. Table 12-1 shows how.

Table 12-1	Proper \<pubDate\> Elements
Day of Week	*Month*
Mon	Jan
Tue	Feb
Wed	Mar
Thu	Apr
Fri	May
Sat	Jun
Sun	Jul
	Aug
	Sep
	Oct
	Nov
	Dec

The day of the week is always expressed in double digits, adding a zero in front of any single-digit numbers (for example, 03 instead of 3), and the year is always expressed in four digits. (Well, at least it will be for the next 8,000 years or so, and then we'll just have to do something different.)

The big stumbling block with \<pubDate\> tends to be the time and zone:

- ✔ **Military time:** The time should always be expressed in 24-hour or military time, (HH:MM:SS). Again, add zeros in front if necessary (for example, 03:07:02 is correct).

- ✔ **Time zone:** The time zone isn't represented by everyday abbreviations such as PST. Instead, it's referenced from GMT, or *Greenwich Mean Time.* (That's a city in England where the International Date Line passes through, not a small village on the east coast of the United States.) Podcasters in California are in either -0800 or -0700 (that's 8 or 7 hours earlier than GMT, respectively) depending on whether Daylight Saving Time is in effect.

Don't sweat the timestamp too hard. You should be changing the date every time you put up a new episode, but even if you had to hard-code the timestamp to 12:00:00 -0800, you wouldn't have a problem with it. Chances are, your RSS 2.0 is generated automatically, so time stamping shouldn't be an issue.

<category> tag

Though the original drafters of RSS 2.0 had standards in mind, the `<category>` tag has become pretty much a free-for-all. If your podcast has an industry-recognized category, use that. If not, make it up! That's what we did in our example:

```
<category>Automotive</category>
```

<image> tag

This optional RSS tag provides a graphical representation of your podcast. It actually contains several elements that further describe the image. They are

- ✔ **URL:** The location of your image (in GIF, JPEG, or PNG format) on a Web server.

- ✔ **Width:** The width of your image, up to 144 pixels.

- ✔ **Height:** The height of your image, up to 400 pixels.

- ✔ **Title:** This text describes the image, but most people just describe their podcast again, because that's what the image should do anyhow.

- ✔ **Link:** The link to your Web site. Just because you needed to put that in one more place. Can you say "overkill"?

All these elements, when used together, result in something very much like this:

```
<image>
  <url>http://mypodcast.com/images/logos/TCCP100x86.jpg</url>
  <width>100</width>
  <height>86</height>
  <title>The Car Collector Podcast</title>
  <link>http://mypodcast.com</link>
</image>
```

<copyright> tag

Here's where you can list the copyright information about your podcast. It's free-form text, so be sure to include all the narrative necessary to get your copyright information across. We use Creative Commons (more on that in Chapter 4) to retain some rights to our podcasts, yet allow for some additional freedom that's difficult with conventional "all rights reserved" notices.

```
<copyright>Creative Commons Attribution 2.5 License</copyright>
```

<language> tag

Although the file itself is written in the RSS 2.0 flavor of the RSS language, the "human language" should also be declared. In our example, we've declared that our podcast is in English:

```
<language>en-us</language>
```

If your podcast is not in English, see http://blogs.law.harvard.edu/ tech/stories/storyReader$15 for the appropriate code to use in this section.

<docs> tag

This is simply a link to the document that describes what RSS 2.0 is all about. This entry is optional, but including it is considered good form. If you do use it, just copy the URL in the example — it's one of the most common. In the unlikely event your feed is picked up by a developer who hasn't adapted his application to accept the RSS 2.0 standard, you're being a good global citizen and pointing him in the right direction. Think of this as the Rosetta Stone of your podcast feed:

```
<docs>http://blogs.law.harvard.edu/tech/rss</docs>
```

<itunes:subtitle> tag

This is what iTunes uses to populate the Description column of its application. It should be a collection of a few choice words about your podcast. We recommend simply mirroring the <title> tag:

```
<itunes:subtitle>The best podcast on the planet. Period. With your host, me!</itunes:subtitle>
```

<itunes:summary> tag

Apple says you have up to 4,000 words in this entry. This content is featured prominently when your podcast is selected by someone interested in your show. Sounds like a repeat of the <description> tag to us:

```
<itunes:summary>This podcast blows the doors off all other podcasts. Have a listen and leave the others in the dust.</itunes:summary>
```

<itunes:owner> and <itunes:author> tags

On the surface, it may seem we're repeating the same thing with <webMaster> and <managingEditor> described earlier in this chapter . . . no, wait. This *is* pretty much a repeat of that.

iTunes uses the <itunes:author> tag to power the *Artist* listing inside of iTunes. <itunes:owner> doesn't publicly display anywhere and is simply a way to identify who is responsible for the feed in the event Apple needs to contact the party responsible for the feed — such as technical issues, non-compliance, directory listings, and so on. <itunes:owner> has two subtags: <itunes:name> and <itunes:email>.

Here's how the two tags work together:

```
<itunes:owner>
    <itunes:email>chuck@mypodcast.com</itunes:email>
    <itunes:name>Chuck Tomasi</itunes:name>
</itunes:owner>
<itunes:author>Chuck Tomasi</itunes:author>
```

<itunes:category> tags

Pay close attention here because this is another area that gets fouled up more times than we care to count. You can't make this one up — it has to follow Apple iTunes categories.

Look at the categories inside of iTunes and find out where your podcast belongs before adding this tag. iTunes is a free download, and you have to install it in order to see what categories you have to choose from. Get it at www.apple.com/itunes.

Some categories have subcategories, and both are handled a bit differently when it comes to tagging. If you find a subcategory you belong to, you have to identify not only the subcategory, but also the parent category. For this bogus feed we've built, we've selected a category/subcategory pair (Games & Hobbies:Automotive/Automotive) as well as a category that has no subs (Society & Culture:History) so you can see how each is coded:

```
<itunes:category text="Games & Hobbies:Automotive">
    <itunes:category text="Automotive" />
</itunes:category>
<itunes:category text="Society & Culture:History" />
```

Notice how "Automotive" is nested between the beginning and ending tags for "Games & Hobbies:Automotive". Because "Society & Culture:History" has no subcategory associated with it, the tag has its ending / at the end of a tag, itself, just as you see with "Automotive".

<itunes:link> tag

Continuing to do its own thing, Apple ignored the RSS <image> tag and came up with its own to better match the album art already used within iTunes.

This tag is made up of several different declarations, all of which you must follow if you want your artwork to show up inside of iTunes:

✔ rel="image": This tells iTunes that the link in question is really an image file. It's not the most intuitive thing in the world, but you work with what you have.

- ✔ `type="video/jpeg"`: With this tag, iTunes knows that the image is a JPEG. Bet you didn't know that JPEG was originally used as a video format. Neither did we. If you decide to use the PNG format, you need to change the statement to `type="image/png"`. Regardless of your format, iTunes recommends images that are 600 x 600 pixels in size.

- ✔ `href="[URL of your image]"`: This is a link to the image.

- ✔ Yet another title-like statement: Make it easy on yourself and just use the name of your podcast.

When it's all over with, you should have something that looks very much like this:

```
<itunes:link rel="image" type="video/jpeg" href="http://mypodcast.com/images/
              logos/TCCP300x300.jpg">The Car Collector Podcast</itunes:link>
```

<itunes:explicit> tag

Apple has a kid-friendly reputation to uphold. And because it already has a huge 20-million-plus subscriber base, it doesn't want to allow any unsavory podcasts to fall into the younger hands. Already having developed the EXPLICIT tag for songs designed for mature audiences, Apple simply extended that tag to the podcasting world.

Three possible values exist for this tag: `yes`, `no`, and `clean`. If you drop the F-bomb on your show, fess up and put a `yes` value in this tag. If you use language like you would with your friends, but it's still safe enough for your mom, go ahead and use `no`. If you're so squeaky clean that people could eat off your podcasting rig, you still include the tag, but your value is `clean`.

```
<itunes:explicit>no</itunes:explicit>
```

Stating that your podcast uses explicit language excludes anyone under 18 years old from downloading your podcast, but we wouldn't want our kids using the same computer as we did for that type of podcast.

Incorrectly marking your tag with `no`, or `clean`, when in fact you drop an F-bomb or other bad language could get you rejected or removed from the iTunes directory listing.

Loading up on <item>s

Now that the channel has been defined, it's time to talk about the individual items contained within the channel. An *item* is (in this case) an individual podcast episode. If you have three shows available for download on your Web site, you have three distinct <item> declarations in your file.

Chapter 10 sums up the pros and cons of making all your shows available. If you have the server space and the bandwidth to handle it, go right ahead. If not, include only the most recent podcasts in your feed. You can control that with the items you include in your RSS 2.0 feed.

True to form, each of your podcast episodes starts off with the item declaration: `<item>`.

<title> tag

Much like your channel, each `item` element also has a title. In this case, it's the title of the episode:

```
<title>TCCP 013 - Experienced restorer, a peek at a Mustang, and driving a true
      classic.</title>
```

Some podcasters prefer to put in some recurring text to identify their podcast (in this case, `TCCP`); others choose not to. It really is a matter of choice.

After you decide on a naming convention for your podcast episodes, try to stick with it. Listeners grow comfortable with seeing your show display on their MP3 players or computer folders in a certain way. If you randomly change how you name your episodes, your audience may no longer recognize the files as yours. Although there's no rule against changing, you might want to warn your audience before you do so.

<link> tag

Earlier in the chapter, we showed you how to provide a link to your main podcast Web site. Here you're providing a link to the specific page where listeners can find your show notes and other information about this particular episode:

```
<link>http://www.mypodcast.com/tccp013.html</link>
```

<comments> tag

If you collect and display comments from your listeners on particular episodes of your podcast, provide a link to that specific page. For many, the `<comment>` URL is the same as the `<link>` tag. In our example, it's slightly different:

```
<comments>http://www.mypodcast.com/tccp13.html#comments</comments>
```

<description> tag

The `<description>` tag works the same way in the `<item>` statement as it does in the `<channel>` statement. It's used to provide detailed information about the episode. This is the place for a teaser of what's in your podcast — bigger than the title, but smaller than the full show notes:

```
<description>Synopsis: Steel Headers is the company that made this trip possible.
Can't recommend them highly enough. Thanks to Dave Wishfield from
San Jose, CA for talking to me about his 1965 Ford Mustang. Listen
and find out how much he got at the auction! Special thanks to
Aiden Somerset from Sun Prairie, WI for allowing me the privilege
to drive the 1957 Chevy Belair. What a ride! Download The Car
Collector Podcast Episode #13</description>
```

<guid> element

GUID stands for *global unique identifier*. Well, okay, *global* may not be the best word here, but that's what it is; don't worry — you don't have to pick something that's one-of-a-kind-in-the-entire-universe. But you should pick something that makes this entry unique to your RSS file. Here's an example:

```
<guid isPermaLink="false">1808@http://www.mypodcast.com/</guid>
```

In this example, a sequential, non-repeating number is added to the beginning of the URL of the Web site. Each time a new `<item>` goes in the file, the number is incremented by one. This helps the podcatching clients figure out whether a file is new. If a podcatching client has already seen the GUID for this particular podcast, it doesn't download the file. If it has never seen the GUID associated with this podcast, it downloads the show.

You can generate a GUID lots of ways. In reality, most people use a program to help generate the RSS file, and the GUID is automatically taken care of. In the event that it isn't, you can just use the URL of the podcast media file for this episode, assuming you use a good filenaming convention and you don't plan on repeating the filename anytime in the future.

<pubDate> tag

This tag shows when the podcast episode was published. Just like in the `<channel>` statement, make sure you follow the right convention. Assuming you have more than one `<item>` in your feed, each item has its own `<pubDate>`.

```
<pubDate>Sat, 31 May 2008 12:02:28 -0800</pubDate>
```

<author> tag

This is simply the e-mail address of the person who created the content. For most podcasters, this is the same in each `<item>` in the feed. But if you're making a compilation where you repurpose content created by others, you may want to put their e-mail address in here. The choice is yours:

```
<author>editor@mypodcast.com</author>
```

<enclosure> element

Chapter 3 provides a brief rundown of how the `<enclosure>` element makes podcasting possible — but now (finally) we come to that sacred piece of code. We hope you're not too disappointed when you see how simple it is:

```
<enclosure url="http://mypodcast.com/media/TCCP013_20080531.mp3"
           length="24849394" type="audio/mpeg" />
```

Hardly seems worth the fuss, does it? Believe it or not, this is the main line that makes your podcasts automatically download to your listeners' desktops and MP3 players. The enclosure tag contains three elements:

- ✔ `url`: A link to the podcast media file.

- ✔ `length`: The length of the file. In this case, `length` is synonymous with file size, expressed in bytes.

- ✔ `type`: The standard MIME type of the media file referenced in the link. Podcasting works with a variety of media types. This example is for audio files saved in MP3 format. You can enclose video files (and even BitTorrent files), but to do that successfully, first determine the appropriate MIME type for your preferred media file. A full list of MIME types is available at `www.iana.org/assignments/media-types`. Rather than make you wade through all that, we'll let you know that most audio files are either `audio/mpeg` (for MP3 files) or `audio/m4a` (for Apple's AAC format used in enhanced podcasts). Video files have a few different formats to choose from. Depending on how the file is encoded, you'll want to look it up on the IANA site.

<content:encoded> tag

Earlier we show you how to put a synopsis in your feed by using the `<description>` tag; this is just straight text, without any images, formatting, or hyperlinks. The best way to include these extras is to use the `<content:encoded>` tag.

You want a good-quality synopsis on your Web site and in your RSS feed — complete with URLs that lead to the various Web sites. So it's time to do something special (okay, sneaky) to avoid breaking any XML laws.

XML is pretty picky about which characters are allowed and which ones aren't. After all, a good synopsis is written to be read by a human being, not an XML program — and human language just has a lot more stuff in it. If (for example) you want to put in quotes, ampersands, apostrophes, and other characters that are considered illegal inside XML, you have to use a Get Out of Jail Free card in the form of this statement:

```
<![CDATA[]]>
```

The `<![CDATA[]]>` statement informs the XML reader that the contents contained within the `[ ]` symbols are *not* XML and should not be treated as such. Some older XML readers just skip such content altogether. But every RSS and XML reader we've seen switches over to HTML mode and displays the information properly — links, images, and all. As it should be.

So if you really want your description to read "'There's trouble & danger ahead,' said the Cap'n" — quirky, isn't it? — you have two options:

XML-Encoded

```
<description>&quot;&apos;There&apos;s trouble &amp; danger ahead&quot;, said the
             Cap&apos;n&quot;</description>
```

Using CDATA

```
<content:encoded><![CDATA["'There's trouble & danger ahead', said the
             Cap'n"]]></content:encoded>
```

Now, which way are you going to choose? Both approaches give you the same results. One probably gives you a headache.

You can go about *escaping* or encoding illegal characters inside your XML in other ways. You can find more information about that in *Syndicating Web Sites with RSS Feeds For Dummies,* or at www.w3schools.com/xml/xml_encoding.asp.

For now, it's easier to tell the XML reader to lighten up and deal with the text as is.

<itunes:author> tag

You guessed it — yet another iTunes tag that looks amazingly like a standard RSS 2.0 tag. Hey, we didn't write the spec. We're just telling you how to implement it. In fact, iTunes will use the standard `author` tag if the `itunes:author` is missing.

```
<itunes:author>Chuck Tomasi</itunes:author>
```

<itunes:subtitle> and <itunes:summary> tags

The same rules apply here as did in the `<channel>` section. In this case, you're describing a single episode of your show in both short and long versions, respectively.

```
<itunes:subtitle>My recent trip to LA's antique car auction, plus my
        adventures.</itunes:subtitle>
<itunes:summary>Synopsis: Steel Headers is the company that made this trip
        possible. Can't recommend them highly enough. Thanks to Dave
        Wishfield from San Jose, CA for talking to me about his 1965
        Ford Mustang. Listen and find out how much he got at the auction!
        Special thanks to Aiden Somerset from Sun Prairie, WI for allowing
        me the privilege to drive the 1957 Chevy Belair. What a ride!
        Download The Car Collector Podcast Episode #13</itunes:summary>
```

<itunes:category> tags

Just as with the `<channel>` section (see the earlier section "<itunes:category> tags"), it's important to get this right. Use the categories iTunes has available, not just any categories. Oddly, we've learned that episode-specific categories (those within the `<item>` and `</item>` tags) aren't used for anything in iTunes — yet. We include them here to be good podcast citizens.

```
<itunes:category text="Games & Hobbies:Automotive">
     <itunes:category text="Automotive" />
</itunes:category>
<itunes:category text="Society & Culture:History" />
```

<itunes:duration> tag

Finally — something brand new with an iTunes-specific tag! Remember that iTunes was originally a music-distribution system. As such, the length of a particular song displays next to the title. Podcasters too are asked to provide this information. It follows the `HH:MM:SS` format.

If you use software to help build your file, you may not be able to figure out the exact duration of your individual podcasts. iTunes has no way to verify this data, so you can just hard-code a ballpark figure of your average podcast length.

```
<itunes:duration>00:45:00</itunes:duration>
```

<itunes:explicit> tag

Here's an implementation from iTunes that makes a lot of sense. If your podcast normally doesn't include any questionable language or subject matter, go ahead and mark the channel with an explicit tag of `no`. However, if a particular episode does get a little on the raunchy side, you can use this tag inside a particular `<item>` and `</item>` pair to mark just the single episode.

Even if you know all your podcasts episodes follow the same explicit label set forth in the `<channel>`, you still need to include it here:

```
<itunes:explicit>no</itunes:explicit>
```

<itunes:keywords> tag

One would think this tag helps people searching in iTunes find your podcast, but in reality, iTunes gets most of that information from the title, description, and summary information. Apple recommends minimizing the use of the keywords tag and using it for things like common misspellings of your name or show. To prevent keyword abuse, Apple only indexes the first 12 keywords in this tag.

Separate keywords by commas and add in as many as you see fit:

```
<itunes:keywords>tomassi,thomasi</itunes:keywords>
```

Wrapping things up

As with any other markup language (and as indicated earlier in this chapter), you have to close those declaration tags. The closing tag looks like this:

```
</item>
```

This tag tells the podcatching client that the end of the episode has been reached. After you close your `<item>` tag, you can immediately add a second, and a third, and so on. There is no limit to the number of `<items>` you can have inside your RSS feed.

After you add all the episodes inside their own `<item> </item>` statement, it's time to finish the file:

```
</channel>
</rss>
```

These two lines of text bring to a close your `<channel>` declaration and mark the end of the RSS 2.0 file itself.

You should have no further text after these two statements. This really *is* the end of your file. If you have extra text hanging around after you close your `</rss>` tag, delete it. Or better yet, figure out where you wanted to put it in one of the elements — and put it there.

Tweaking the Contents

The main function of your RSS 2.0 file is to distribute your media files to the various people who have subscribed to your feed. However, it's a smart podcaster who recognizes that a well-formed RSS feed can be employed for a wider range of needs.

Adding keywords and tags

Although all the elements of a well-formed RSS 2.0 file are important, it's the <title> and the <description> content that are the most useful for listeners — be they current or potential. As a podcaster, it's your job to create descriptions and titles that are both relevant to your content and intriguing to your listening audience.

As discussed in Chapter 11, keywords are important. Rather than making stuff up again, this time we use real-world examples to illustrate the point. One of your humble authors hosts several podcasts. One of the shows features topics about tech, science, sci-fi, and other nerdy subjects. Another show deals exclusively with a popular online mail application; yet another is really more about . . . well, whatever fits the podcaster's mood.

Understanding that each of these shows appeals to a completely different audience, the podcaster employs very different strategies when providing information about these shows. But as different as these strategies are, they follow a similar theme: Tell listeners what they want to hear.

No, we're not suggesting you lie or stretch the truth about the content of your podcasts. Instead, practice thinking like a listener. What do you think listeners want to hear? Then consider why you did this episode in the first place: Who would be interested in listening, and why? After you figure all that out, it's time to start writing descriptive keywords and adding them to your <title> and <description> declarations.

Whether or not you heard it here first, the ability to change the contents of your RSS file is critical to your success as a podcaster. Before you select a hosting company or blogging software that manages your RSS 2.0 file for you, ask some important questions about modifying that file. (By and large, we'd say take a pass on companies that don't allow do-it-yourself changes to your RSS 2.0 file or template.)

Making newcomers feel welcome

Think back to when you were a new podcast listener or, perhaps, consider the last time you added a podcast to your podcatching client. Did you know what you were getting yourself into? Perhaps someone recommended the show to you, and you already had a feel for what it was you could expect. But maybe not.

For a lot of new people just starting out as podcast listeners, there is a large gulf of uncertainty and concern they have to get over before subscribing to a new podcast. By subscribing to your feed, a listener is putting a significant amount of trust in you, the podcaster. Don't forget that podcasting means your subscribers automatically receive *any and all* podcast media files you make available, regardless of what's in them or how big they are.

How large will these files be? How often will they be coming down? What can I expect out of the content? Can I listen in front of my kids? Will the file size overload my hard drive?

These and a slew of other questions invade the mind of every person thinking about taking the plunge and subscribing to your podcast. And these concerns stay on the minds of those who bit the bullet and subscribed for at least the first few weeks. Your job, then, is to find ways to make those listeners feel comfortable so they keep listening. Stay tuned (as it were). . . .

You have two options to address these concerns:

- ✔ **Place a short audio file or block of HTML on your Web site:** Describe what the show is, the run time, and how often you expect to offer a new show. This is commonly referred to as "episode 0" and released as the first show in the feed.
- ✔ **Address these same items as part of your show:** "Listen every week for an exciting hour of outdoor news, product reviews, and discussion from the man who's been in the business for over 30 years." Within 10 seconds, the listener knows exactly what to expect.

If you find your listeners still have questions, try to provide answers. Sometimes this comes in the form of e-mail, sometimes blog or forum replies, or adapt your show description content mentioned earlier. If you want to be a little more proactive, you could also set up an FAQ (frequently asked questions) page for Web visitors to read and review.

Make your RSS feed easy to find

Podcast still has a "geek factor" to it. As a result of that, you're going to have to do whatever you can to make it easy for people to find, and subscribe to, your show.

If you want to convert casual listeners in to loyal subscribers, make it as easy for them to subscribe to your show as possible. A little link in an obscure place on your Web page just isn't going to do the job. Remember, podcasting is as much about marketing you and your podcast as it is about the technical details. iTunes and Zune now offer a way to put an icon/link on your Web site so that people can subscribe with a single click — once your podcast is listed in those directories. Now that's simple!

Make it easy to listen

One strategy used by many podcasters is to have an audio player on the site. You can do this in a variety of ways — plug-ins to your blog software or Flash players. These players allow people to listen to your material without the bother of a podcatching client. For some podcasters, it's difficult to comprehend that despite the fact that they've spent a lot of time setting up an RSS feed, a fair percentage of listeners are still listening straight from the Web site. Don't be like those podcasters: Make it easy for listeners to click and listen. One popular way is to use the PodPress (www.podpress.org) plug-in to WordPress. Adding the podcast file is trivial and includes a Flash player for each episode.

To add a link on your Web site, follow these steps:

1. **Search for your podcast in the iTunes Store or in Zune.**

2. **When you have the screen with just your show's details displayed, right-click your podcast icon and choose Copy.**

   What you're copying looks kind of like this:

   ```
   zune://subscribe/?MyPodcast=http://mysite.com/myfeed.xml
   ```

3. **Paste your show's URL i.nto the HTML for your Web site.**

   Now, you've given listeners a simple way to find your show.

You can make a one-click subscription for iTunes listeners by changing your URL slightly. After copying and pasting the URL, change the `http` to `itpc`. Now when someone clicks the link, instead of being taken to your podcast listing in the iTunes Music Store, your podcast will automatically be added to their iTunes podcast list.

For most other software packages besides iTunes or Zune, a standard RSS badge with a link to your feed works well, but you rely on the user to copy the URL manually in to a podcatching client.

Multiple-Show File Strategies

You may just catch the podcasting bug *hard.* It's so easy to create a podcast that you'll want to do more. Soon you may find yourself doing three shows a week, each with slightly different content and topics, each appealing to a different audience.

One possible situation might be that you have diverging content — you begin to hear from your listeners that Monday's show is right up their alley, but Wednesday's coverage of different material isn't their cup of tea. You get plenty of e-mail and voice mail with the opposite viewpoint, and a good many listeners say they love everything you're doing.

Another situation might be to offer special content. Give the listener something above and beyond your regular content for those die-hard loyal fans who are willing to contribute a little information such as demographics or e-mail address for your members-only newsletter list.

How can you make all these people happy? Simple. Multiple feeds.

Manager Tools (`http://manager-tools.com`) is one example of a podcast with multiple feeds. Its primary feed of useful management advice is available to the public without obligation. It also offer a "members only" feed with a monthly extra. To receive this separate feed, the subscriber needs to give his or her e-mail address — that's it. In addition to the members-only audio content, the subscriber also gets a regular newsletter, pre-announcements to conferences, and other items. *Manager Tools* also has something called "premium content," which is available for an annual fee.

When you've figured out how to customize your feed, it should be easy to break out a second (or third) feed, isolating the content as appropriate. You need to check the documentation of your blogging software or RSS-generation tool to see what steps are necessary.

Part IV

Start Spreadin' the News about Your Podcast

The 5th Wave   By Rich Tennant

"This is number 271 of the podcast show, 'Help! Get Me Off This Stinking Island!'"

In this part . . .

When you've finally managed to put your show "out there," you may find it's a cold, dark place. You need a beacon on your podcast that tells everyone you're here — and what your show is all about. In this part, you find the tips and tricks successful podcasters use to attract a wider audience. Additionally, you find ways to communicate better with your fans (yes, fans!) and keep your show fresh.

Chapter 13

Speaking Directly to Your Peeps

Communication can be defined in a multitude of overly complex ways. For the sake of argument (and not to copy each and every dictionary entry we can find), we define the term as

> *The exchange of information between two points.*

Note that last part — *between two points*. To us, this implies a bi-directional flow of information, to and from both parties.

If you've had the pleasure (note how well we can say that with a straight face) of attending any productivity or team-building seminars, the presenters really drive the message home: Effective communication is not a one-way street.

Over the past few years, podcasting has evolved as a more effective communication than traditional media (such as radio or television). We all have same tools to communicate at our disposal — e-mail, Web sites, phone lines — so why do podcast listeners seem to get more involved with podcasting? Two simple reasons

✔ There seems to be a closer bond between podcast listener and podcast producer. The simple fact that anyone can do this makes the producer seem more like a real person than a personality and easier to relate to.

✔ The podcasters are asking for the feedback — and getting it. Audience size doesn't matter. We've seen some instances of shows with a couple hundred loyal followers where the podcaster has to spin off a second show just to handle the listener feedback. When was the last time you heard of a "listener feedback show" for American Idol?

In this chapter, we show you some real-world examples of how to foster communication between you and your audience, touching on a variety of methods and venues you probably haven't considered.

Gathering Listener Feedback

It must be a natural human reaction to fear the opinions of others. Perhaps it's insecurity, but we think it has more to do with our culture's constant reinforcement of the "How are you?" — "I'm fine. You?" — "Fine." meaningless chatter that precedes most of our conversations.

That cultural crutch, however, is left next to Tiny Tim's seat when it comes to podcasting. Listeners, for whatever reason, are compelled to actually give real and meaningful criticism. And podcasters, for the most part, take to heart those responses.

Of course, we're speaking in general terms. Yes, there are flamers and jerks out there with less than helpful answers at the ready. Podcasting can't change basic human nature for the ill-evolved, unfortunately.

You can foster good communication with your listening audience in a multitude of ways, such as

- ✔ Allowing and responding to comments on your blog
- ✔ Creating and visiting online discussion groups and forums
- ✔ Responding to listener e-mail
- ✔ Exploring online social networks
- ✔ Leveraging voice mail

All of these avenues are discussed in detail in the sections that follow.

Fostering Comments on Your Blog

In an ideal world, all communication, feedback, rants, and raves about your show would take place in a neat little box, keeping things nice and tidy for you. But because that won't happen, your best bet is to build a Web site that both enables and encourages the communication in your own backyard.

In Chapters 11 and 12, we demonstrate how much simpler adding show notes and generating RSS files are for those podcasters who use blogging software, rather than those who try to do everything by hand. Well, here's one more feather in the cap of blogging software such as WordPress, Blogger, and even Movable Type: Feedback mechanisms come pre-installed.

In the world of blogs, this feedback mechanism is referred to as _comments_. Visit just about any blog you can find, read a post, and you're likely to find a small Comments link at the bottom. Figure 13-1 shows one example, though the treatment varies widely from site to site.

If you're already using a blog, you usually don't have to do anything special to turn on the comments feature. Most software comes configured to accept comments by default. If you decide comments are not for you or your podcast, turning off that capability is simply a matter of finding the right check box.

Some podcasters get dozens of responses per episode. Some get none. Although there is some relation to the size of your listening audience and the number of comments you're likely to receive, it really has more to do with the connection users feel they have with your podcast.

Figure 13-1:
The Bitterest Pill gets quite a few comments on each episode.

Much like two co-workers chatting about last night's *The Daily Show with Jon Stewart,* two or more listeners using your Web site to talk to each other about your show speaks to the attachment they feel to what you have to say (or play). From the very first moments of attachment, you can nurture for your podcast its own community. Here are some simple ways we recommend to foster your following:

- ✔ Mention that you have comments on the blog either as a standard practice as part of the show — part of the intro, outro, or break perhaps.
- ✔ Include a line in your e-mail signature.
- ✔ Ask questions during the show and direct listeners to your blog to leave their comments or opinions.
- ✔ Actively respond to received comments.

Communication develops amongst the listening community itself. Rather than talking to you, listeners start talking to each other, and the conversation takes on a life of its own. If this happens to you, don't fret over it; encourage it! For example, on *Jack Mangan's Deadpan Podcast* (http://jackmangan.com) blog, the comments on *individual blog posts* consistently reach well into the hundreds, and the comments may begin on one topic from the show only to break off into a tangent of their own. Other times, it may become quick banter between listeners. With Jack at the helm, the activity has become so lively the podcast now has a regular segment where Jack uses a 20-sided die to pick several comments at random to read on the show. This kind of interaction between host and listeners has now created a Deadpan community that meets regularly on this blog to share links, feedback, and random thoughts.

Sometimes, the comments that take on lives of their own mutate into hostile takeovers, and the conversation is lost amidst an onslaught of personal attacks either to other posters or to you, the podcast's and blog's host. Neither your community nor you need this kind of conversation. You may want to consider *moderating* blog comments. Moderating still allows people to post comments, but you get to approve those comments for public consumption. When someone posts a comment, you get an e-mail. With a couple mouse clicks, you can chose whether to approve it. You have to do a little more work, but moderating ensures all comments meet your quality standards.

You may find your name or podcast mentioned other places on the Internet via search engines (discussed later in this chapter). We recommend you get engaged with those discussions as well. Be sure to check back in a couple days for additional follow-ups, or if you are responding to a blog comment or forum, check to see if they have an option to alert you to replies.

Starting an Online Discussion Group

Community forums, groups, and discussion lists — also known as e-mail lists, mailing lists, or distribution lists — allow for easy virtual community building, enabling disparate people to share their thoughts and opinions on a wide variety of subjects. You can find many free services to create a place where listeners can post, share, and discuss their thoughts and ideas online.

As easy as it is to create places for these types of conversations to occur, someone else may have already done it. Spend some quality time searching the Internet for your name and your show. Maybe a devoted fan has already done the not-so-heavy lifting for you.

Although the number of free online discussion groups is legion, we've decided to focus on two of the larger offerings: Yahoo! Groups and Google Groups. Both are free to join and create, but both are supported by various forms of advertising. There ain't no such thing as a free lunch, as Heinlein said.

Remember when we said podcasting has an element of marketing with it? Here's another opportunity to take your name to the people. Using a large service like Yahoo! or Google means your information is available to a lot of potential listeners. They may find your discussion list and become interested in your podcast, rather than the other way around.

Yahoo! Groups

Yahoo! Groups has the distinction of being one of the oldest and most widely used free discussion groups on the Net. Although it may not have been first on the block, it has stood the test of time, and many consider it the 800-pound gorilla on the block. Yahoo! Groups also boasts of a huge user base, which can help your fledgling group swell in size rapidly.

Setting up a group is quick and easy; just follow these steps:

1. **Log in to Yahoo! Groups at** `http://groups.yahoo.com`.

   If you already have an account, enter your Yahoo! ID and password.

   If you don't have a Yahoo! ID yet, click the Sign Up link and follow the simple instructions to get your free Yahoo! account.

   When you're logged in, you can find a list of all the groups you've either created or belong to on the left side of the page. Of course, if you're in Yahoo! Groups for the first time, this area is empty.

2. **To start a new group, click the Start Your Group link near the top of the page.**

3. **Select the appropriate category and subcategory for your group. Then click the Place My Group Here button.**

   As you select categories, you're presented with subcategories to refine your group's placement. You can stop after the first subgroup or continue selecting links until you find the appropriate categorization for your group.

4. **Enter the appropriate information in the Group Name, Group Email Address, and Describe Your Group text boxes. When you're finished, click Continue.**

   See Figure 13-2 for an example of a page that's been filled out.

   The Group Email address is the e-mail address members of your group will use to send messages to the entire group. You get to make up this address; we suggest making it something simple and easy to remember. Acronyms are a good idea here, as are any abbreviations or secret words that your group members are likely to remember.

5. **Select which Yahoo! Profile and Email Address you want associated with this group.**

   Because you're setting up the group, you are the *Owner* (which gives you phenomenal cosmic powers like kicking people out if they get out of line). If you have multiple Yahoo! IDs, you need to associate one with this group. And if you have more than one e-mail address, Yahoo! needs to know where to send the mail.

6. **In the Word Verification text box, type the letters that are displayed in the accompanying image.**

   Yahoo! Groups asks you to type the letters to help prevent e-mail spam — which is a good thing, right? Oh, and it's case-sensitive, so make sure you use capital letters where appropriate.

7. **When you're done, click Continue.**

   That's it! You've just created your group.

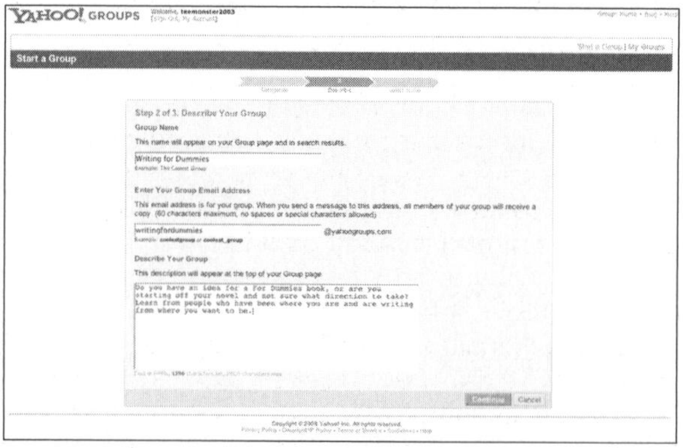

Figure 13-2:
Yahoo!
Groups
allows you
to describe
your group
with a little
text or a lot.

From here, you can set how much control and flexibility you want to have over the group, as well as the ease at which others can join. Yahoo! leaves some things pretty open, yet locks down others. Be sure to follow the Customize Your Group link to make sure that the settings are to your liking. If not, change them! If you need to make changes later, start at http://groups.yahoo.com, click your group name in the My Groups, and then click the Management link.

When you're happy with your group, click the Invite People to Join link and tell everyone you know about your new group. Well, maybe not everyone. But you should tell the folks who might be interested. You can also send an e-mail — or better tell listeners in your podcast about your new group.

An invitation is something you send to notify people about an event or new service, in this case your Yahoo! group. Sending an invitation to 1,000 people is likely an unsolicited e-mail. Chances are good that recipients aren't expecting this mail from you. That makes it look suspiciously like spam, and people are likely to just delete it. When you send your invitations, don't send them to folks you don't know and make sure the mail is personal enough to let them know the message is not spam from some faceless person.

Google Groups

Not to be outdone, Google has released a service similar to Yahoo! Groups. Google is quickly becoming the dominant player in many online initiatives after its successful Gmail launch in early 2004. Here's how to create a Google group:

1. **Sign in to your Google account at** http://groups.google.com.

   If you're already registered with Google, enter your e-mail address and password to log in to Google.

   If you don't have a Google account, the sign up process is free and easy.

2. **Click Create a Group on the right side of the screen.**

3. **In the corresponding text boxes, type the Group Name, Group E-mail Address, and Group Description.**

   The group e-mail address is the e-mail address members of your group will use to send messages to the entire group. Google helps by suggesting an e-mail address based on the name of your group. You can change the e-mail name if you're not happy with it.

4. **Set the Access Level for your group.**

   If you want the maximum usage of your group, select the Public level. Of course, you may have reasons to select a more restrictive access level, and we're certainly not going to stand in your way. One of the options also allows you to deem your group Adults Only or open to all ages.

5. **Click the Create My Group button.**

   You've now created your group and are all set to invite new members. Google Groups makes this an integral step in the creation of the group, whereas Yahoo! Groups makes it more of an option.

6. **In the large text box at the top of the page, enter the e-mail addresses of the people you'd like to have in your group. Then select the Add or Invite option button, depending on what action you want to take.**

   It's a better idea to invite people than to automatically add them to your new group.

   If you choose to automatically add members to your group, e-mail messages from the group will show up unannounced in the recipients' mail boxes, unless you told them in advance. That's spam, pure and simple. Unless you know beyond a shadow of a doubt that the person you intend to add wants to be a member of your group, invite that person instead. That gives them the option to join or not and makes you a better netizen.

7. **Select a subscription type and write a welcome message. When you're finished, click Done.**

   The default subscription type is to have e-mail sent individually to members that have joined your group. We suggest leaving this setting right where it is and allowing the members to change it to their personal preference at their discretion. Some prefer the Digest Form option, and some prefer No E-mail at all. Leave it up to them.

To access your group in the future, simply go to http://groups.google.com and your group is listed in the My Groups section. To make changes, click the Manage link next to the group title.

Publicizing your group

After you create your online discussion group and send your initial invitations, it's time to spread the word! In Chapter 14, we go into a longer conversation about publicizing you, your podcast, and everything you do to support that. But for now, here are a few tips on how to increase membership in your discussion group:

✔ **Publish the group information on your Web site.** Log in to your Google or Yahoo! account to find the URL for your group home page and/or your subscription e-mail address. Post this information prominently on your podcast's Web site.

✔ **Add the group information to your signature line on outbound e-mails.** Let each e-mail you send out act as a mini-advertisement for your discussion group. Provide a link to the home page as well as the subscription e-mail address.

✔ **Promote the group on your podcast.** Find time to mention the group on each episode of your podcast. Don't make an entire show about why someone should join the group, but do talk about the ability to have stimulating conversations with other listeners as well as yourself.

Focusing on Online Forums

While quite useful in some situations, discussion groups can be a little confusing to follow, especially when the topic of your show is complicated and multifaceted. This is compounded by the time-shifting nature of podcasting, causing your listeners to be a week or more behind the listening schedule from one another. How are you going to handle conversations that span timelines and topics? We suggest giving forums a shot.

An *online forum* allows individuals to post their thoughts and ideas on a variety of topics — at their own choosing. Through a concept known as *threading,* multiple discussions can exist independently of all the others. Topics can get buried quickly in a mailing list like those mentioned in the previous section. Forums work differently, keeping all threads and topics available for clutter-free commenting at any time.

Finding free, hosted forums

Using a hosted forum, like a hosted blog, takes away much of the burden of downloading, installing, and configuring the software. On the other hand, you don't have quite the flexibility with a hosted solution as you would with a package you host yourself. One of the easier hosted forums to use is ProBoards. To get started, just follow these steps:

1. **Browse to** www.proboards.com.

   If you have a ProBoards account, enter your username and password.

   If you don't have an account, click the Sign Up link.

2. **Create a username.**

   Choose carefully. Your username becomes part of the URL that followers will navigate to. We suggest using your show name as the username.

3. Enter the remaining information in the form.

Provide a password, your name, e-mail address, and category for your topic.

4. Click Sign Up.

Information regarding your newly created forum will be displayed including the URL to publish, your administrator account, and password. That's it! You've created a new forum, like the one shown in Figure 13-3.

5. Customize the forum.

Click the Admin link at the top of the screen, and you can create new boards, categories, and other customizations to create a framework around which discussions can happen. For example, visitors will find it easier to find information about where to get car parts if that discussion is kept separate from auction values for classic vehicles.

6. Send invitations.

Using the same etiquette as a distribution list, let the world know your forums are available. You can send an e-mail or announce it on your podcast.

Again, keep in mind the issue of how some people might see invitations as spam. If you missed that discussion, check out the "Yahoo! Groups" section, earlier in the chapter.

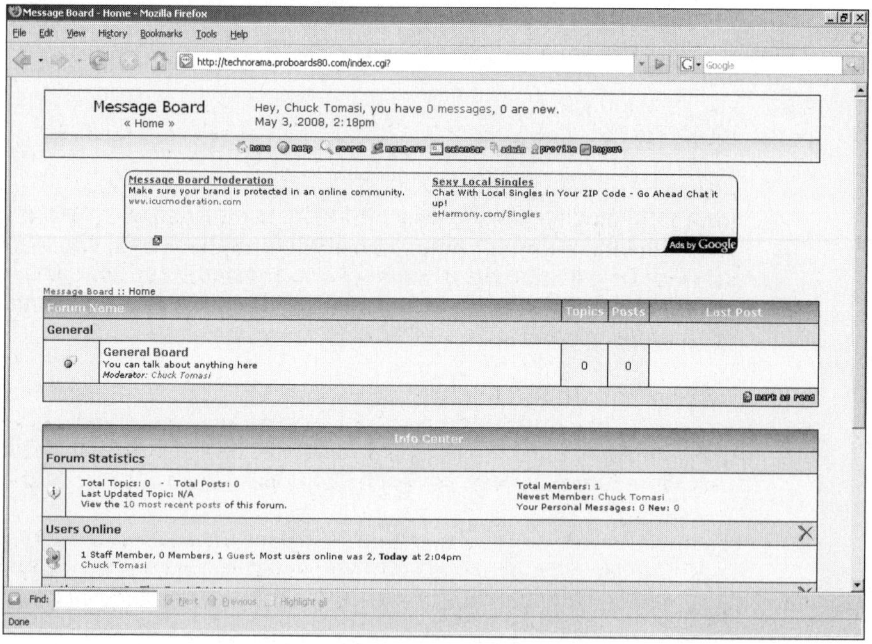

Figure 13-3:
ProBoards offers free forum hosting that you can use for your podcasts.

That's it! You can now customize your forum, start new posts, and spread the word of your newly created forum. Much like discussion groups, you can promote your forum by

- ✔ Posting the address on your Web site
- ✔ Adding the address to your e-mail signature line
- ✔ Mentioning the forum on each of your podcast episodes

Other hosted forums are available. You can find plenty of options by entering **hosted forums** into a Google search. Most are supported by Web ads or voluntary donations.

Like discussion groups, forums take some time to build steam. Be persistent, post every day, and constantly encourage your listeners to interact with you and your podcast in this manner. But above all, be patient!

Now, although your forum performs admirably — for free — it most likely doesn't have *The Look* (and you know what we mean by *The Look*) of other online forums. Popular podcasts also host forums that sport a spit-polished look, interfaces that make posting and replying easy-peasy, and little details peppered throughout that make you think "Wow, I'd love to have a forum that does that!"

You can . . . but a bit more effort (and investment) is needed. See the following section.

Gaining more control of your forum

After a time, you may find yourself wishing for more control of your lively forum. Perhaps you'd like to implement the look and feel *(branding)* of your Web site on the forum, eliminate the advertisements you get with the free service, or more tightly integrate your forum into your overall Web presence. When that happens, it's time to think about installing some forum software on your Web site.

Here we go with the tech stuff again. We're not going to go into great detail on how to install and configure forum software on your Web server. But we give you some things to think about when wrestling with the decision of using free forum software or dropping some cash on one you can purchase.

There's the old saying: Why should I pay for the cow when I get the milk for free? Choosing between a free or paid solution depends on many factors, at the top of which are your level of technical prowess and tolerance for down time. Like anything in life, there are tradeoffs with each option. Consider this checklist:

- ✔ Are you comfortable editing PHP or Perl scripts?
- ✔ Do you have the ability to create new MySQL databases?
- ✔ Can you change the permissions of files and directories on your Web server?
- ✔ Are you willing to continually seek out patches and updates to keep the hackers out?
- ✔ Can you handle having your forum down for days on end while you research problems?
- ✔ Do you want to field "I can't remember my password" questions from your listener base?
- ✔ What is the capitol of Estonia?

If you answered *No* to one or more of the preceding questions, you probably aren't ready to tackle installing your own forum software.

If you answered *Yes* to all the preceding questions — except for the last one, and, by the way, the answer is *Tallinn* — you don't mind getting your hands dirty. We recommend finding out what forum software your hosting company already has pre-configured on your Web server, if any. If your hosting company doesn't have a forum pre-configured for your system, start searching through the multitude of options out there ready for downloading and installing. You can also visit some existing podcast sites that use forums and ask them what they use, what they like (or dislike), and perhaps some of the technical details.

One option for your own forum is to look into open source solutions that many podcasters implement on their sites. For the *Fear the Boot* guys of www. feartheboot.com, their forums are powered by phpBB (www.phpBB.com), a download that needs only your Web host to support PHP (a programming language that gives site developers methods of creating dynamic content that interact with databases) and databases in order to work. Although knowing PHP helps you use phpBB to create a better forum, it isn't a pre-requisite. With its built-in GUI (graphic user interface), phpBB can do quite a lot for you, even if you know nothing about PHP. It's a bit like working with the WordPress blogging software in that you can use what phpBB provides or go beyond it with a background in PHP.

Adam Pinilla carries the responsibility of making sure the *Fear the Boot* forums are online and running (see Figure 13-4). He says, "Forums are a direct link to the fans. While podcasting in itself is one-way communication, forums are a direct avenue for fan interaction, and it keeps people around." For him, moderating a forum takes only three to four hours a week for troubleshooting, answering user requests, and keeping the spammers and forum troublemakers at bay. Four hours is a modest investment considering the return is a strong community of *Fear the Boot* listeners.

As far as his investment of time as a forum participant, Adam clocks in anywhere between 20 to 25 hours on a weekly basis. "I have grown quite fond of our community," he admits.

Like blog comments, you might find your name or podcast being thrown around other forums. We highly suggest you sign up and participate in the discussion. Respond to the comments — positive or negative. (See the section about not-so-positive comments later in this chapter.)

Like many other things on the Internet, the most popular software is often the biggest target of attacks from spam and hacking — that includes phpBB. You might want to choose a "path less traveled" like Simple Machines Forum (http://www.simplemachines.org) that is very secure and easy to set up.

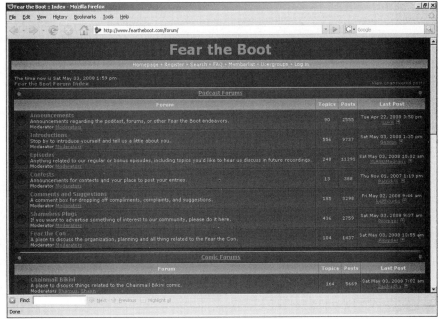

Figure 13-4:
Fear the Boot hosts a forum with sizzle, powered by phpBB.

Online Social Networking

Social networking Web sites are online communities that are made up of online profiles and pages for individuals. They can serve as one-stop shops for when you pay a visit, or combine popular forms of communication into a hybrid that gives you all the best features. These sites have been online longer than podcasting has been in existence, but the podcasters have now taken these sites to new levels of application.

We cover only a few of the networks available. Yes, there are many more than the ones highlighted here, but these are the ones getting a lot of the attention.

You can find plenty more social networking sites out there, and many more will probably appear (and disappear) in the time it takes this book to reach your hands. What's important is finding the network or networks that can get the word of your listeners back to you, help you create a better show, and make you a better podcaster.

MySpace

If iTunes is the King Kong of the podcasting clients, MySpace (www.myspace.com) is the Mighty Joe Young of the social networking sites. With a staggering membership of over 200 million users, MySpace remains the social networking juggernaut. What makes it so popular is what it offers in one location: a blog, an instant messenger, a bulletin board, a comment board, an online forum host, and a mail service. If you don't feel like monitoring numerous applications or maintaining various Web sites, and do like to keep everything in one location, MySpace is your economic space saver online. You can cultivate communities, set up your own group, and keep in touch with your listeners using MySpace.

If you choose to set up a MySpace account, check out *MySpace For Dummies* by Ryan Hupfer, Mitch Maxson, and Ryan Williams to really get the most out of MySpace.

Facebook

At first glance, Facebook (www.facebook.com) may strike you as a MySpace version 2.0, but Facebook goes beyond offering a blog, bulletin board, a mail service, and an online scrapbook. Facebook gives registered users the ability to create online groups where comments can be circulated across others' networks as well as your own. You can also customize your Facebook with add-on applications that promotes an even greater interaction with your community. You can even set up a Facebook account to be an online, one-stop bulletin board of events that your listeners can check to not only see what's coming up next on your podcast but also give feedback on previous episodes.

For more information on Facebook, pick up a copy of *Facebook For Dummies* by Carolyn Abram and Leah Pearlman.

Ning

What sets this new player apart from others is that Ning is not as all-encompassing as either MySpace or Facebook. With the other two services opening their doors to the great big Internet out there, Ning (`www.ning.com`) allows a moderator to start up a meeting place for a specific community. This site combines the power of forums with the invitation-only exclusivity of an online discussion group. Figure 13-5 shows the Podiobooks.com Community powered by Ning; the feedback and discussion are geared for only the interested (and invited) members of the podcast novel listeners. So instead of creating a community in the Podcast directory, you can set up a community specific for your podcast. After you have an exclusive network created, you can then open discussions specific to issues pertaining to your topic.

Figure 13-5:
Ning communities combine the benefits of forums with the security measures of an online discussion group.

Twitter

Twitter (http://twitter.com) is the unassuming service that is a fantastic and instantaneous way of beginning conversations, garnering feedback, and getting word out about your podcast while not becoming a distraction or time-sink from your productivity. Twitter, either through its Web site or through a third-party application, such as TwitBin (www.twitbin.com) or Twitterific (http://iconfactory.com/software/twitterrific), gives you 140 characters to say anything. You can use Twitter to direct people to your blog when a new show posts. Listeners can post (or *tweet*) what they're listening to and comment on it. From various tweets, topics can be created on the blog or forums, resources can be cited, and quick announcements can reach a wide variety of listeners in moments.

Twitter is best described as a nanoblog, giving you the instant gratification of posting a comment but giving you only 140 characters to do it, keeping you from losing your intent in a drawn-out posting. It's based on the premise of answering the question "What are you doing?" If you find someone is listening to your podcast, ask them for feedback. Good or bad, begin a simple chat and ask for the opinions of others in your network. Feel free to post teasers on the next episodes, ask for validation from comments found elsewhere, and tweet links back to other comments and URLs sent in from listeners.

Using Voice Mail

One of the strengths of podcasting is that the content is so portable. That means your listener is quite likely to be away from a computer while listening to your podcast — making the interaction more difficult. Plenty of people, including your authors, listen to podcasts during their commute to work or on road trips. How do you get comments from those listeners? Simple, have them call in.

Mobile phones are very ubiquitous. It's a fair assumption that if your listener has a portable media device, they likely have a mobile phone also — sometimes they are the same device. If you want those listeners to give you feedback, give them a number to call. Many podcasters have set up a number through K7 (k7.net). K7 lets people call and leave a message. A copy of that message is then e-mailed to you.

To set up a "listener line", follow these steps:

1. **Go to** k7.net **and click the Sign Up link at the top of the screen.**

2. **Give the e-mail address you want your messages sent to (twice for validation).**

3. **Provide a security code in the event you cannot login.**

4. **Check the options for how you want your messages.**

   Messages can be e-mailed to you, saved on the server for you to retrieve later, or both.

5. **Choose your file format.**

   We recommend you choose PCM. The files are a little bigger, but quality is a bit better too.

6. **Click Submit.**

   You are issued a phone number. Now get the word out! Post that puppy on your Web site, include it in your e-mail signature, mention it in your podcast. You know the drill!

K7's service is based in Seattle Washington (United States). While it isn't free to callers outside the local Seattle area, most mobile plans have more minutes than a person is likely to use in a month.

K7 numbers are disabled after six months of inactivity. If you set up a number, and don't get a lot of feedback you could find yourself advertising a phone number for someone else. We recommend calling your own number every month or so if you find you're not getting a lot of calls.

Okay, K7 is fine and dandy if you're calling from the United States, but let's not forget that podcasting can reach anyone anywhere. How do you get in touch with the listeners from Australia, South Africa, or Tierra del Fuego? For about $1 per month, you can add a service to Skype to get voice mail. Listeners can use their computer to call your Skype voice mail from anywhere in the world for free — well, free for them.

You may find yourself with so much voice mail that you'll have to do what several podcasters have done and create a separate show for their listener feedback. Listeners, including your authors, often get a kick out of hearing their comments aired before the world.

Seeking Out the Comments of Others

There's an old saying about the best-laid plans of mice and men (and how they often go awry). Although some doubt exists in our minds as to the reality of rodents podcasting, we can say for certain that listeners of your show, both fan and foe, will communicate about your show to others in a variety of formats and places of which you have absolutely no control.

There are likely existing forums, chat rooms, and mailing lists that deal with your particular podcasting topic. At some point, those people will find out about your show and start listening. Current research shows it takes these people exactly 3.7 seconds to post a review to the rest of the masses. Welcome to the community of the Internet.

There are a variety of ways to keep your eyes and ears on these groups and to find comments regarding your podcast. Doing so will give you valuable, direct feedback from listeners and let you respond quickly and easily. See the following sections for the details.

Trying a general search

Is it just us, or don't most people do a Google search for their own name at least twice a week? Could be just us. But that's a great way to see whether people are talking about you. Google has a gazillion pages in its search database and constantly crawls a good percentage of the Web, finding interesting tidbits and adding more data with each pass.

When you search, try various combinations. If your name is a common one, such as *John Smith,* you're probably going to get a lot of hits unrelated to you. Try adding the topic of your show to the search for more relevant results. For example, if your name is John Smith and you're podcasting about underwater basket weaving, type **John Smith underwater basket weaving** in the Google search box. If your show name is unique, or at least uncommon, try using the name of your show as a search term.

We realize that there are other search engines besides Google. Yahoo! produces fine results, as do a few others. If you have neither the time nor the inclination to experiment with a dozen search engines, we suggest these two. Both syndicate their results to other lesser-known (but equally valid) search engines. Together, they cover the vast majority (by some estimates, about 90 percent) of the indexed pages online. But as we've said countless times before, your mileage may vary. The same techniques we outline work well on just about any search engine you prefer.

Using specialty search engines

Search engines are great tools, but sometimes they search a bit too far and wide for your tastes. Many specialty search engines have cropped up in the past few years to cater to the needs of people looking to search a more narrow set of criteria than "all Web pages on the entire planet." Researchers, academics, and students have had this level of access for a while. Now, several services that have been made public may be of use as you're trying to find communications about your show.

Google Alerts

In what might be the most narcissistic activity on the planet, Google allows you to easily do a daily check of who is talking about you and your podcast on the Internet with *Google Alerts* (www.google.com/alerts). With this feature, you receive an e-mail when a news article, blog posting, or Web page containing text matches a text string of your choice, which is likely to be your name or the name of your podcast.

Here's how to set up Google Alerts:

1. **Go to Google Alerts at** www.google.com/alerts.

   If you have a Google account, you can save yourself a couple steps at the end by clicking the Sign In link and providing your credentials.

   On the right side of the page is a Create a Google Alert interface.

2. **Enter the search terms for the topic you want to monitor, the type of results you want, and how often you want to receive results.**

   Just for example, you might want to type **Tee Morris** and have it perform a comprehensive search, covering blogs, Web sites, news, and any other connotations of online media. If you want to change the parameters of your search to more than once a day, you can change these default settings.

3. **Enter your e-mail address.**

   If you're already logged in to Google, you won't see this step. Google Alerts work with any e-mail address. If your e-mail is not part of the Google system, you receive an e-mail validating your request. Check your e-mail and click the link to validate your request.

When Google finds matching terms, it sends you an e-mail notification along with a link to the article. Each alert that comes in offers you the ability to cancel the Google Alert at any time.

Technorati

Technorati (http://technorati.com) is really more of a "buzz engine" than a search engine. It focuses its concentration and power on blogs and news services and does an exceptional job of ferreting out conversations about hot topics of nearly any size.

With Technorati, you can search for keywords, key phrases, or specific URLs. Many bloggers have found ways to pass the URLs of their blog posts to the Technorati search engine, allowing them (and others) a quick way to take the pulse of the community reaction to their words. Although Technorati won't search through podcast audio yet, it's a great way to find out whether bloggers are discussing the ideas and comments you put forth on your show.

Podscope

As of this writing, many podcasts talk about . . . other podcasts. Many don't adequately use show notes, which makes it difficult for search engine spiders and bots to find the content. (*Spiders* are programs that follow links around the Internet and report back on what they find, and *bots* are automatic scripts that act a lot like spiders but usually don't crawl so far.) However, the fine folks at Podscope (`http://podscope.com`) have figured out a way around that difficulty — searching the actual audio (and when it applies, video) entry of the episode. Figure 13-6 shows a recent result on searching for *Yo Yo Ma* at Podscope. If the service finds any show notes, they are brought back as search results.

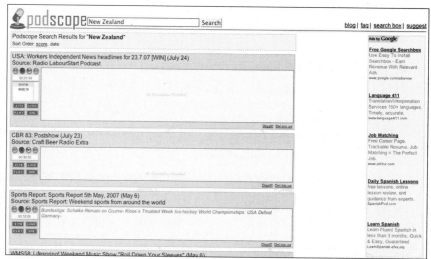

Figure 13-6:
Audio
and video
search
results are
displayed on
Podscope.

However, the true coolness lies a bit deeper. Click the little + button to expand your results and then click the green Play button to listen to a 10-second audio clip that contains the search phrase in question. How very cool! You can amuse yourself for hours on this little feature. And rather than spoil it for you with a technical description of the technologies involved, we're sticking with "magic" as the most relevant explanation.

Will you find everything you look for with Podscope? Doubtful. Will you turn up some interesting results? To quote the Magic 8-ball — future uncertain, try again later.

Searching within a site, blog, or message board

As extensive and cool as search engines are, they can't cover everything on the Net. Not only are there physical limitations as to how wide of an area the spiders and bots can cover, there are also self-imposed limitations set up by Web site owners that inhibit a good indexing of the site.

Take forums for example. Some forums are set up in a manner that renders their internal pages invisible to the spiders and bots of even the best engines.

But most forums have an internal search engine that you can use to find the content within the forum — though you may be required to register with the forum to access its search engine. Figure 13-7 shows the search results we found by doing an internal search on a popular discussion board that prohibits spiders and bots from indexing its individual pages. None of these pages were indexed by Google or Yahoo!.

Figure 13-7: Results of a search on "podcasting" at Serenity Movie.net.

When the Comments Are Less Than Good

First, don't panic.

Second, don't respond. Not yet.

Third, let your blood pressure come down to a normal level.

Let's face it. Anytime someone has any critical comments about us, we get an emotional reaction. We call that being human, and it's perfectly understandable and impossible to suppress. Following that impulse of replying right away only leads you to discover the two reasons why it's called a *knee-jerk reaction*: It's a reflex to clashing viewpoints, and you come across like a real jerk when you don't think about your response before riding the emotional roller coaster. (The classic wooden ones like the *Rebel Yell, Beast,* or *Grizzly.* Yeah. Roller coasters. Cool.)

When you're calm and feeling a bit more detached, reread the comment and plan your course of action. Here are some suggestions:

1. **Reflect on the comment.**

   What does the comment say, really? Does the person make a valid point? Is there an area of improvement you should make? If the comment was specific, re-listen to the show in question. Did you say what the person said you did or stumble as bad as the person made it out to be? You may need a different perspective, so feel free to get someone else involved.

2. **When you fully understand the criticism, decide whether or not you want to respond.**

   Obviously, if a comment is in any way libelous, you may want to seek legal counsel before proceeding. If a comment is simply pure vitriol, your best course may be to ignore it and go about your business.

3. **If you decide to reply, consider sending an e-mail.**

   If you send an e-mail, count on that e-mail being posted right alongside the negative comment. There's no guarantee the person will keep your correspondence private. In fact, count on the opposite. Whatever you say in a private e-mail should be something you would be willing to say in a more public forum. Keep your rebuttal rational, civil, and, above all, professional.

Just like any argument, it's best to keep things on a professional level with your words and mannerisms. Although it may be hard to not put it on a personal level, try to refrain. It's not going to help the situation.

Negative feedback is never an easy thing to stomach, but look at the positive aspect of this: People are listening. They're listening, and now they're most assuredly talking, blogging, and podcasting about you. We're not saying to rush out and say something completely irrational simply to drum up controversy, but we're saying that people will disagree with you now and then. It should be expected, and you should be ready to face that tough love when it comes your way.

More than anything, grow from the experience. Understand that anything you say in your podcast will be heard by a variety of people, with different backgrounds, experiences, and expectations of the world. We've been on both sides of this and can count many times where the negative comments we received turned out to be some of the best feedback. We think we're better podcasters for it.

Feedback, good or bad, is only as constructive as you make it out to be.

Avoid The Baiting Game

Tee recalls, after watching a scene in *Bull Durham* where an umpire goads Kevin Costner into insulting him, saying, "That's so Hollywood." His dad, a highly respected umpire in college and semi-pro baseball, said, "Actually, that's not. That's *baiting*." Although you may not think there is a common trait between baseball umpires and podcasters, there is: The Baiting Game.

Fast-forward to Tee's Web site (and podcast) *Survival Guide to Writing Fantasy*, where he posted a tribute to a friend lost to breast cancer. Billed as a "Special Edition" this show was simply to raise awareness. An anonymous poster came on to the show's blog and left a long comment that said in so many words, "We don't care about you. We don't care about your friend dying of cancer. Stick to the content of the show." While Tee did not reply, his community of "Survivalists" did, to which the anonymous poster rebutted with a lot of contempt and very little reason. On his following *Survival Guide,* Tee asked the poster to stop listening if he found the show so distasteful. The anonymous poster returned to say "You can't make me stop listening . . ." and then listed other writing podcasts he found better than Tee's.

At this point, Tee recognized this for The Baiting Game that it was.

There are people out there who live to pick fights. They can be "listeners" of your podcasts or, sometimes, other podcasters looking for a thrill in bucking the community. A way to tell it's The Baiting Game is to look closer at the criticism with (pardon the pun) a critical eye. Usually the feedback from baiting is comprised of personal attacks, misconstruing of facts, flawed reasoning (if there's any reason present), spin control, and a healthy dose of verbal insults akin to punching someone in the ear and then running away. When this happens, don't reply. Ever. By not replying, the words sent to you are a waste of time and effort on the sender's part, not yours. Not replying isn't a guarantee that the baiter will simply disappear. You may need to moderate your blog just to be sure people don't post comments that you deem inappropriate.

The high road has a better view than the low. In some cases, like The Baiting Game, the best response is none at all.

Chapter 14

Fishing for Listeners

- -

In This Chapter

▶ Getting your podcast ready for advertising

▶ Using paid advertising

▶ Taking advantage of free advertising

▶ Generating buzz about your podcast

- -

As of this writing, there are tens of thousands of podcasters. By some estimates, the number of people who listen to various podcasts range in the millions. However, that pales in comparison with the potential audience, which is somewhere in excess of 300 million people worldwide with a broadband Internet connection. Although the audience is large, the options for listeners are legion. But how do you attract an audience to your podcast?

In this chapter, we show you a variety of options that you may want to use in an effort to gain a larger listener base. Some cost you money; others cost you time. But the end result is exposing your podcast to the right people at the right time.

Getting Your Podcast Ready for Advertising

Whether you plan on spending real money or expending real energy, you need to do some prep work before you start your campaign. You shouldn't rush your advertising campaigns, but take the time to carefully plan and execute them. Failure to do so can not only be a huge waste of time and money, but it may also result in turning off potential listeners to your show, making it many times more difficult to attract them back for a second chance.

Polishing your presentation

Most podcasters need a few shows under their belts before they hit their stride. If you're on podcast episode number three, you likely haven't fleshed out your show. Granted, you may have been planning your podcast for months on end, or have previous experience behind the mic on another medium, or have nailed it from the beginning. If so, great. But understand you're in the minority.

Even though each person is different, we suggest giving yourself at least five full shows to find the sweet spot. Experimentation is part of the format, so play with a few things along the way to see where your strengths as well as your weaknesses are.

Checking your bandwidth

In Chapter 10, we talk about the negative aspects of too large an audience. Each new listener means more of your precious bandwidth being consumed. For podcasters with limited bandwidth, getting more listeners can be an expensive proposition.

If you're using the services of Liberated Syndication (http://libsyn.com) or another unmetered bandwidth podcast hosting company, you don't have to worry about your bandwidth and can safely skip ahead to the next section. See Chapter 10 for more information about these very affordable services.

Many podcasters start out using the standard Web hosting service to host their podcast files and are quickly surprised when they run out of bandwidth. We're more surprised about how poor their math skills are. Suppose that you have 100MB of monthly transfers allowed for your site. On the 10th of July, you log in to your bandwidth stats page and see that you're already at 60MB for the month. Will you make it? Here are the formulas to figure this out:

Bandwidth consumed / number of days so far this month = Daily bandwidth rate

Daily bandwidth rate 31 (the total number of days in the month) = Total bandwidth needed

Now you plug in your numbers to find out your daily bandwidth rate:

60MB / 10 = 6MB

You're consuming about 6MB per day. Now multiply this number (6MB) by the number of days in the month (31) to get the total bandwidth you need for the month:

6MB × 31 = 186MB

It's inevitable; you're not going to stay within your 100MB limit. You will be roughly 86MB over your 100MB plan.

That sounds — and is — simple. As a real-world example, Chuck checked his bandwidth usage on July 18th and found that he had used 256.65GB in the first 17 days.

First, he needs to find out his daily bandwidth:

256.65GB / 17 days = 15GB average daily transfer rate for July

Then, he has to find out his total bandwidth for the month:

15GB × 31 days = 465GB

As you can see, he needs 465GB of bandwidth to get through the month, assuming his traffic stays steady and doesn't increase. If his bandwidth ceiling was 500GB, he'd need to think twice before starting an advertising campaign, as he'd likely hit that ceiling, and his hosting provider would likely shut down access to all those brand-new podcast listeners he just worked so hard to get. Not a good way for anyone to spend his or her time.

As a good rule, you need to be using less than 50 percent of your monthly allotment of bandwidth before starting an advertising campaign. If you're using any more than that, you'll run out of room and will have to seek alternative hosting options before proceeding. We cover some of these alternative options in Chapter 10.

Figuring out your USP

USP is a marketing term, and it stands for _unique selling proposition_ — a message that sells your podcast to potentials listeners. Although you probably aren't charging money to listen to your podcast, make no mistake that you need to "sell it" to potential listeners if you're considering advertising.

Why should a potential listener listen to your podcast? And more importantly, how can you, as the podcast advertiser, present a message that makes a potential listener want to listen?

Plenty of books, Web sites, seminars, and post-graduate degree programs are dedicated to the subtle nuances of advertising. We're not suggesting you go that far, obviously. But we do suggest you take a good, hard look at what you produce every week and come up with a concise and consistent message with which to promote your show.

For example, when Chuck was looking at advertising for his ChuckChat *Technorama* podcast, he found that the market for another tech podcast was pretty saturated. Several dozen shows repurposed the same news about Microsoft, Google, and Apple. Instead, Chuck chose to spotlight the strange, bizarre, and unusual items that are typically passed via e-mail from geek to geek — the steam-powered Nintendo DS, the motorcycle that folds in to a briefcase, and who can forget the device made of wood that adds binary numbers. Thus, the USP for *Technorama* goes like this:

> *Technorama* takes a light-hearted look at the world of tech, science, sci-fi, and all things geek.

Is advertising right for your podcast?

Before launching your advertising campaign, apply some *Jurassic Park* logic. In that movie, Jeff Goldblum's character chastises the dinosaur-resurrecting mogul with "your scientists were so preoccupied with whether or not they could, they didn't stop to think if they should." Good advice for podcasters and mad scientists alike.

For many, podcasting is a labor of love and not a money-making proposition. As such, spending too much money or time on advertising may make a passion seem a heck of a lot more like a job — and you probably already have one of those.

If you're interested in making money on your podcast, you might also consider the Return on Investment, or ROI — oh, now we're starting to sound like a corporation so bear with us a moment. Simply put, is the money you spend on advertising going to generate you any additional. . . anything? It doesn't make sense to spend $5 or $5,000 if you won't get more. . . something — listeners, advertisers, sponsors, money — in return. Spending money just to spend money doesn't sound like a lot of fun to us.

Some of the podcasts we enjoy the most, such as Dave Slusher's *Evil Genius Chronicles* (www. evilgeniuschronicles.org), are very vocal about not advertising and not working toward a huge listener base. Dave makes a podcast for one person — Dave Slusher. If other folks hear about the podcast and decide to listen, great, so long as they enjoy it and don't expect him to be something he's not. Fame is a double-edged sword — even the moderate fame a popular podcaster can achieve. Before long, e-mails and voice mails are flying in with ideas, suggestions, and even mandates of how you can make the show better — for the listeners. Don't forget that *fan* is short for *fanatic,* and fanatic people don't always behave rationally.

So choose this path with caution. In reality, "doing it for the love" probably means you can (and should?) forgo advertising your podcast. It's not a fast way to get more listeners, but it is a fast way to burn through money without a lot to show for it.

Sometimes calling in help from the outside can be a good thing. Ask your friends and family, or even your listeners, to come up with some key points of why they listen to your show. We're not talking about a catchy slogan or jingle of the sort a Madison Avenue marketing firm might designate as the "perfect" thing to attract new listeners, but plain English (or your language of choice) ways to tell interested folks what your show is about and why they should be listening.

We can't give you a step-by-step outline on this one. Spend a few days on it. Try it out on some folks first. When you find a message that fits, you're ready to proceed on your advertising quest.

Exploring Various Advertising Options

In this section, we discuss some of the many ways you can advertise to give your podcast exposure to a larger audience.

Google AdWords

When it comes to exposing yourself to the largest possible audience, you simply can't beat the power of Google. More than just a search engine, Google allows you to reach over 80 percent of all active Internet users with targeted and relevant advertising. With Google AdWords (`http://adwords.google.com`), you can keep your advertising costs under control and reach a very specific audience.

How it works

Google AdWords allows you to place text ads or *sponsored links* at the top and right side of Google search results pages, based on keywords that you (and others) bid on. Additionally, its content distribution network allows your text ads to appear on various Web sites related to the keywords for which you have placed bids. The trick is to pick the keywords and phrases likely to be used by people interested in listening to your podcast. Here's how it works:

Google charges advertisers on a cost-per-click basis, — that is, you're only charged when a user clicks your advertisement. Knowing that this cost-per-click system appeals to lots of small advertisers with small budgets, Google allows you to cap your daily spending. There may be the chance for a thousand people to click your ads on any given day, but Google pulls your ads once you've reached your limit. And Google scales to your budgetary requirements, happily serving ads whether your budget is $5 per day or $500,000 per month. Evo has been a power user of Google for years, both personally and on behalf of his clients, and has always found Google delivers great results.

All Google ads are bid-based, causing those who pay the highest amount of money for a click to (usually) rise to the top. If you are only willing to spend $0.25 to get a click, yet the top bid on that keyword is already $4.50, you're going to be way down the list of advertisers, and probably see little to no clicks.

When you sign up for AdWords, Google provides a Traffic Estimator so you can see how much traffic you might expect from a given set of keywords. Then you can evaluate how much you need to budget to get a decent showing on the page, or whether a set of keywords is worth the price of the clicks or not.

Using the service

The signup process for the AdWords product is simple and straightforward, so we don't go in detail about it in this book. Simply access http://adwords.google.com, and Google takes you step by step through the signup process.

When you first sign up for Google AdWords, start with a small investment. Even if you represent a large company that's starting a podcast, don't go overboard on spending real dollars on advertising campaigns right off the bat. Pick a modest number to start with, evaluate your results, and refine your technique. After you have it figured out, then you can go hog wild!

After you decide on a budget, you need to find keywords that fit within that budget. Say, for example, your podcast is about fishing. For the keyword *fishing,* Google estimates approximately 2,600 clicks per day for ads in the top positions. That's a great traffic number that any fledgling podcaster would love to have hitting his or her site each day.

However, to get all those 2,600 clicks for *fishing,* Google says you'd need to set your maximum bid at $2.50 per click so that your ad shows in the top position against other people and companies advertising on the page. That's a lot of money. You can choose to not bid for that top position and just set the bid at the average price of $0.62 for each click. You ads won't always be on top, but should be in the top three spots. You'll end up paying a bit over $1,600 for all the clicks Google can deliver to you. Per day. Wow.

To help bring this cost down to a more manageable level, you need to get more targeted with your keywords. *Fishing* is a rather broad term, so try a few other combinations to see whether you can find a cost within your budget. Here are a few examples you might consider:

✔ **salmon fishing:** If you enter **salmon fishing** in the Traffic Estimator, you get a more reasonable estimate of a daily cost of $46.19 per day. However, at that price tag, you're only attracting 20 clicks. *Salmon fishing* has a much higher average cost per click ($2.31) than *fishing* ($0.62).

> ✔ **fishing advice:** Not as many big outfitters and organizations are willing to give advice away, so they aren't bidding on those types of keywords. Daily traffic isn't much more than 1 or 2 clicks per day, and the cost estimate is only $0.44 per click. Now you're on to something. Less people are viewing the ads, but you're reaching a much more relevant audience than the thousands who may or may not see the more generic "fishing" ad. Now you're into the world of reality.

What happens after the click?

So now you're happily spending money for clicks. It's within your budget, and Google provides you a nice and easy-to-read interface that shows you exactly what Google is giving you for your money.

But what are you getting?

Any online advertising campaign that doesn't come with clearly defined goals and extremely unambiguous ways to track them isn't worth the money — at any price. Earlier in this chapter we mentioned Return On Investment (ROI), and in this section, we discuss how you measure it.

To measure your ROI, you have to have a good handle on the current performance of your podcast. How many subscribers do you have? How many visit your Web site? How many listen to your show from the links straight off your page? You have to know these data. Any ad campaign you put in place is designed to improve one or all of these metrics, so you had better know where your starting point is.

When you have a handle on the number of subscribers you have, figuring out what your ads have done to improve those is a relatively trivial matter, as long as you are good with simple math. Find out how your show is trending prior to your campaign and compare it to the trending after the campaign has launched. This will be different for each podcast, so we can't be a whole lot more specific.

Want an even easier way to measure success? Install Google Analytics (www.google.com/analytics). It's free, it's easy, and it ties in to your Google AdWords campaign seamlessly. It also works with any of the other ideas we talk about in this chapter. Pretty slick. With the click of a few buttons, you can see how the campaign has impacted your site, for better or for worse.

Blogads

Advertising on blogs requires a different mindset than advertising on a search engine. Blog readers, for the most part, have little love for advertising.

They're looking for content they can't get from the mainstream media outlets or are caught up completely by the cult of personality surrounding their bloggers of choice.

Sounds like a perfect place to attract listeners to your podcast!

Blogads (`http://blogads.com`) is a fine example of a company that makes advertising easier for you. Blogads has created a network of sorts, allowing you to place a single ad on a multitude of blogs. That's a whole lot easier than researching blogs, negotiating prices individually, and creating and tracking ads for each one.

According to Blogads: "Warning: ads you'd run on sites like MSNBC.com may underperform on blogs. Smart blogads join a community's conversation rather than shouting over it." If you're an independent podcast producer, you should have no trouble creating ads that really speak to why people should listen to your podcast. If you're podcasting for a corporation, getting your advertising department to speak in this language may be more difficult. Blogads has some great examples of what works, as well as what doesn't work, on its network of sites.

Signing up for Blogads takes only a few minutes. You're guided through the process of creating a compelling image and using supporting text within the ad. Prices range from $20 per week to over $5,000 per week, putting Blogads in a price range for nearly anybody who is ready to spend some money advertising his or her show.

There are other services similar to Blogads to help get your message out — another popular one is called Project Wonderful at `www.project wonderful.com`.

Writing press releases

Some podcasters have had enormous success attracting new listeners with press releases. When you release a press release, it's available to be picked up by a variety of news sources. On the positive side, you have a lot of room inside a press release to talk about your show. On the negative, you have no guarantee of whom — if anyone — will pick up and run your press release.

Writing an effective press release is a true art form. It has to appeal both to the managing editor of the publication considering your release for building a story around it, as well as being worthwhile reading to John Q. Public in the publication.

Here are some ideas to help you write a good press release:

- **Tell a story.** Your press release should convey a condensed version of what it is you want to say. Three or four paragraphs made up of two or three sentences each is a good guideline to follow. Try to answer the most common questions people will have about your announcement. Start with the basics of good journalism — who, what, when, where, and why.

- **Target the press release**. Write the press release suitable to your target audience. You will likely have to write more than one version — and send your story to those likely to run it. A story about "*hometown boy writes successful book on podcasting*" is more likely to get published in the college alumni school paper than *USA Today*.

- **Hook them early**. This is also known as B.L.U.F. — stating your bottom line up front. Whatever you have to say, be sure to say it first and grab their attention.

- **Give the tag line.** Use your USP. This is the perfect place to give someone that 30 second pitch about your show.

- **Give some quotes.** Include a couple lines from the people involved. Keep them positive and upbeat.

- **Provide appropriate URLs.** Don't forget to provide links to your site(s). This should go without saying, but sometimes you may get so wrapped up in the wording of the press release that you forget the point of the press release — to get people to come to you site and try your content.

We recommend reading a number of press releases to get a feeling for the marketing aspect.

If you know people who have written press releases in the past, see if they can lend some help — if not, reach out. Remember that podcasting can be a very helpful network.

PR Newswire

PR Newswire (`http://prwire.com`) is the cream of the crop when it comes to online and offline distribution of your press release. PR Newswire has the ability to send your press release to thousands of media outlets, ranging from newsprint, radio, Web sites, television, and more.

The company also provides editorial services for your press release, as well as tips and tricks on how to write an effective release that's more likely to get results. If you're serious about getting the maximum exposure to your show and are thinking about using a press release as part of your strategy, PR Newswire is worth looking into.

However, many independent podcasters may find the cost prohibitive (around $300 to start) and the registration process somewhat daunting. In a world where online registration and upfront disclosure is commonplace, PR Newswire follows a more traditional approach. Gaining access requires you to contact your local bureau either via e-mail (`information@prnewswire.com`) or by telephone. You can find a list of bureaus at `www.prnewswire.com/services/resources/bureaus.shtml`.

PRWeb

Considerably less archaic is PRWeb (`http://prweb.com`). This organization offers paid and donation-based services, and it boasts of a good number of media outlets. The main difference between the two organizations (other than cost and the hassle-factor) is the quality of the distribution. PRWeb works to put your press release in front of thousands of online media outlets. Offline media sources may subscribe as well, but the primary distribution is online.

Not that that is a bad thing. After all, your podcast is an online service, and you're likely most effective reaching an audience who is already online. All three of us have had various write-ups in both online and offline media, and we've always received more traffic and attention to our Web sites from the online sources.

We don't want to make PRWeb sound somehow inferior to the traditional sources of press release distribution. Far from it, actually. Although the service may not be as full featured, it can still be a great way to get your word out, and one that is quite cost effective.

For $80, PRWeb distributes your press release (among many other things) in Yahoo! News, a huge news source that's often referenced in the online community. Additionally, press releases at this level are reviewed by the PRWeb editorial team, providing valuable feedback on ways to make your press release more meaningful and more likely to be picked up by various other news organizations around the Internet.

Promoting Your Podcast

Before you start throwing money toward an advertising campaign, consider all the things you can do to spread the word about your podcast that don't require a financial investment. In fact, you probably should be doing these things even if you plan on tossing out some cash for effect.

Optimizing your site for search engines

In Chapters 11 and 12, we give you several tips on how you can make your RSS listings, as well as your show notes, more appealing to search engines. You can employ similar methods to your entire Web site so that it receives the maximum exposure and visibility to search engines.

For more information on optimizing your site, we highly recommend *Search Engine Optimization For Dummies* by Peter Kent (Wiley Publishing, Inc.). Additionally, Cre8asite Forums at `http://cre8asiteforums.com` is an invaluable discussion board to keep up on the latest techniques on keeping your Web site search engine friendly.

Submitting promos to other podcasts

Podcasting has been called by critics (even us) to be a great hall of mirrors, as it seems that nearly every podcast spends a ridiculous portion of its time talking about . . . other podcasts!

We think this is normal for an emerging medium, and something that is, for the most part, accepted by the general podcasting audience. The podcasting landscape isn't shrinking anytime soon, and it's so fractured that many listeners are looking for their favorite podcasters to help steer them toward other podcasts they may find interesting.

Not all podcasters do this. In fact, the majority of the corporate podcasts must see other podcasts as competition and are as likely to talk about another podcast as a traditional broadcaster is to talk about another station across town. Even some of the independent podcasters make a point not to talk about other podcasts, simply because they don't want to add to the hall of mirrors effect.

One of the more widespread ways podcasters talk about other podcasters is with promos. A *promo* is a short (or long) audio clip that describes your show. Other podcasters then insert this clip into their shows — play it on the air so to speak — thereby presenting your message to their subscribed and downloading audiences.

Promos are a great way to let other folks know your podcast exists. Spend some time listening to other podcasts and see whether they're playing promos. When you find one that does, see what the average time for the promotion turns out to be and what type of content is being presented. Is it all serious business, or is more light-hearted humor involved?

Some podcasters are really good at making promos and even offer to make promos for free for other podcasters. A whole promo exchange industry is cropping up, allowing podcasters to trade time with other podcasters, each agreeing to run the other promo for a certain number of weeks. Check out `http://promos.podshow.com` and `http://podcastpromos.com` for details.

One final note on sending out promos: Ask. Unless the show specifically says "submit your promos to us at . . .", be a good podcasting citizen and send the podcaster a note asking whether she'd like to run your promo. Requests that start off with "I listen to your show every week because you . . ." are likely to get a better response than those starting (and ending) with "Please run my promo."

Recording your promo

Recording your own promo isn't difficult, and we tend to enjoy the ones that come from the voice of the podcaster. You've done the hard work by figuring out what makes your podcast special; now you need to sit down and record your promo. Here are a few tips:

- ✔ **Write your script.** Or don't. Some folks are happy flying off the cuff. But in the interest of time, we highly recommend putting some thoughts down on paper and running through them out loud to see how long it takes. Most promos are under a minute long, unless you have lots of great stuff to say.

- ✔ **Add effects and music from your podcast.** If you use the same music (see Chapter 7) in your show each week or have some special sound effects that brand the show as yours, include them in your promo. Effects are a great way to tie in your promotion to your show, giving new listeners assurance they have subscribed to the right place.

- ✔ **Don't forget your Web site URL!** Too many podcasters provide the link to their podcast feed. Useless, in our opinions. Instead, repeat the URL of your Web site, where it should be painfully simple to subscribe to the RSS feed for your podcast. Now here's to hoping you picked an easy-to-remember domain name!

- ✔ **Include a link to the promo on your Web site.** Recording one and sending it out to a few podcasts is great, but what about all the other folks who you inspire to make their own podcast? Chances are good that if you put a link to your promo file on your Web site, others will grab that file and include your promo in their shows. It's also a good repository for when you find another podcast you think might want to run your promo.

When you send other podcasters your promo, save some e-mail bandwidth and send the link that's on your Web site, rather than the file itself.

Giving interviews

Don't forget that podcasting is the fastest growing medium we've seen . . . ever! If your podcast covers a brand-new area of the world or addresses an underserved market, folks are out there who want to talk with you about it.

Contact the publications, radio shows, Web sites, and other outlets that cover the industry your podcast falls under. Send them your press release, along with a personalized note telling them about your show and stating that you're happy to do an interview.

Interviews can be done in person, but most today are conducted over the phone. A handful are conducted via e-mail. Preparing for an interview can make the difference between a poor interview that never sees publication or airtime and a well-delivered interview that keeps the audience — as well as the interviewer — engaged and entertained.

Here are a few tips to make your interview go swimmingly:

- ✔ **Eliminate the BS factor.** If you have only a passing interest in the subject for which you're trying to pass yourself off as an expert, you'll quickly be discovered, thrashed repeatedly, and left out for the buzzards. The people who are interviewing you likely are already experts in their fields, so don't try to come off as something you aren't. Be open and honest about your experience and focus on why you're doing the podcast. Even if you're considered a subject matter expert, remember that your listener may not be. You might want to consider simplifying things on behalf of the listeners new to the subject. Of course, this depends on your listeners and the subject being covered.

- ✔ **Mention your Web site over and over again.** Remember that the listeners, readers, or viewers you are being interviewed in front of have no idea who you are and what you are about. This is your chance to sell yourself and your podcast. If your interviewer is good, he'll give you ample opportunity to mention your Web site and podcast. If not, it's up to you. Look for chances to drop the name and URL if necessary.

- ✔ **Stay positive.** If the interviewer knows anything about podcasting, he'll likely ask questions on the future of podcasting, the death of radio, amateur versus professional, and all sorts of other controversial topics. Unless your podcast is about podcasting, we recommend rising above the din. This conversation doesn't serve you or the listening/reading/viewing audience well. Point out how your podcast addresses the issue and resist the temptation to get into an argument. Unless your podcast is about arguing with interviewers; in that case, go right ahead.

Generating buzz

All the processes we outline in this chapter are geared toward one thing: generating buzz for your podcast. The more folks you can get talking about your show, the better off you are. We don't buy the "any publicity is good publicity" line, but we do think that "Hey have you heard about . . .?" conversations amongst real people are the best form of advertising you can get.

Sometimes, you need to take the message to the masses. Find a discussion group or an online forum germane to your podcast's area of interest and start posting.

When you post, don't start out with "Hey, I'm new to the group and have this great podcast!" Instead, listen in to the conversation, comment on a few threads, and get folks used to your voice before you hit them with the come-listen-to-my-podcast pitch. In fact, the best way to pitch your podcast is to never utter those words at all. Instead, offer up things like "Last week on my podcast, I covered the very thing you were talking about, Jill." It shows you're paying attention to the conversation and not just looking to spam a newsgroup or mailing list with your podcast URL.

A very fine line exists between tasteful self-promotion and outright spamming. Generating buzz isn't the same as advertising. Advertising has its place, but most forums don't welcome it. If you can't decide whether your post contains too much advertising or not, it probably does. Discretion is the better part of valor, in this instance.

For more ways to generate buzz we recommend *Expert Podcasting Practices For Dummies* by Tee Morris, Evo Terra, and Ryan Williams (Wiley Publishing, Inc.).

Part V
Pod-sibilities to Consider for Your Show

"What do you mean you're updating your videocast?"

In this part . . .

As you can see in the parts and chapters leading up to this one, podcasting is a breeze when you know the right steps. But now comes the moment of truth: We move away from the "how" questions and tackle "why" you might want to podcast. Fame and fortune? Strength and honor? Therapy and philanthropy? Fun with computers? An alternative to a real social life? These all sound like good reasons to us.

Chapter 15

Show Me the Money

*T*hroughout this book, we show you novel and interesting ways to toss significant amount of coinage into the proverbial black hole of podcasting. Throwing money at your podcast can easily become a habit — and it likely should come with a warning from the Surgeon General or perhaps your accountant.

Hosting fees, bandwidth overages, shiny new microphones, music royalties and licensing fees, phone charges, travel expenses . . . the hard and soft costs of this little hobby of yours just might add up quickly.

That's why this chapter shows you some ways to offset a portion (or all) of these costs and perhaps even add a few dollars to your pocket while you explore your newfound passion. In case you anticipate a large following, we cover some ideas you can use to make this your paying gig.

Being a podcaster is a lot like being an actor, a writer, or a movie star. A few select individuals may make it big, but most folks just get by — and that can be okay. If you're reading this chapter first in hopes of getting a crash course in how to "get rich quick" with your podcast, you're about to be disappointed. If not, we can talk.

How Much Money Can You Make?

Most podcasters fall into one of three categories in terms of their audience size: small, medium, and large (well, yeah). Because of the very low barrier-to-entry — in effect, almost anyone can create a podcast — the smaller variety of podcaster will likely make up the bulk of the community for the foreseeable future.

Here's a closer look at the moneymaking opportunities for these three podcast categories:

- ✔ **Small:** Roughly, a small podcast has under 1,000 listeners. Having a small audience size doesn't exclude you from drawing a revenue stream from your podcast. It likely limits the size of your potential revenues, but it doesn't mean you can't bring in at least some income.

    Small is a relative term, and we're not about to start tossing out audience-size statistics to draw a clear demarcation between small and medium. Small is also not a derogatory term; many podcasters enjoy the idea of keeping their cast small. There's a certain comfort in the small podcasts, a charm that some would say is diminished as the size of the podcast's audience increases. Small can actually be an asset — some podcasts are so niche that they draw a small, but extremely loyal following. To a potential advertiser, you have a target audience.

- ✔ **Medium:** When you have more than a handful of dedicated listeners (in the four-digit bracket with over 1,000 listeners), you find yourself in the medium category. This category affords you additional opportunities. For instance, corporations and advertisers may be more willing to consider placing ads or providing sponsorships.

    However, you also find yourself in a more competitive marketplace, as other podcasters start fishing for monies to help offset their costs. Stepping upward in the ranks also means stepping up your game, and you may find yourself in an unfamiliar place — trying to develop a media kit that boosts your podcast above the din raised by all the other podcasts chasing the very same advertisers.

    Creating an effective media kit, especially for a newly discovered marketplace such as podcasting, is actually a pretty important task. (For more about the why, what, and how-to, see "Developing a media kit," later in this chapter.) We highly recommend the *Podcast Brothers* podcast (`http://feeds.feedburner.com/PodcastBrothers`) to anyone looking for ideas and ways to make money with podcasting. Tim and Emile Bourquin produce this weekly show, covering the ins and the outs of making money with your podcast.

- ✔ **Large:** Breaking the barrier at the far end of the size spectrum is an elite set of podcasters who occupy the *large* category and are in the five-digit bracket with over 10,000 listeners. When it comes to making money with your podcast, size really does matter. With a huge audience base, you'll likely find advertisers a lot easier to approach; you can present listener numbers that are more like what the advertisers are used to seeing in their more traditional media buys.

    Outside the mainstream media (like NPR, CNN, and ESPN), there aren't that many really *large* podcasts out there — yet — so thus far the playing field is still fairly open. Still, it's no picnic for large podcasters; after all, they're still targeting a very narrow audience on typically one topic (or show), and they probably won't rake in as much as a nationally syndicated radio program. Don't be surprised, however, if you see that paradigm change. Podcasters have much more flexibility than broadcasters and arguably a closer relationship with the audience.

Does your podcast need to pay for itself?

"You spent *how much* on a new microphone?" You'll soon be hearing that or a question just like it with a different gizmo attached to the question mark. Your non-podcasting friends, colleagues, and perhaps even family will gaze in wonder at your apparent lack of good judgment as you seemingly spend money as if it grew on trees, *trees we say,* adding just one more piece to your previously professed "perfect" podcasting setup.

How can you, in good conscience, justify this outlay of cash without the financial backing of someone else? Surely if no one is willing to pay you to do this podcasting thing, you shouldn't be doing it at all, right?

In a word, wrong.

(Evo here) As I write this, my 14-year-old son is busy bouncing back and forth between his PS2 and his PC, about $3,000 in total investments. My wife is on her laptop ($1,500) cropping recent images taken with her new top-of-the-line prosumer digital camera ($2,000). Next door, my neighbor is up to his elbows in grease, changing the rear seals (whatever those are) in his "family fleet" of ATVs before a trip to the dunes this weekend. He wins the prize, having no less than $15,000 invested in his passion.

Each of these non-podcasting individuals, all of whom are involved in the healthy pursuit of liberty and happiness, constantly spend money on their hobbies. My son thinks nothing of dropping $50 of his (read: MY) money on a game every two months. My wife now goes through at least two color ink cartridges every month. And Jerry next door has to burn through a few

hundred dollars of fuel, parts, and doctor bills each month.

If I were to poll each of these people, asking them whether they had ever considered getting someone to help pay for their various addictions, they'd look at me as if I were from another planet. Well, except my son. He'd just grin and say, "But isn't that *you,* Dad?"

Think of the amount of money you spend eating out each week. Or for movie tickets, theater presentations, concerts, and/or bar tabs. These are things you love and enjoy, not things you're trying to find others to pay for. Most podcasters will spend no more than a hundred bucks a month on their show — average over time — and that's stretching it. And for such a small investment that has such a high personal payoff . . . do you *need* to be paid off in cold hard cash to do it?

(Chuck here) To follow-up on Evo's thought, there is an incredible non-monetary value in podcasting. It was through podcasts that I have found a wealth of information to help my professional career. Heck, if it weren't for doing a little bit of volunteer work writing and voice-overs in the podosphere, I may not have landed this gig — writing *Podcasting For Dummies.*

(Tee here) And of course, never underestimate the power and value of *SPUs: Spousal Permission Units.* Flowers, a surprise trip to a spa, and cooking dinner and cleaning house for a month . . . it will surprise you how many SPUs a little TLC can earn you for some killer podcasting hardware!

Convincing Advertisers to Give You Money

If the idea of begging for money sounds rather repulsive, good. If you have to resort to begging, you shouldn't be asking at all. People will only part with their cash if you give them a compelling reason. "Because I'm a poor pod-caster" is not a compelling reason.

Whether your goal is to gain sponsors or sell advertising spots, you have to answer a very important question: What's in it for them? Why should some-one else make a financial contribution to your show? There are a multitude of good reasons that you'll need to uncover, understand, and be able to explain if you hope to be successful in asking for funds to support your podcast.

Contrary to popular belief, there aren't nearly enough corporations so bursting-at-the-seams with unused advertising dollars that they'll welcome you with open arms when you approach them and say, "Hey! Wanna adver-tise on my podcast?"

Most corporations have an advertising *budget* (as in, a limit on what they can spend). In nearly all circumstances, this budget is significantly smaller than the range of potential places they might be advertising — so they're looking for the most bang for their buck. As one of the would-be venues for their ads, you're competing with other forms of media — including outlets that already have well-established pitches and presentations at the ready.

Before you start cold-calling possible advertisers, do a little homework. Spend some time, energy, and money developing something your poten-tial advertisers can touch and see: a media kit and a rate sheet, which we describe in the next sections.

Sometimes all you can do is put your best foot forward and make your pitch. Talk to the advertiser about your dedicated audience, and how loyal it is to your show. Breaking down the costs into per-listener numbers might help as well. Whatever your approach, don't try to compare your numbers with those of traditional outlets the advertiser is already working with. Instead, talk about how *adding* podcast advertising to the mix can enhance its current efforts, allowing the company to reach an audience that has turned away from tradi-tional media sources in favor of this new medium.

Developing a media kit

A *media kit* is, in effect, a collection of marketing tools designed to awaken potential advertisers to their crying need to shell out big bucks to support your product (in this case, your podcast). The size of your media kit depends on many factors, among which are how much you want to spend and how much important stuff you think you have to say. It's not size you're striving for here; it's a compelling argument that you can present to your potential advertisers.

Media kits are most certainly not one size fits all. Your media kit should be representative of the actual feeling you try to produce on your podcast — competent and real, not over-the-top glitzy. Consider it like a job interview: It's okay to comb your hair and put on a fresh shirt, but you wouldn't send your good-looking-but-ignorant roommate as a stand-in, would you? (Look what happened to Cyrano.)

The big fish are very well armed in this pond. Large media outlets tend to have large media kits that were developed with the assistance of large advertising agencies that charged large sums of money for their expertise. The small- to mid-size podcaster need not go this far. But you need something more than just a burned CD of your latest episode.

So here's a practical list of dos and don'ts to keep in mind when considering what to put in your media kit.

First off, the "Yes, go for it" list:

- ✔ **Include accurate listener statistics.** Well, as accurate as you can, anyway. Include the total number of subscribers to your podcast feed; estimate how many direct downloads an episode of your show attracts. If your podcast is seeing great growth, include a chart that shows the increasing numbers. (For more about listener statistics, see the handy nearby sidebar, "Can you ever really know the size of your audience?")

- ✔ **Display your show schedule.** If you update your podcast several times a week or once a month, include a calendar or schedule of when your updates happen. If your show has no set schedule, be prepared to explain your methodology of updates. Many advertisers expect some sort of consistency (read: reliable exposure) from the places their ads are running.

- ✔ **Provide demographic information.** Some advertisers want to know the general make-up of your audience. The more detailed you can get, the better. At a minimum, show a breakdown of gender, age range, and household income level. These statistics can be difficult to gather, but doing so increases your chances with many advertisers. Consider asking listeners to take a voluntary survey. There are many sites like `http://surveymonkey.com` that cost a few dollars — remember sometimes you have to spend money to make money.

- ✔ **Showcase your popularity.** If you get 50 comments on each of your show note entries, talk about it. Technorati (`http://technorati.com`) and Google (`www.google.com`) can support any claims for the popularity of your site. Print any great testimonials showing your knowledge and expertise in the field. Favorable comments from other known experts go a long way, too!

And in the "No, no, a thousand times no" corner, we have . . .

- ✔ **Don't artificially inflate your statistics.** Grandmother always used to say that lies just cause you to make bigger lies. Eventually you find yourself with an advertiser who wants you to explain how you came up with your numbers. Make sure you can support your claims.

- ✔ **Don't offer reduced pricing.** Podcasting is a new medium, and you likely haven't had time to put things on sale yet. Pick a price you're comfortable with and justify why it's worth it. If you're not sure of a starting price, ask other podcasters. Avoid discounting right off the bat; it implies that you're over-valuing your product. You can always negotiate the price, but don't try that in a media kit. We talk about putting together a rate sheet in the following section.

- ✔ **Don't include a copy of your entire show on CD.** People like to know what they're getting themselves into. You have a great opportunity to offer that courtesy to potential advertisers — to let them listen enough to sample the wares. Remember, however, that their time is limited. You may include entire episodes if you like, but you may find better success by stitching together "best of" clips from your show; these take less time to consume.

- ✔ **Don't make a halfhearted effort.** Okay, you don't have to create a full-blown presentation that would make the mavens of Madison Avenue envious of your skill set. But we're not talking Elmer's glue and crayons here, either. Treat it like a business; invest the right kind of time and money to make your media kit look (and sound) as professional as you can.

When you have your content figured out, go buy a nice, pretty binder. Or better yet, order some custom ones online that feature your podcast logo, slogan, and Web site address. You can get them online from VistaPrint (`www.vistaprint.com`) if you want large quantities. For smaller runs, see what your local office-supply or copy center can provide.

Establishing a rate sheet

A *rate sheet* is simply a table of what you charge for ads and other services — this could include things like audio or graphic production. And you thought you were headed into uncharted waters by just creating a podcast? How about figuring out a fair price to charge for running advertising? That's by no means a science. Heck, it's not even an art form at this stage! It's total guesswork — picking a number, throwing it out there, and seeing what sticks.

You can start by reviewing rates of other podcasts — hopefully podcasts with similar topics or audience sizes. Ask them for their media kits and rate sheets — if they are separate items.

TECHNICAL STUFF

Can you ever really know the size of your audience?

Tracking down listener statistics is elusive — and that's quite an understatement. Although many of the podcasting pundits will tell you how important understanding your audience size is (especially when you're trying to attract advertisers and sponsors), it's difficult for them to agree on the best way to snag those numbers.

Web server analysis tools are wholly unreliable in this regard; after all, they weren't designed for this purpose. They can tell you how many times your podcast episodes were requested, but not how many of those requests were successful. They can tell you how many times your RSS 2.0 file was accessed, but they provide no tool to filter out requests made every five minutes by the same obsessed podcatcher.

The most widely used model of determining audience size is the *bandwidth-division method*. This requires you, the podcaster, to know two pieces of data: the average size of your podcast media files and the total amount of data transferred in a given month. For example, suppose your ISP reported that you transferred 350GB of data in the month of May. Convert that to MB by multiplying by 1,024 (the numbers of megabytes in a gigabyte) to get 358,400MB of data transfer.

Okay, suppose that during that month, you put up four podcasts, each with a size of 10MB.

Divide the total number of transfers (358,400) by the average size of your file (10MB) to get the "total" number of accesses to that file — in this case 35,840. Finally, divide that number by the total number of podcast media files released (4, in this case). The answer (in theory, at least): You have approximately 8,960 listeners to your show.

This number, however, does not take into account the data transferred by your Web server simply to run your Web site — say, images and text. Nor is it helpful when your podcast media files vary widely in size. And it still doesn't factor in those folks who downloaded 90 percent of your show before the connection broke.

Another method is counting the unique IP addresses. This involves using the raw Web log data and using a script for unique download sites. The "podstats" script might do the trick for you — you can find it at: `http://forums.friendsintech.com/index.php?board=7.0`. Check with your hosting provider to see whether you have access to the raw logs.

Our advice is to find a method that seems to work for you and stick with it. It's the best you can do . . . for now.

A rate sheet can be as simple as a fixed price for a given ad segment — we like to think podcasting is more flexible than that. Can you offer cheaper prices for shorter ads? Can you offer prices for different placement within the show, keeping in mind that the closer to the top of the show, the more valuable the ad placement? You can offer decreasing rates based on how many shows carry an ad. How about giving better pricing if there's an ad in your show along with a link on your Web site? Are you capable of offering production services for an audio or video ad? All of these options can be combined in a variety of ways to complement each other.

Getting a Sponsor

Sponsorship and *advertising* are often used as interchangeable terms, but they're actually distinct approaches with different requirements. For the purposes of this discussion, we consider sponsorship as a relationship you (the podcaster) have worked out with an organization that regularly funds — and has a vested interest in the success of — your show. (Obviously, you can't say that about all advertisers.)

Sponsorships were popular — almost to the point of exclusivity — in the old days of radio in the early 20th century. During that time, corporations would actually create the various radio programs as an advertising vehicle — they could even censor content if (for example) some writer goofed and had the villain using the sponsor's product. Modern-day advertising deals, which allow a station or program to drop a 30-second ad into its already-established programming, came into play much later; these days, such deals dominate the scene.

Traditional media sponsorships have all but disappeared, and their last bastion can be found in the world of daytime television: They have morphed into . . . the dreaded infomercial. We're not suggesting that you turn your podcast into an infomercial. However, if you're catering to a niche audience and a corporate entity can service the needs of your audience, that angle may be worth considering.

Understand that obtaining a true sponsor for your show likely means you give up some creative control. Instead of paying you a few dollars to run a pre-produced ad, your sponsoring corporation underwrites your entire show, or at least a significant portion of it. Rather than getting you to take a break from your content while you talk about its product for a few moments, your content becomes *dedicated to* talking about its product.

Two examples of the "pay-for-podcasting" model are *Disneyland Resort* podcast (`http://disneyland.com/podcast`) and the (albeit short-lived) *Heineken Music* podcast (`www.heinekenmusic.com`). In both cases, the corporations underwriting the programs are heavily involved with (read: *own*) the content.

If you're thinking about approaching a corporation to underwrite your show, you need to provide much of the same information necessary for securing advertisers, as discussed earlier. In addition, however, you need to demonstrate how your show can help bolster the success metrics of the corporation. "It's a cool show that your customers will love" probably won't cut it.

There's no secret sauce that irresistibly attracts corporate sponsorship. Each corporation has distinct goals and objectives. Any podcaster trying to solicit sponsorship would be well served to understand these goals and objectives inside and out, and be prepared to clearly demonstrate how sponsoring a podcast can help the company achieve those goals.

Asking Your Listeners for Money

There is one group of potential financial backers out there who could care less about your fancy media kit: your listeners. They couldn't give a hoot about your anticipated growth curve in subscribers or your ratio of direct downloaders to feed-based audience. They do have a vested interest in your continuing to produce the very best possible show, each and every episode — and they are (usually) content to let you take the show in the direction you feel it should go.

Sometimes your show is important enough to them that they're willing to pony up. That's why the following section discusses some novel ways you can go about soliciting your listeners for funds to help offset some of the costs of creating a podcast.

Please don't turn your podcast into a weekly telethon. Most people tolerate the time when NPR goes into pledge-drive mode, but no one looks forward to it. If you're going to ask your audience for money, do it tactfully and as rarely as possible. Please.

Gathering listener donations with PayPal

Some of your audience will so love your show that they'll happily hand over some of their hard-earned money — if you'll only ask.

Asking for listeners' support is a two-step process: First you ask for the money, and then you provide an easy and convenient way for your listeners to send you money. PayPal (www.paypal.com) has been handling small and large Web-based transactions for years. A PayPal donation link can be fully integrated into your Web site with minimum hassle. Here's how:

1. **Log in to PayPal.**

   If you don't have a PayPal account, click the Sign Up link and follow the simple instructions. You need a valid credit card to sign up.

   PayPal, like much of the Web, is subject to change. The flow of these steps might be slightly different at the time you're reading this. Regardless, the steps you need to follow will basically be the same.

2. From your Account Overview page, click the Merchant Services tab.

The Merchant Services section allows you to set up a variety of ways people can send you money.

3. Click the Donations link in the Create Buttons section on the right side of the page.

You may also find this link under Website Payments Standard elsewhere on the page.

You're taken to the Donations page, shown in Figure 15-1.

Figure 15-1: PayPal makes accepting donations as easy as filling out a few fields.

4. Enter a donation name and donation ID in the appropriate text boxes.

We recommend using the show name, and perhaps a suffix such as "– Donations" to help you identify your donations if you have other types of income to your PayPal account.

You can also use the ID field to denote multiple types of donations or donations for different shows in the event you produce more than one podcast. You can put anything you want in this field, but keep in mind that it will be visible to those making donations — so make sure it isn't something confusing.

5. Enter a set donation amount if you want in the Amount text box. Also, change the designated country if you'd like your currency to be something other than U.S. dollars.

If you want your listeners to donate a set amount, choose that amount now. If you leave the Amount field blank, your users will have to enter an amount before they donate. You decide which is best for you.

If you're familiar with using HTML forms, you can later add a suggested donation amount, and allow your listeners to change the amount if they desire. Get a copy of *HTML 4 For Dummies* by Ed Tittel and Mary Burmeister (Wiley Publishing, Inc.) if you need help with editing forms.

6. **Select the style of Donation button you would like to use from the Choose Button Style section.**

   If you have a custom button, here's the place to change it. If you don't have one, don't worry. The default button works just fine on your Web site, and you can always change it later if you want.

7. **Set the encryption to No.**

   If you're confident you won't want to change any of the settings given so far, you can set the encryption to Yes. We prefer to leave it unencrypted, so we can later edit any options without having to re-create a button from scratch. Also, turning encryption off allows PayPal to create a simple-to-use URL for your donation page that you can add to e-mails and show notes.

8. **After you fill in the fields on the Donations page, click Create Button Now at the bottom of the page.**

   PayPal whisks you to the Add a Button to Your Website page.

9. **You have some decisions to make about the custom HTML code for your button:**

   If you're comfortable doing some minor editing of the HTML that makes your Web site work, copy the HTML in the first box and add it to your page.

   If you think editing HTML is a little beyond you just now, then simply copy the text in Link for Emails and include it in your show notes. You'll want to make it a hyperlink, so don't just leave it like this:

```
https://www.paypal.com/cgi-bin/webscr?cmd=_xclick&business=chuck%40chuckcha
          t%2ecom&no_shipping=0&no_note=1&tax=0&currency_code=USD&charset=
          UTF%2d8&charset=UTF%2d8
```

   Instead, you want to enclose it with an `<a href=""></a>` tag and include some descriptive text, like this:

```
<a href="https://www.paypal.com/cgi-bin/webscr?cmd=_xclick&business=chuck%4
          0chuckchat%2ecom&no_shipping=0&no_note=1&tax=0&currency_code=USD
          &charset=UTF%2d8&charset=UTF%2d8">Donate to my show</a>
```

   That should do it for the donation link.

Curious about what your donation page looks like to those who click the link? Cut and paste the link into your browser and press Enter. If you want to change the color scheme or add a logo, simply return to PayPal, choose My Account⇨Profile⇨Custom Payment Pages, and set up a new style. It's all very point-and-click.

Selling stuff

Some podcasters offer merchandise for sale as a way to support their show financially — T-shirts, hats, mugs, CDs, autographed pictures, you name it. If it's sellable, chances are good that some podcaster out there is selling it.

If you're contemplating selling merchandise via your podcast, you fall into one of two groups:

- ✔ **You have merchandise to sell.** Musicians, authors, artists, and craftspeople fall into this category. For these podcasters, offering CDs, books, prints, or other items to the listening audience can bring in significant revenue. (Down the road, there's no reason why it shouldn't be possible to make a living via podcasting.)

   Once again, PayPal (www.paypal.com) can be very helpful in taking away the technical hurdles for selling items online and integrating them into your podcast and Web site. If you can master the process for setting up online donations, you aren't far from having PayPal work as your entire online shopping cart. But this book is about podcasting, not about PayPal. Luckily for you, Victoria Rosenberg and Marsha Collier wrote *PayPal For Dummies* (Wiley Publishing, Inc.).

- ✔ **You need merchandise to sell.** If you need stuff to sell, CafePress (www.cafepress.com) is more than happy to step in and offer its assistance. Remember the T-shirts and other stuff mentioned earlier? You can go to the trouble of making those yourself, carrying an inventory, and shipping the orders out as they trickle in — or you can let CafePress take care of all that for you.

   Setting up a CafePress storefront is a breeze, though it's a highly configurable task, and how you set it up depends on what you want to sell. A basic shop is free to set up and to use. Your listeners buy the T-shirts and coffee mugs (or whatever), with your logo or design on them from the CafePress store, and CafePress pays you a commission. It's very simple and requires only some quick setup information from you to get started. Figure 15-2 shows a CafePress store for *Technorama*. It took about five minutes to set this up; CafePress takes care of the rest.

Figure 15-2:
Listeners
can buy lots
of good-
ies from a
CafePress
store.

Don't expect to make tons of cash via CafePress. Unless you can convince a large group of your listeners that they simply *must* have an $18 T-shirt with your logo on it, we wouldn't recommend quitting your day job just yet.

Handling Fee-Based Subscriptions

Getting your listeners to donate a couple of bucks to you or buy your latest CD is one thing, but getting them to *shell out money for the privilege of listening to your show* is another matter altogether.

If you don't have a pre-established following, a fee-based subscription approach likely won't help you. If you do have a following but have never required anyone to give you money, you may find yourself with less of a following afterwards. Use this option sparingly — and only if you really think others are willing to give money to listen to your podcast. You'll need to come to the decision whether you want x listeners for free, or $1/10\ x$ listeners to pay — okay, we made that number up, but it will definitely be far less than your current listener base.

One way to get your listeners interested in parting with their money would be to give them a sample of what to expect. Offer the first episode or two for free download and in them, mention how to get the rest. (We knew podcasting was addicting, but this is ridiculous.)

Securing your feed

Okay, we're sure you're wondering just how you prevent giving away your podcast to anyone who cares to download it, not just to those who pay for it. The answer is to create a secure RSS feed with logins and passwords.

It's time to be blunt — setting up and maintaining a secure feed is a little ugly. The good news is this is a *For Dummies* title, so we don't expose all the technical warts and scars here. We keep the process simple but still manage to get you in touch with the inner code monkey that lurks in everyone.

To start, there's nothing special about a secure feed. The Web server handles prompting for the login and password. You are responsible for setting up the feed and a configuration file. If you're using a Web server based on Apache — which a lot of hosting providers are — the high-level technical bits look something like this:

- ✔ Create a separate RSS feed for your "protected" content in a separate directory — we'll call it `members`.

- ✔ In the new `members` directory, create a file called `.htaccess` with some special instructions. These instructions tell the Web server where to look for accounts and groups allowed access to this directory.

The authentication process works like this:

1. The Apache Web server receives an instruction from the podcatching client to download the new feed file. It peeks inside the `.htaccess` file to find the logins and passwords.

2. The podcatching client presents a prompt for a login and password.

3. The user types his or her information.

4. The podcatching client sends the info back to the Web server. It checks to see whether a) the information provided is correct, and b) that the account is in a group with permissions to the directory.

5. If both of those are correct, the feed is downloaded and processed by the podcatching client like any other feed.

A sample `.htaccess` file looks like this:

```
AuthType Basic
AuthName "Members Only"
AuthUserFile /www/users/chuckchat/html/security/passwd
AuthGroupFile /www/users/chuckchat/html/security/group
Require group members
```

The first line (`AuthType`) tells the server what type of authentication to use — for now, stick with what it says. The second line (`AuthName`) is the text that appears when the login/password prompt appears. The `AuthUserFile` line points to a file with login names and passwords. The `AuthGroupFile` file is a simple list of accounts associated with a group name. It's important that the files indicated in `AuthUserFile` and `AuthGroupFile` are placed where the file says they are or this doesn't work.

The contents of the `.htaccess` file are case-sensitive — with the exception of the text between quotes. It's extremely important you get the case right for this to work. One of your authors spent many hours trying to figure out why things didn't work because he had `Group` instead of `group`.

A sample line from the `AuthUserFile` file looks like this:

```
chuck.tomasi:2nyp44rex
```

In this example, the login name is `chuck.tomasi`, and the password is encrypted, so nobody can download your file and find out all the passwords. You, the podcaster are responsible for creating and maintaining the `AuthUserFile` (and `AuthGroupFile`). For a small list of user accounts, it's fairly easy to maintain the password file by hand, using a command-line utility called `htpasswd` — commonly provided as part of the Apache Web server.

Not all hosting accounts provide access to a command-line interface. You should check with your Web hosting provider to see whether you have this capability. If not, you may have to resort to creating and maintaining these files on another system and uploading the files. For Mac OS X users, you already have Apache installed and can access these tools from the Terminal window. Windows users have to download Apache (`http://apache.org`) to install them.

If you find yourself with a runaway hit podcast on your hands with lots of accounts, managing them can be a bit of a pain. In such a case, take a look at a product like aMember at `www.amember.com`, which is a PHP Web interface that runs on your Web server. Make sure your hosting account allows you to upload and run PHP programs beforehand, though.

A typical line from an `AuthGroupFile` file might look like this:

```
members:tee.morris,chuck.tomasi,evo.terra
```

The format is pretty straightforward — first is the group name (`members`), then a colon (`:`), then a list of comma-separated names from the `AuthUserFile` file. You can name the group anything you like — as long as it corresponds to the `Require group` line in the `.htaccess` file. The `AuthGroupFile` can also manage multiple groups with each line following the same format described earlier.

The path less traveled

When you have your `AuthUserFile` and `AuthGroupFile` files set up, you must designate the *physical path* to them. You get the physical path to your password and group files from your hosting tech support.

Be sure to ask for the physical path and not the virtual path. A *virtual path* is a shortcut that the Web server gets from the browser on the other end in a URL to get to your files, for example, */security/passwd*. The *physical* is how the operating system on the Web server gets to the same information, for example, `/www/users/chuckchat/html/security/passwd`. Most modern podcatchers and RSS readers support basic authentication. If you would like more information on configuring an Apache file, refer to the Apache Web page (`www.apache.org`).

If all else fails, seek out an experienced Web geek and offer pizza, extra cheese, and a six pack of Red Bull!

Chapter 16

Podcasting for Publicity

"True" podcasters bristle at the growing commercialization of podcasting. With iTunes stepping into the podosphere and spotlighting many corporate podcasts, the independent podcasters have voiced many concerns that boil down to one: A "true" podcast is done for passion, not for profit. The movement towards podcasting as a moneymaking venture goes against the grain of a "true" podcast. The words, opinions, and emotions should all be aimed for the listeners' hearts and minds, not their wallets.

Well, yeah — and even as we cheer the sentiments of the purists, we have to observe that sheer love of the medium isn't all there is to it. Truth be told, podcasting has proven itself a great way to reach the consumer. It's economical, unobtrusive, and can be a great way to connect with your potential audience.

With the new buzz word in business being "Web 2.0," blogging, social networks, and the still-mysterious podcasting are all finding themselves becoming integrated as part of a business' marketing and promotion machine.

Podcasting has come a long way since the first edition of this book, but for larger corporations (such as Coca-Cola, Nike, and others), podcasting still remains an unproven medium when it comes to promotions. Because podcasting is "audio-on-demand," there's still no formal way to measure numbers, feedback, and response in the same way radio and television advertisements are tracked. However, statistics from WordPress plug-ins like pod-Press, online services like Google Analytics, and service providers like LibSyn and Podango continue to develop new methods to do so.

This doesn't mean the change is taking its time. With Apple iTunes and its podcast subscriptions going from zero to 1 million in *two days* — match those numbers, J.K. Rowling! (oh, wait, you did) — the corporate world is wanting to know more about podcasting, realizing that some independent podcasts are actually discovering new audiences for their products (and broadening their existing audience) one MP3 at a time. If the end goal of your podcast is publicity, this chapter is for you. We go through several examples of where podcasting has paid off — maybe not in dollars and cents, but in good word-of-mouth buzz.

Podcasting and Politics

In the political arena, innovation can be a political candidate's best strategic option in winning an office. The "podcasting fad" that some of the old guard snickered and scoffed at is now catching the attention of major political players. Individuals interested in holding office — be it local, state, or national — are side-stepping conventional media and adding to their platform the people who listen in the podosphere.

What we're defining in this section as a *political podcast* is a podcast hosted by a political figure or an individual seeking a political office. (We're *not* talking about podcasts where the host discusses current affairs, rants about the state of the world, or cracks jokes about the latest scandal.)

So, what can a podcast do for you, the tech-savvy politician?

- ✔ Podcasting (and its companion blog, if you use a blog as part of your delivery) connects you directly with your constituencies.

- ✔ Podcasting can reach young voters, the elusive demographic that can easily make or break a victory at the polls.

- ✔ Podcasting avoids the bias that creeps up in media outlets, allowing you as a candidate to present agendas and intentions uninterrupted.

When going political with a podcast, whether you're running for the U.S. Senate or podcasting your term as School Board representative, here are a few things to keep in mind:

- ✔ **Keep your podcast on a consistent *weekly* schedule.** Monthly podcasts don't cut it; the tide of politics is in constant flux. Daily updates are less than practical, but weekly podcasts work well for ongoing political issues, and you can shape their content to remain timely enough to fit the podcasting medium. Set a day for delivering your weekly message and stick to that schedule.

- ✔ **Focus on the issues, not the opinions.** A political podcaster will always walk a fine line between public servant and political commentator. You need to stay focused on the issues. If you suddenly start hammering away with opinion and commentary, you'd become more like Hannity, O'Reilly, or Franken (whom nobody elected). If you want politics as your podcast's subject matter, ask yourself whether you're looking to help listeners understand the issues accurately and take meaningful action, or whether you're just ranting and venting to entertain people who want their opinions reinforced.

✔ **Give your listeners a plan for action.** When you cover the issues in your podcast, provide possible solutions to the pressing matters of your community and your constituents. Whether you're detailing blood drives or fundraisers, or launching an awareness campaign for cancer research, increase that divide between *political figure* and *political commentator* by offering listeners ways they can get involved in the community and make a difference.

Anytime a podcast goes public on the issues, its creator walks a fine line between public servant and political commentator. The following podcasters all keep their content focused on the issues and less on what they "feel" are the issues.

The first politician to use a politically themed podcast was North Carolina Senator John Edwards. Following the 2004 election, he launched the *One America Committee Podcast with John Edwards*. Found at `www.johnedwards.com/media/podcasts`), the podcast covers poverty, Internet law, and environmental issues and encourages youth involvement in politics. Also featured in this podcast is Elizabeth Edwards' update on her current fight against breast cancer and her efforts to raise awareness about the disease.

Edwards invited the world into his home with an intimate podcast that not only gets political, but personal as well: "Elizabeth and I are both sitting here at our kitchen table. The microphones are sitting on my youngest's, Jack's blanket that he sleeps with every night, so we feel very much at home, and I hope you enjoy this discussion."

To make his connection to the podosphere even stronger, Senator Edwards — on the success of his podcast — enlisted the help of two accomplished podcasters, Mur Lafferty and Rob Walch, to assist in its recording and production. The success of the *One America* podcast caught the attention of the govern-ator himself, Arnold Schwarzenegger, who is now podcasting his weekly radio addresses (found under iTunes Podcasts⇨News & Politics). Also in this iTunes category is Senator Barack Obama, reaching out to voters with both audio and video podcast. And the White House also joined the podosphere with President Bush being the first American president to host a podcast (`www.whitehouse.gov/podcasts`).

Podcasting is definitely an avenue to explore if you're venturing into the political area, but this is not your sole means in reaching out to voters. You will need to campaign, of course. Get out on the road, shake hands, kiss babies, and the like. Unless you are recording said baby-kissing and hand-shaking, campaigning will mean your podcast goes on the occasional break (as John Edwards' has at the writing of this edition). Make sure to communicate to your listeners that changes in the posting schedule are upcoming. When you can, give a podcast from the road to keep the communication lines open.

In an interview with *BusinessWeek,* Democratic strategist Joe Trippi sees a time when podcasting will carry the same impact and influence as blogs. "Podcasting is growing even faster than blogging. I think podcasting is going to have a huge impact on the next election cycle."

If you're a politician and you want to get in touch with the people (as a way to respond when voters complain about poor communication with their representatives or the candidates running for office), why not invite them into your kitchen, offer them a cup of virtual coffee, and ask them to relax a bit? Instead of dishing up prepared statements from professional speechwriters, you can offer voters (and worldwide listeners) impromptu, candid, sincere opinions on issues facing the country and the world.

Telling the World a Story, One Podcast at a Time

The whole point behind promotion — be it for books, film, or other forms of entertainment — is to win prospective target audiences (or build on existing ones) with something new or to give a different take on a familiar commodity. For a fraction of the cost of print advertisements and broadcast-media commercials, podcasting opens markets for your creative work — and can even start to get your name into an international market. If you're an established presence in the writing market, or any entertainment field, the fans you have nurtured, with time, will not only eagerly support your podcast, but also introduce your MP3s to reader groups, friends, and enthusiasts of the subjects you're writing about.

Podcasting can introduce your writings or your music to audiences worldwide. For artists in more visual arts such as film, dance, painting, or sculpture, podcasting can serve as an audio journal leading up to the premiere of your work — or as a venue to promote your career. It's an instant connection with your audience, and a great way to build an audience by getting them to know you on however intimate a level works best for you and your work. Planning a strategy for this kind of promotion only helps your agenda:

✔ **When podcasting for visual media, briefly describe the action for the audience.** In his podcast for the SciFi Channel, Ron Moore adds in his commentary on whichever episode of *Battlestar Galactica* happens to be airing (www.scifi.com/battlestar/downloads/podcast). He doesn't take for granted, though, that people will always be watching the episode along with its companion podcast. In only a few words and a few seconds, he sets the scene for what's happening in the episode, for the sake of listeners who may listen to his podcast independently.

If you're documenting your visual art, it will take only a moment to describe what you're doing. For the painter: "I am using green with just a hint of black so we can make the eyes appear more unearthly, unnatural." For a dancer, "In reconstructing the Australian Aboriginal dance, you must remain grounded and deep in your squats, more so than what is normally seen in modern dance." You don't need to go into every minute detail. Only a few words are needed to create a picture.

Another option is to take advantage of enhanced and video podcasting. Although you may not reach as many listeners, you can take advantage of incorporating visuals with your audio. For the basics of video podcasting, take a look at Chapter 8.

✔ **For writers and musicians: Edit, edit, edit.** Awkward pauses, stammers, and stumbled words are obstacles for a writer introducing his work to the podosphere: They've gotta go! The approach is no different from that of an independent musician who podcasts a rehearsal session or a recording: You don't want off-key instruments and vocalists missing the high notes. Your podcasts need to sound sharp and clean.

Musicians, no matter if it takes five takes or 50 takes, should have their instruments in tune, lyrics clearly pronounced, and all notes sung on key. Writers should enunciate, speak clearly, and (most importantly) enjoy the manuscript. Each piece, whether music or printed word, should be a performance that serves as your audition to a worldwide audience. (While that may sound a bit nerve-wrecking, don't think of it as walking out on stage so much as building something fine to send into the world. Just have fun, and your audience will enjoy the ride with you.)

If you need a refresher on the basics of editing, skip back to Chapter 7 for the primers on editing with Audacity and GarageBand.

✔ **Open or close your podcasts with a brief, off-script commentary.** Before beginning your latest installment or after your latest chapter concludes, a brief word from the author is a nice (and in many cases, welcoming) option for a podcast's audience. This commentary gives the author a unique opportunity to connect with readers, sharing ideas about what inspired a scene, to promote an upcoming book-signing, or to give an update about what's happening in the next book's production.

The first author to do this was Scott Sigler. Along with keeping his listeners on the edge of their seats with his science fiction/horror podcasts (available at www.scottsigler.com), he chats with his fans at the beginning and end of each episode. In these messages, Scott assures listeners he wouldn't hold last chapters hostage, announces release dates, and shares his plans for world domination.

This approach added to the intimate experience of podcasting a novel, and other podcast novelists like Mur Lafferty, Philippa Ballantine, and J.C. Hutchins followed suit, inviting listeners into their real world after sharing the world they imagined. Let your audience members know who you are, and they'll show their appreciation through their support of your current and future works.

Where it all began . . .

Allow us a personal account of the journey from podcasting fan to full-fledged podcaster. When *Podcasting For Dummies'* own Tee Morris was in the final rewrites of *Legacy of MOREVI,* his publisher contacted him and said, "Okay, Tee, start thinking of neat promotional ideas." Around this time, Evo Terra and Michael R. Mennenga, hosts of *The Dragon Page* (www.dragonpage.com), had just started podcasting. The more Tee found out about podcasting, the more he began planning to podcast *MOREVI* as a way to get word out about *Legacy of MOREVI.* After all, he'd been complimented several times on his live readings. And as an actor who loved playing around with his Mac's audio and video features, he figured . . . *why not?*

The Prologue of *MOREVI: The Chronicles of Rafe & Askana* (www.morevi.net) dropped into the Dragon Page's feed on January 21, 2005, and so began a completely new kind of promotion, different from what The Dragon Page had ever done before: a chapter presented every Friday, as read by the author. The feedback was nearly instantaneous. Within weeks of Tee's first episode, two other authors stepped up and offered their works for podcast as well. One of them was Mark Jeffrey, author of the science fiction/fantasy young adult adventure, *The Pocket and The Pendant* (www.podiobooks.com/title/the-pocket-and-the-pendant). The other author was an adrenaline-hepped, in-your-face, über-intense conductor of mayhem, chaos, and carnage, Scott Sigler, and the book was *EarthCore.* The idea was apparently working with other authors.

Listeners' answers came after the conclusion of *MOREVI* in the form of a review from SFFAudio.com: "Swashbuckling action takes the main, and heart-rending romance builds slowly, culminating right at the end . . . it is daring-do adventure set in a world that would fit well on a shelf next to Eric Flint's *1632verse* alternate history series."

Along with a glowing review, orders for *MOREVI* and pre-orders for *Legacy of MOREVI* spiked in sales (which included a few international readers) via Amazon. Scott Sigler went on to see the *EarthCore* novel finally in print, had the novel of his second podcast *Ancestor* debut at #1 in Amazon's Science Fiction and Horror section when it premiered in print, and took the novel of his third podcast, *Infection,* to a hardcover debut with Crown Books and topped the Amazon charts in 2008.

Podcasting fiction continues to prove itself as a viable means of promotion for authors unable to fund their own coast-to-coast tour. It may make conventional writers shake their heads at the idea of giving their works away for free, but the numbers and individual successes of authors taking this chance is the proof in this publicity. Now, before ink even hits the page, authors are building fan bases and getting their names out into the public. (And some of the really lucky ones get to write books for the *For Dummies* people!)

Keeping Good Company: Community and Sound-Seeing-Tour Podcasts

Slice-of-life podcasts that encourage community among listeners and among fans are podcasts that *promote*. They can promote a show cancelled too soon into production, an issue affecting the well-being of a community, or a cause such as breast cancer research. The promotion comes from word-of-mouth advertising (*buzz*) that these podcasters generate from their thoughts, comments, and opinions on their subject — be it traveling across Spain, daily life in New York City, George Lucas's *Star Wars,* or Joss Whedon's *Firefly.*

Slice-of-life podcasts let the world into locations and clue people into possibilities that listeners may be curious about. After a few podcasts, you can even encourage listeners to experience that corner of the world, that idea, or join the community.

Do you have a cause you want to give attention to? Do you want to raise awareness in your county or district? Do you want to share the experience of preparing for a wedding or anniversary? Consider sound-seeing tour podcasts in order to build an online community through your podcast.

Putting together a sound-seeing tour of your favorite destination

Sound-seeing tours are "virtual walks" down sidewalks and side streets of wherever you happen to be in the world. These audio getaways, just by the sounds (and if you're doing video, the sights) of the people and things around you, can promote the community of a city, region, or country better than any brochure found in a travel agency.

The atmosphere of a marketplace, the rumbling of a train and various announcements to its commuters, and even the traffic passing by builds the world (or the part of it you are presently occupying) around you. Peppering this atmosphere is your commentary. The podcast becomes a grand bay window to your world with you as the walking, talking frame of reference.

Don't rely on the environment to *be* the podcast. Part of a sound-seeing tour is the ambient noise. A sound-seeing tour shouldn't be you simply walking through your local downtown or social hot spot, recording the world passing you by. The world is your backdrop, and you are the podcast's host. Your thoughts, opinions, and observations will continue to drive this podcast; your environment is working with you to create a complete picture. Feel free to comment on what you see and allow yourself a chance to explore.

Rich Pav is your average, ordinary blogger, making his way through the not-so-average, ordinary Land of the Rising Sun. In the podcast *Herro Flom Japan* (www.herroflomjapan.com), Rich frames his various travels and encounters with the history, culture, and people of Japan in his own unique point of view. According to his companion blog, Rich doesn't consider his podcast to be a true *sound-seeing tour* — but his glimpses into Japan were compelling enough for listeners to nominate *Herro Flom Japan* for the First Annual People's Choice Podcast Awards in that category. Now, with the ease and popularity of video podcasting, *Herro Flom Japan* also offers the occasional video podcast, a logical evolution for a sound-seeing tour that's now a *sight-seeing tour* via your iPod.

Creating a podcast to bring together a community

Community is synonymous with podcasting. This book talks a lot about the power of community through podcasting, establishing a connection between you the podcaster and your audience which is waiting impatiently for the next episode. Podcasts can also bring an existing community — a group with a shared interest, a community of homeowners, or a group dedicated to a cause — together and keep its members informed. The podcast can reach audiences in and outside of your community, sharing your interests and concerns with others, making your community even stronger in the long run.

The Disney Podcast Directory (Figure 16-1, found at www.disneypodcast directory.net) is a *Yellow Pages* of podcasting that features shows by either the Disney Corporation or Disney fans. What started off as a simple portal to all thing concerning Mickey, the *Disney Podcast Directory* has become a central hub for fans. There's even a behind-the-scenes podcast of things going on at this directory called *Inside the DPN*, a podcast that spotlights new arrivals and old favorites to the directory. *Inside the DPN* also interviews podcast hosts, comments on the state of Cinderella's Castle (and other franchises), and shares personal anecdotes on everything from a favorite amusement park ride to tips on planning the best Disney vacation. What makes *DPN* more of a community than just another directory is in how its podcast keeps everyone in the know on who is joining the network, which shows have *podfaded* (gone away), and what is happening in the Disney fan community based on content contributed by the directory's members.

The podosphere takes great pride in its sense of community, but the podcasts showcased here are set apart because the community is encouraged to take a more active role in the issues, concerns, and points of focus the podcast is centered around. More than chiming in with feedback, the community takes an active role in participating with increasing awareness over the podcast's main subject. In some cases, the producing of the podcast brings the community together, either through listener contributions, listeners directing the course of the show, or listeners coming together for a common cause.

Figure 16-1:
The Disney Podcast Directory encourages community by keeping its members and fans of the Mouse in the know.

Thirty days, 50,000 words, and a podcast for each day . . .

Having a podcast keep its community focused on a goal is seen clearly in *The NanoMonkeys*, a daily podcast that happens in November. Why November? It coincides with NaNoWriMo (National Novel Writing Month), which takes place in November. Participants in NaNoWriMo commit to writing a novel of 50,000 words in a month.

To help NaNoWriMo writers, P.G. Holyfield, Chris Miller, and Kris Johnson started *The NanoMonkeys* (www.teampodcasts.net/ nanomonkeys) podcast. From November 1 to December 1, these three podcasters post a daily podcast ranging from 3–10 minutes,

offering advice for the struggling participant or for the NaNo player who is on a tear.

With *NaNoMonkeys*, the community is dedicated to a goal: Producing 50,000 words in a month. Not only the producers, but the listeners themselves, are all driven by the daunting task of creating a novel in a month's time. The success of *The NaNoMonkeys* can be seen in its kudzu-like growth in listeners and participants, as well as the feedback from its subscription base who gave K.J., P.G., and Chris a lot of credit in getting their work (and they themselves) to the Finish Line of Midnight, November 30.

Community podcasts cover a wide range of audiences. However, all communities share a similar mindset, and you can apply these "sound" production principles:

- ✔ **You are the host, but it's not all about you.** Community-based podcasts should be *about the community.* Yes, there is room for personal thoughts and commentary, but in small doses.

    The podcast is about the community and how it interacts with the world around you; that is what the content should focus on. Your podcast can feature other members of the community who share the same opinions as yours or even take opposing viewpoints (a spirited debate can up your show). Just remember that the community-based podcast is not about you personally, but about how you see the world, how that connects with the people around you in the community, and how all that comes together in the pursuit of a common interest.

- ✔ **Avoid the negative.** Particularly with community-based podcasts such as *Jack Mangan's Deadpan* (www.jackmangan.com) and *The Signal* (http://signal.serenityfirefly.com/signal.php), it would be easy to turn a podcast into a gossip column or a personal rant against the very concept that brought the community into being. While there is no law or ethic barring you from speaking out or voicing concerns, a community is based on support. Whether you consider yourself a fan of Harry Potter, Apple Computers, or Prince William County, your goal in a community podcast is to remain positive and celebrate the benefits of being part of the cooperative spirit. If there is a matter of concern in your community, then there's room for debate and action, as with a political podcast — offer some possible solutions to these issues.

Regardless of the kind of community you're chronicling, your podcast should work much like glue — helping to keep supporters together in the face of problems (instead of just crying in your collective beer) and celebrating what gives them joy. Reinforce that sense of community and keep your podcast strong.

Chapter 17

Podcasting for Passion

*O*ur mission from the beginning of this book has been to fill you in on what a podcast is, demystify the technical aspects of getting your voice heard on media players around the world, and assure you that those with the drive to make their message happen can do it, with the right tools. But a podcast is empty if you don't have that drive, that passion to get your podcast up and running and keep it running, whether the episode goes out every week, every other week, or every month. We drop that word a lot in the previous chapters: passion. What do we mean by "podcasting with passion"?

Okay, if you take the dictionary as a starting point, *passion* means "a keen interest in a particular subject or activity, or the object of somebody's intense interest or enthusiasm." You can have state-of-the-art audio equipment, hire the most engaging vocal talent, and employ the best engineers, but that isn't what makes a podcast a podcast. The artists and creativity behind a podcast make an investment — not simply financial or physical — and collect the windfall in listener feedback and download stats.

Yes, a podcast can make money, promote a cause, or bring attention to social issues, but without that passion, you might as well sit behind a microphone and read the instruction manual to your mobile phone. Passion is what motivates relative unknowns to slip on the headphones, step up to the microphone, and let their words fly.

This chapter won't presume to teach you how to create, cultivate, or conjure your own passion. It's something you have, or you don't, for a given topic — and we suspect everybody has it for *some* topics. Instead, we offer some real-world examples of how others apply their passions to podcasts — and we tell you about some tools to apply a little passion-power of your own.

The Philosophical Question for All Podcasters: Why Do We Do It?

It's going to come up sooner or later: Someone will question your motives, rationale, and even sanity at your investment of so much time and energy into this newfangled thing called podcasting. We highly recommend deep nonsensical answers such as "It's because of the cheese" be returned to these people. Then watch their eyes start to twitch. That never stops being funny.

The following sections tell you some of the ways you can take that passion and channel it in to a truly effective force behind your podcast.

Gaining perspective on passion

"Get some perspective!" they say. Well, we agree with them (whoever they are). As a podcaster, you need a firm idea of what your show is about. If you're not sure what your point is, your audience isn't going to be sure, either!

Mur Lafferty entered the podosphere in December 2004 with *Geek Fu Action Grip*. The podcast featured witty essays about growing up geek and remaining geek in adulthood. *Geek Fu,* in its way, was a lynchpin to Mur's plan to make a living at writing, and hopefully selling her first novel for publication. She used the podcast to discuss the tribulations of writing full-time, and also the frustration of getting fiction published amidst her non-fiction accomplishments.

Noticing episodes of *Geek Fu* leaning towards her writing pursuits, Mur decided to launch *I Should be Writing* (shown in Figure 17-1). This podcast focused less on essays and witticisms from a geek's perspective and more on the business, the frustrations, and the momentary highs of writing. The podcast was her own journal of what she went through to get that first novel on bookshelves. Mur's perspective of "a writing podcast by a wanna-be fiction writer" became a source of inspiration for writers.

"I wanted to contribute something to the podosphere that wasn't there already," Mur says in response to a question about her inspiration. "There were already podcasts from writers, but to my knowledge, there wasn't a podcast by a published writer who was not published in fiction. In all honesty, I was doing this podcast more for myself. I podcast because it's a good outlet for my thoughts and my writing. That's what I was doing with *I Should Be Writing,* but I didn't expect the reaction it got."

Figure 17-1:
Mur Lafferty
(inset)
invites writ-
ers present
and future
to join
her in the
journey to
publication
in *I Should
Be Writing.*

The reaction Mur speaks of was the outpouring of encouragement she received from around the world as feedback to her setbacks. Listeners thanked Mur for inspiring them to write again. There were outcries for Mur to continue development and work on her fiction, eventually leading her to featuring previews of her Parsec-nominated series *Heaven* and the popular superhero adventure *Playing for Keeps* (`http://playingforkeepsnovel.com`).

What makes the Parsec-winning *I Should Be Writing* a delight is Mur's enthusiasm. For the Durham, N.C. mother, gamer, writer, and all-around-geek, her podcasts serve as a catharsis for the struggles in getting her fiction published: "I was so stunned when people told me it was *I Should Be Writing* that made them pick up writing after years of nothing. The knowledge that people are looking forward to my podcast really means a lot and does a lot to motivate me. I know a lot of podcasters have had the problem of not receiving sufficient feedback. A nice e-mail here and there really means a lot to keep people going. It's that kind of encouragement that motivates me to podcast my fiction."

Whether Mur's wisdom was planned from the start or not, it offers some good take-aways for the budding podcaster:

✔ **Look for a unique angle.** The last things your listeners need are carbon copies of other podcasts or (perish the thought) radio shows based on a template. If your passion is commonplace, focus on a niche or small aspect that you have the most knowledge about.

✔ **Step beyond your comfort zone.** No one expects you to be a trained voice actor. All they expect is for you to talk about your passion with authority and sincerity. Remember, you're only trying to appeal to people who care.

✔ **Don't get preachy.** Passion and authority are fine, but don't cross that line into assuming you know more than everyone else. Unless you're putting together a sermon or series of lectures, speak in the common tongue and with respect to your audience. If we want to be talked down to, we can always tune in certain talk-radio hosts.

Podcasting passion with a purpose

Podcasting with a purpose is an essential. By doing so, you have a destination. It doesn't matter if that destination is to educate, showcase your material, or entertain. Pick something as your core reason for speaking and don't be afraid to have fun with it and make it exciting.

Speaking of fun and exciting (and, okay, escapist) rides, the *EarthCore* podcast (http://scottsigler.net/earthcore) might have escaped notice had it not been for the passion behind its host: the high-octane, in-your-face podcasting personality, Scott Sigler. Sigler found a terrific hook in describing his science-fiction thriller as "*24* meets *Predator*" — but even his promotions convey the deeply rooted passion he nurtures for his genre and his own adventures.

Scott Sigler — who has, hands down, the most successful of the podiobooks initially offered by www.podiobooks.com — set out to show that a book in audio format didn't have to be a guy in a soundproof booth simply reading the manuscript. "I podcast because it's the perfect vehicle for serialized fiction," Sigler says of his decision to podcast his debut novel. He seeks not only to hook listeners with the format, but also to keep them in suspense till next week's episode: "My novels are long, with cliffhangers at the end of each chapter. That's designed to keep you turning the pages. With podcasts, you just have to wait for the next episode."

Scott's nostalgia for radio-style serials is not the only motivation behind his podcast. "The amazing reaction I get from the listeners is the motivation," he adds, acknowledging his loyal fan base, also known as "Junkies" as they became hooked on his podcasts. The fans showed Scott (along with print publishers, Dragon Moon Press and Crown Publishing) exactly how hooked they were when the podcast of *Ancestor* premiered in print. The book shot up Amazon charts to hit #1 in both Horror and Science Fiction. That was enough for Crown to approach Scott with an contract for another one of his podcasts, *Infection*, which the publisher retitled as *Infected* (shown in Figure 17-2).

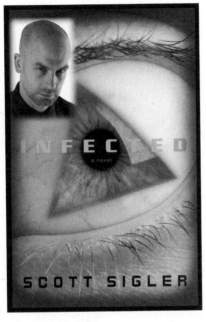

Figure 17-2: Scott Sigler (inset) took his podcast-exclusive novel *Infected* to print, and it became a major blockbuster, thanks to podcasting.

For Scott, the passion had a purpose; but even on meeting his goal, Scott continues to deliver. "To know that my fiction has entertained thousands of people, helped them escape from their day-to-day lives, and just plain have some fun means the world to me. Is it a power trip? Sure! But knowing that I've delivered a great story and entertained someone is a fantastic feeling."

Scott showcases some excellent attitudes and approaches that would serve many podcasters well:

- ✔ **Cultivate feedback.** Don't sit on your heels hoping someone will e-mail you. Put together a contest, solicit information, and generally get out there and ask people what they think.

- ✔ **Respond in a timely manner.** If you're going to ask, you can't ignore the responses. When someone takes the time out of his or her busy schedule to e-mail you feedback, positive or negative, respond. Sooner rather than later, please.

- ✔ **Have your audience spread the word.** Who better to seek out people who might like your podcast than those who already love what you do? Assuming these people have friends, have them toss a little love your way by getting their friends to listen. Ask them to burn your show onto a CD and pass it around. Make it easy for others to listen!

Planning out your passion

Equally important to having a purpose is having a plan with your passion. The purpose is the *why* of your podcast, and the plan as the *how*. If you can plan out your podcast, you're more likely to achieve your goal or purpose. This is what happened with Lanie James of Oklahoma State University.

As part of her Masters in Mass Communications and Media Management, Lanie turned to podcasting. "It was something no one else was looking at and I saw the potential in it," she said. The plan she outlined was a strategic implementation of podcasting as a way to offer interview and résumé tips for soon-to-be OSU graduates looking to enter the professional sector. Her boss at OSU's Career Services (http://hireosugrads.com) took a look at her plan and saw the same potential Lanie did. As Employee Development Coordinator, Lanie served as liaison between recent OSU grads and potential employers. The podcasts outlined in her Masters' creative component ranged from interview tips for graduates to background for employers to consider about potential job candidates. Lanie kept her podcasts short (between 5 and 15 minutes) and easily accessible. "I was pretty excited about OSU wanting to give podcasting a try, and now part of my job is producing these podcasts. I'm helping students and employers, and doing it in a manner that I have a lot of fun and creativity with."

Lanie is also the podcasting oracle of OSU as Student Affairs turned to her to run workshops and clinics for their podcasts. OSU is now turning to video podcasting and has plans to implement enhanced podcasts as part of its program. Lanie said, "I really find OSU embracing podcasting so rewarding, and I know we're doing something good as I was checking our stats and discovered a new subscriber from the University of Toronto. That means our podcast is helping more than just OSU grads, but reaching out to a wider audience."

If you come up with a cunning plan for your podcast, here are a few tips to keep in mind:

- ✔ **Make sure your plan is clear.** Coming up with a plan is more than just saying to the people you work with "We should do a podcast because it's cool. Here's what we talk about in Episode One." A plan for your podcast will be more than the show's posting schedule, content outline for the first five shows, and who will be the guests on Episodes 3 and 5. Your plan will go into detail. Who is your target audience? What is your goal? How do you plan to obtain your goal? What other tangible benefits will the podcast generate? Ask the tough questions when writing up your plan so when others ask them, you have the answer in front of you with the facts to back it up.

✔ **Keep the plan close by and easily accessible.** The plan that you have slaved over and put your time, effort, heart, and soul into is now complete (and approved if approval is required), and your podcast is underway. It would be a good thing to have a printed copy of your plan so you have a roadmap to get you, your co-hosts, and your show guests to the planned destination of the episode and of the podcast on a whole. The plan, within reach of you, will keep your podcast on track and in sight of your eventual goals.

Passion comes in all shapes and sizes

Passionate people are usually easy to find. One guy started a podcast because he knows a lot, and loves to talk about rugby. Another husband and wife team feel comfortable sharing their stories about their children. And another person goes on and on about the English language. What they all have in common is they have opinions and want to share them.

Also never short on opinions — or providing glimpses into his corner of the world(s) — is science-fiction author Paul S. Jenkins. (Or would he call what he writes *speculative* fiction?) His bimonthly podcast *Rev Up Review* (www.rev-up-review.co.uk), launched in March 2005, provides listeners with a review of magazines, books, podcasts, and music. The *Rev Up Review* is not only a review of all things speculative, but also a revue of music available at the Podsafe Music Network, sound-seeing tours around his village and around his home, and even a serialized presentation of his previously published short stories. Is Paul trying to generate new interest in his own published works? Does he have an agenda in promoting the Podsafe Music Network? There *has* to be an agenda here, doesn't there?

Well, we don't believe so. The *Rev Up Review* (or "Revue," depending on your take on Paul's approach) comes across as an hour with an old friend over a pint at your local pub. Paul Jenkins' passion comes through in the sincerity behind his podcast — seasoned with a whimsical, almost mischievous, approach. In one episode, Paul presented an alternative to the beercast: a breadcast. The RevMaster (as he calls himself) welcomed the world into his kitchen for a ten-minute segment of baking fresh bread, starting from the beginning with measuring of water and breaking out the flour. Paul knows this kind of sound-seeing theater may not rivet action-addicts, but he isn't pressured to be aggressively entertaining all the time. You can hear in his voice a genuine delight — in not only recording this culinary experience, but also sharing it with the world.

Paul's approach to podcasting is easily adaptable for many:

✔ **Don't be afraid to explore new areas.** Just because your podcast is about fishing, it doesn't mean that you can't meander to rock climbing, pickup-truck repair, or even the secret to marital bliss. Exploring new areas can breathe new life into stale podcasts and even help you find new areas of interest and expertise you didn't even know you had.

✔ **Keep it personal.** Consider talking to one person — because in most cases, you are. You're likely to build a closer relationship with that person by using terms like "my friend" or "my faithful listener" — yeah, those are cheesy examples, but you get the idea — rather than "folks" or "ladies and gentlemen" like you're addressing an arena. We don't know of many podcasts that get played before a large audience on a regular basis.

A passionate love for the podcast

All successful podcasters share in common a true love for the podcast. Something about getting behind the mic and producing quality content is satisfying. That passion can tax you, especially if the podcast is an emotional ride; and if a podcast reaches an "end," it would make sense if the podcast's host decided to step away from the mic.

Podcast sensation J.C. Hutchins, however, after concluding his roller-coaster thriller, *7th Son* (http://jchutchins.net), came to a conclusion he shared with Tee in an interview: "I've forgotten how to sit still."

Hutchins, a journalist who always nurtured a love for the art of the interview, on wrapping up his trilogy, took a breath and then launched *Ultra-Creatives,* a podcast that includes interviews with innovative minds in technology, business, and arts. (Check out Figure 17-3.) "The world could be coming to an end outside my window," Hutch says, "and I wouldn't care because Charlie Rose is interviewing Spike Lee!" With that passion for the interview — equaled only by his passion for his own fiction — Hutchins developed a brand new podcast simply so he could stay connected to the community of fans he had developed but also to actively stay connected to the podosphere. "I do *Ultra-Creatives* because I love podcasting so much."

The desire to continue recording, producing, and uploading shows simply for the love of the podcast is not uncommon. Many podcasts are created out of that need. These shows and their hosts stand out in their dedication, infusing raw enthusiasm for this medium into every new show. It is this passion that brings the podcaster back to the microphone and invites new podcasters (like you!) to take the host's chair.

Figure 17-3:
Author J.C. Hutchins returned to his journalist roots, offering on his podcast fiction feed the interview show, *Ultra-Creatives.*

Holding Interest: Keeping a Podcast's Passion Alive

You have your podcast underway. You're planning to have a weekly show. The first month in, you feel strong, confident. But this is all in the first four episodes. How do you keep the momentum going?

In the early days of a podcast, you can easily see yourself continuing banter a year from launch date — but remember that schedule you planned? Have you taken into account sick days? Vacation? The occasional stumbling block of inertia ("Do I really want to do a podcast today?")? Even the best podcasters need to step away from their mics, recharge their batteries, and then jump back into their recording. Personal health, well-being, and time to edit episodes if your episodes need editing (and if you're human, sometimes they do) are factors you also must consider. Add in dealing with conditions such as background noise and having to tax the strength of your voice, and podcasting can become less of a joy and more like a chore or a second day-job. Plenty of podcasts begin strong out of the box, only to have their feeds go silent, and remain so.

Even with passion, momentum is difficult to sustain. How do podcasters keep that spark alive? Well — as with the answers to "Why do we do it?" — podcasters have a myriad of opinions and thoughts. Each show applies different tactics to keep each new episode fresh; even amid diverse topics, you can find common threads between all podcasts that provide the momentum to forge ahead 50 episodes later.

Podcasting on puree: Mixing it up

After you've racked up a few episodes of your podcast, take a look at its format. How do you have it set up? Is it all commentary? What can you do to vary the content?

Just because this is your first, second, third — or seventeenth, eighteenth, or nineteenth — episode, that doesn't mean you've set your show in stone. (That's where you find the fossils of all sorts of creatures that didn't manage to evolve.) In this section, we look at ways to dodge that asteroid and keep your show from suffering an extinction-level event.

Don't be afraid to try different things with your podcast's format. For example, you might

✔ Talk about a product, a service, or an idea that's only loosely related to your normal focus.

✔ Interview a guest with a unique perspective on the focus of your show.

✔ Experiment with adding a co-host, even if only temporarily.

✔ Podcast from a remote location or from a studio if you normally do remote shows.

Technorama, hosted by one of your illustrious authors, has been in a near-constant state of evolution since inception in May 2005. It started with a single host and acquired a second after the initial kickoff. Things stayed constant for a while, and then its hosts — Chuck Tomasi and Kreg Steppe — added an "On This Day in Tech History" segment to the show to review tech, science, and geek events that happened in history on the day the show is released.

With the addition of "On This Day in Tech History" segments, Chuck and Kreg started experimenting with production elements and other kinds of regularly occurring features in the podcast. Soon the show, described as looking at the lighter side of technology, started covering odd news in the "Hacks and Strange Stories" segment and began scratching their heads at how silly people can get over tech with the "What the Chuck?!" segment. Following the wacky wake-up morning show format, *Technorama* became a favorite in the podosphere.

Fast-forward through the years (time travel saves belaboring the point), and the award-nominated show continues to offer something different than its normal fare. While taking pride in their lighter look at tech, *Technorama* has also featured interviews with Grant Imahara and Adam Savage of *Mythbusters,* oceanographer and *Titanic*-discoverer Dr. Bob Ballard, John Chatterton and Richie Kohler of *Deep Sea Detectives,* and renowned physicist Dr. Michio Kaku. The guys have also started to experiment with video podcasting, on-location recordings, and elaborate audio spoofs ranging from "How You

Tell He's a Geek" (inspired by Monty Python's "How You Can Tell She's a Witch" sketch) and "The Beta Bunch" (a mash-up of *The Brady Bunch* and JC Hutchins' *7th Son*).

Your show may not have to go to elaborate lengths to stay fresh, but it does need to heed the creed: *Evolve or die.*

If you decide your podcast is going to be in a constant state of flux, keep in mind that the risk of alienating your listeners is ever present. Podcasting for podcasting's sake is like improvisational comedy: It's a skill. You can keep your passion alive by continuously changing the format of your show, but you run a gambit of making your show an acquired taste.

Starting a second podcast

Keeping the passion alive and well in one podcast can be found in variety and in allowing yourself to follow another passion in a second podcast. Okay, that may double your workload, but it also keeps your perspectives fresh and excited about what to focus on in upcoming podcasts.

If you have enough content to warrant a second podcast, don't overload one podcast with this new content; why burn out? If your gut instinct is telling you to begin a second podcast, go for it. Variety, not only in a podcast's original content but also between the different podcasts you create, can benefit both shows. Now, instead of the same old podcast every week, you can allow yourself different avenues to explore — and maybe a whole new audience.

After focusing on books and authors for so many years, the hosts of *The Dragon Page: Cover-to-Cover* (http://dragonpage.com) wanted to expand into new areas in order to attract new listeners. They found a willing audience with the unfilled niche (more like a huge hole in the podosphere) of sci-fi TV and movies.

Attaching themselves to arguably the most enthusiastic of all fan crowds — *Star Trek* geeks — the hosts of *Cover-to-Cover* created *Slice of SciFi* (http://sliceofscifi.com), a podcast that quickly grew to become an overnight success in the podosphere and one of many offerings on XM Satellite Radio.

If you're thinking about branching out with a new show, consider these tips:

✔ **Take your audience with you.** If you're podcasting about triathlons, yet hold a secret passion for seventh-century Gaelic text, expect only a handful of folks to subscribe to both shows. However, if you move from triathlons to a podcast on sports medicine, they may find the new topic an easier pill to swallow.

✔ **Cross-promote.** Even if your podcasts are quite close in scope, there will be listeners to one who aren't aware of the other. Although we caution against turning one podcast into a giant commercial for the other, plug the heck out of your other show. Within reason.

✔ **Look for the niche within the niche.** If your main topic is broad, break it out into chunks and see what needs further exploration. Granted, a deep dive into the minutiae of a niche topic may reduce the size of your listening audience. But so what? This is about exploring your passion, not about gaining market share. And (we promise) there's always someone else out there who will want you to delve even deeper into the obscure topic you've just built an entire podcast around.

✔ **Keep trying.** Don't expect to hit your stride in the new show by Episode 2. You have to try different formats, flavors, and ideas, just the way you did to make your first podcast perfect. (Or is it? Maybe it's getting a little stale. Time to spruce that one up, too. See the following section.)

When enjoying the journey of your first podcast, keep in mind that your *next* podcast may be closer than you think. Keep a close eye on your feedback; look for recurring themes that your audience likes to hear. If it's a broad enough topic and you can speak on it with authority, you may be able to craft a show around audience suggestions instead of having to sweat bullets to come up with something brand new every time.

Moving forward with a plan

Reinvention for the sake of reinvention isn't a bad idea, but it's so 20th century. You may find it a better idea to move forward with a plan. So here are a few do's and don'ts — with the don'ts first.

What NOT to do (ack! run away! run away!):

✔ **Don't use shock-radio techniques.** Hearing a podcaster drop a few words that would make most grandmothers blush isn't anything new, and it's a cheap way to get a laugh and attention. We personally don't have any moral compunction against the more colorful aspects of the English language. If that's your style, don't change it; otherwise, try to use them sparingly, okay?

✔ **Don't swing between kid-friendly and adults-only.** If you're unhappy being a family show, give some advance notice so folks can unsubscribe. Hell hath no fury like a mother scorned (or even unpleasantly surprised).

✔ **Don't get angry when you get dissenting e-mail.** Not everyone will be happy with your decision to change things around or to add a new segment. Deal with it and move on. You can't please everyone — or "correct" their opinions — so don't even try.

What to DO with all your might:

- ✔ **Cast your net wide.** Be open to a variety of new ideas and concepts and don't be afraid to try them out on your audience. Your loyal listeners will likely forgive you a few miscues along the way.

- ✔ **Have a purpose for the change or addition.** Find the common connection with what your show has focused on before and talk to your audience about it. You can do this before or after the "newness" goes in the show, but your listeners will enjoy knowing the method behind your madness.

- ✔ **Encourage feedback about the change.** When you do this, ask more than "do you like it?" Find out whether your audience members feel differently about your show, if they think it's "fresher" or perhaps more appealing — and ask why. The changes you put in place are designed to give your show a boost; be sure and ask for confirmation that it actually happened!

If you find yourself in need of a break, there's nothing wrong with taking some time out. As a courtesy to those who are listening, however — whether it's 20 or 20,000 — let them know you're holding off on new episodes for a few weeks so you can reorganize priorities, goals, and the whole momentum of your podcast in order to make it even more rewarding for them to listen to. The same courtesy applies when you've had an unexpected illness: Give your listenership a quick update on what happened; reassure them that your voice is back and that your podcast is back. As passionate as you may be about a podcast, always remember your health and your voice must come first. There's nothing wrong with missing a week or two of a podcast while you get back up to par.

Truth and Honesty in Podcasting

"To me, ultimately, martial art means honestly expressing yourself. Now it is very difficult to do. I mean it is easy for me to put on a show and be cocky and be flooded with a cocky feeling and then feel, then, like pretty cool . . . and be blinded by it. Or I can show you some really fancy movement. But, to express oneself honestly, not lying to oneself — and to express myself honestly — that, my friend, is very hard to do."

—Bruce Lee, from an interview on The Pierre Burton Show

When Tee was writing the first draft of this particular chapter, he had playing in the background *Bruce Lee: The Way of the Warrior,* a (really cool) documentary featuring recently discovered footage from Bruce Lee's then-work-in-progress *Game of Death,* rare commentary from The Dragon himself, and interview footage. In one of the interviews came the preceding quote — a compelling moment when Bruce Lee sums up, in his own words, what the martial arts mean from his perspective. As Tee pondered his words, it struck him that Bruce was basically saying, *Martial arts are all about keeping it real.*

And (for whatever reason) he blurted out loud, "If Bruce Lee were alive today, he would have a podcast!"

Part of the passion in a podcast is cultivating honesty with yourself and your audience, and that honesty in your podcast is what keeps listeners coming back. "To thine own self be true . . ." — one of Shakespeare's most-quoted lines from *Hamlet* — holds as true for podcasting as it has for every other intensely personal creative activity; let it serve as a mantra that fires up your drive to produce a terrific podcast. Honest passion, and honesty in general, cannot be faked in a podcast because many podcasters are producing their audio content without any other compensation save for ratings on Podcast Alley and Podcast Pickle, some feedback from listeners, and perhaps a dona-tion. On the larger scale, podcasters, regardless of their agendas or goals, are on the podcasting scene because they want to be there, and if that honesty in wanting to deliver new content is even remotely artificial, listeners will lose interest in your podcast.

It's okay to ask yourself, before hitting Record, "Do I know for sure what I'm getting into?" — or, more to the point, "Do I really want to do this?" — but never ask yourself whether you *can* do this. That isn't even a question to consider. Podcasting welcomes voices of all backgrounds, all professions, all experience levels (be they professional, semiprofessional, or amateur). You can do this — and you have as much right to as any of us. All you need is a mic, an application, a feed, and a server host. From there, it all rests on you. And once you start podcasting, produce your podcast because you *want* to, not because you *have* to.

Podcasting is a commitment of time and resources — to yourself and to your listeners. It's a promise you make to bring to the podosphere the best content you can produce — and with the right support, passion, and drive, your pod-cast will evolve, mature, and move ahead with the same zeal that inspired the first episode. Accomplishing this feat rests on remaining honest in your desire to sit behind the microphone and produce your next show. If you're not sure about the answers to "Do I know for sure what I'm getting into?" or "Do I really want to do this?" ask yourself, "If I don't want to be here, then why would lis-teners want to hear my latest episode?"

"To express myself honestly — that, my friend is very hard to do." Oh yeah, Bruce Lee would have produced an incredible podcast.

Part VI
The Part of Tens

The 5th Wave   By Rich Tennant

OUR TECHNOLOGY HISTORY:
Radio during the Silent Era

In this part . . .

Like any *For Dummies* book worth its weight in compressed MP3 files, this book contains a Part of Tens.
Because podcasting is an evolving medium, this particular
Part of Tens provides lists of ideas, thoughts, and philoso-
phies from the authors to take along on your podcasting
trek. Chapter 18 helps to guide you in your selection of
podcasts to listen to for ideas, inspiration, and fun.
Chapter 19 covers some of the most influential people in
podcasting. Chapters 20 and 21 are diametrically opposed
views of how podcasting will, or will not, influence the
future of traditional radio. (Isn't life on the unexplored
frontier exciting?)

Chapter 18

Top Ten Types of Podcasts to Check Out

. . . .

A h yes, narrowing down the thousands and thousands of podcasts out there to an elite ten: the Top Ten Podcasts You Should Be Listing To. The Best of the Best. In the podosphere, these higher planes are commonly referred to as The Pod Squad, Podcast Pickle's Favorites, and Podcast Alley Top Ten List.

Where to begin? Where to begin? We sat down and put together our own top ten lists of podcasts. What we found was that one of us swore by some podcasts the others had never heard of, and vice versa. We started wondering, "How are we going to narrow down this list and eventually get it to ten?" Then we took a closer look at our lists and realized "Hey, we've got a pattern going on here!" Amongst us, we had a solid cross-section of *types* of podcasts, not just in the way of genres but in production values. So with a quick edit of the outline and a change of mindset, we present the Top Ten Types of Podcasts to Check Out.

There are other kinds of podcasts that are, perhaps, not showcased here, but with these ten kinds of podcasts as a starting point, you can easily begin to fill playlists and media player space. When you're comfortable with what you hear, you can then follow the Favorite Podcasts links that your podcast's companion blog offers. From this list given here, you can sample a wide cross-section of audio content. Relax, download, and give your eyes and ears a treat.

 Always check your favorite podcasting directory to see how active these shows are before you subscribe. The podcasts in this section are constantly changing. They were actively producing content when we wrote this book, but printed material is never as up to date as a good podcast directory.

Tech Podcasts

If you're thinking about podcasting, you likely have a comfortable knowledge of computers, Web-surfing, and blogging. But regardless of how technologically savvy you are, like any aspect of life, you can never stop learning. That's why your aggregator should be catching at least one *tech podcast.*

The agenda for a tech podcast is (surprise!) technology — usually computer-oriented. All geek, all the time. Geeks, nerds, wizards, and Tech Help gurus sit behind a microphone and pull back the curtain on how your computer works, how a podcast's RSS feed can be better, and how to make your time behind the keyboard more efficient.

Tech podcasts come delivered to you in a variety of skill levels and on a variety of topics:

- **Macs:** Some excellent podcasts for Mac users include *MacCast* (shown in Figure 18-1 and available at `www.maccast.com`), *Typical Mac User Podcast* (`www.typicalmacuser.com`), or *Mac OS Ken* (`www.macosken.com`).

- **PCs:** *Windows Weekly* (`http://twit.tv/ww`), as the name implies, focuses on Microsoft Windows topics, trends, and technology — whereas the *Mike Tech Show* (`www.miketechshow.com`) is a bit more end-user/consumer focused to help you be more productive on your PC.

- **General computing:** Many of the tech podcasts out there like *This Week in Tech* (or TWiT, as it is so lovingly referred as by its hosts and listeners, available at `www.twit.tv/twit`) or HomeNetworkHelp.Info, are generic in their approach to operating systems, following a mindset that a computer is a computer and the rest is mostly bells and whistles.

- **Technology perspectives:** *Tech Talk for Families* (`http://techtalkforfamilies.com`) and *Technorama* (`www.chuckchat.com/technorama`) give personal and (in many cases) light-hearted perspectives on technology in society and go beyond the geek-speak, giving their own perspectives on issues and how technology can affect just about everything.

Whichever podcast you feed into your podcatching client, find a tech podcast that's right for you and either enjoy the new perspective or allow yourself to grow into your geekdom. There is a lot to learn about computers, PDAs, Bluetooth, and other cool Q Branch gizmos that are available at your local electronics store. When you have the basics down, these podcasts allow you to unlock their potential and go beyond your expectations.

Logo by Tim Madden, courtesy of Adam Christianson

Independent Music Podcasts

Podcasting is audio content on demand, and after taking a listen to what is being offered on the radio, that is a very good thing. Maybe it's a hazard of getting older, but some of us just aren't hearing anything on the air that's all that interesting or exciting . . . unless we happen to find an alternative station that has a few up-and-coming bands we haven't heard of, or independent musicians who are looking for the big break.

The good news is that those maverick sounds are alive and well and doing just fine in the 21st century, and they're finding a new promotion channel with podcasting.

Independent labels, where the artists also work as promoters, producers, and holders-of-all-rights, have control over where their music plays, how often it is played, and how much it will cost you. Many indie musicians who are having trouble getting exposure and radio airplay will grant permission for podcasters to use their music. What does this cost the podcaster? A few moments of time and a spot or two, such as, "This music is brought to you by . . ." and "Visit this band online at w-w-w-dot . . ." And in return, the musician is exposed to a worldwide audience.

Musicians such as The Gentle Readers (featured on *Evil Genius Chronicles* at www.evilgeniuschronicles.org), Moanin' Michelle Malone (featured on the podcast novel *Serve It Cold* at www.dancingcatstudios.com), and Fumitaka Anzai (featured on the *Rev Up Review* at www.rev-up-review.co.uk) have all enjoyed the benefits of associating themselves with a podcast. Now indie musicians are turning to podcasts that not only are dedicated to the broadcast of podsafe music, but also spotlight independent musicians whose sound goes against the corporate music industry's notion of "what the public wants." Here are few such podcasts you may want to check out:

✔ *The tartanpodcast* (www.tartanpodcast.com): Podcasting from Glasgow, Scotland, Mark Hunter showcases unsigned or independent label music.

✔ *LoveHouse Radio* (www.lovehouseradio.com): Based out of Richmond, Virginia, host P.D. Love took his love of music, his appreciation for the independent artist, and his everyday life and turned it into a podcast that highlights featured artists on the Podsafe Music Network.

✔ *Podrunner* (http://podrunner.com): *Podrunner* is a great place to get an hour's worth of great workout music every week. DJ Steveboy's compositions (which happen on account of his master mixing skills and Beatport.com) are great for everything from bicycle riding to Karate.

Science Podcasts

The approach to science made popular by Bill Nigh the Science Guy, Mr. Wizard, and the *Mythbusters* Adam Savage and Jamie Hyneman, is rampant in the podosphere. Here are some science podcasts that we recommend:

✔ *Astronomy Cast* (http://astronomycast.com): If you've always wondered about what's really going on beyond our atmosphere, take a listen to a podcast descendant of the Carl Sagan *Cosmos* concept. For those who would never leave the planet without their attitude, Fraser Cane and Pamela Gay dubbed the show *Astronomy Cast*.

✔ *Skepticality* (http://skepticality.com): This Parsec-winning podcast (shown in Figure 18-2) looks deeper into the news too weird for mainstream media, and it takes a critical microscope to the pseudoscience of the paranormal, the supernatural, close encounters, and urban legends.

✔ *MedSqod: Podcasting for Medical Professionals* (www.podcastingformedicalprofessionals.com): Hosted by Peter Beck, *MedSqod* is a podcast for medical professionals, a streamlined production focusing on the changing issues of healthcare, using both podcasting and blogging to keep medical pros relevant in rapidly developing social media.

What makes the MedSqod's podcast and blog so cool is how other science podcasters (like Dr. Ginger Campbell of *The Brain Science Podcast*, `http://brainsciencepodcast.blogspot.com`) will chime in from time to time, making MedSqod a great venue for networking with other medical professionals.

Figure 18-2:
The Parsec-winning *Skepticality* takes a harder look at pop and pseudo science, debunking what some pass off as scientific fact.

Science shows are good for you — like vegetables, only better. Not only can you learn something new or broaden your scope in a field you may regard as a hobby, but you can marvel at how the hosts demystify concepts once comprehensible only to Ph.D.s and keep the ideas easy to grasp.

Educational Podcasts

Why not broaden your horizons with educational podcasting? For example, say you've always wanted to learn Spanish. You could shell out some bucks for the "Teach Yourself Spanish" series, or you could to listen to the free *Spanish Connection Podcast* (its companion blog is located at `http://myspanishconnection.com`). Instructor David Spencer takes a conversational approach (mastered over an 11-year teaching experience) and turns his podcast into a survival guide series to help you navigate situations at the restaurant, at the bank, or if your car breaks down.

If you aren't interested in learning another language, take a look at some of the other subjects offered in the podosphere. Here are just a few examples of what's available:

- **History:** *HistoryPodcast* (http://historyonair.com) is completely devoted to history for the lovers of history. Or if you do want for a more specific era of discussion, my most gracious lord, check out the *British History 101* (http://bh101.wordpress.com).

- **Professional development:** Whether you're a CEO of a multibillion dollar company or an aspiring new hire for an upstart with your sites set on leadership, *Manager Tools* (http://manager-tools.com) is a "must listen" to increase your effectiveness in the workplace.

- **Personal development:** Are you looking to change your eating habits or maybe just find calm within the stress of daily life? Podcasting can bring a healthy alternative to your current digital lifestyle, and maybe even lower blood pressure and cholesterol points in the process. To find a bit of focus and flexibility in your life, give *Elsie's Yoga Class: Live and Unplugged* (www.elsiesyogakula.com) a listen. Get more background on the martial art you study (or are thinking about studying) from the video podcast *Inside Martial Arts* (www.insidemartialarts.tv). Finally, visit *Personal Life Media* (www.personallifemedia.com) for a wide array of "life management" podcasts to choose from.

- **Money management:** If you're looking for advice on managing your money, check out *Money Girl* (http://moneygirl.quickanddirtytips.com). Or if you have a friend or family member getting ready for that next step in education, try *Financial Aid Podcast* (www.financialaidpodcast.com).

There is a lot to learn from the world, and whether you're tuning in to one of numerous podcasts sponsored by universities and colleges or to an enthusiast who wants to share and swap resources with you, all this continuing education is available online, in audio, and at no charge.

Comedy Podcasts

There are times in life when you just need a good laugh. One of the joys of podcasting is having those good laughs categorized, digitized, and waiting for your call, whether it's on the computer or your favorite MP3 player.

Humor, though, is in the eye of the beholder — or in this case, the ear of the listener. Performing a search on "Comedy Podcasts" will offer you many, many choices, ranging from kid-safe comedy to adults-only. Some podcasts (such as *Technorama* and *Skepticality*) pepper their podcasts with humor (always good to add), but straight-up comedy podcasts are not intended to do anything other than entertain and perhaps make you think.

The way these podcasts make you laugh covers a wide spectrum of how humor is defined. Here are a few comedy podcasts that we enjoy:

✔ *The Bitterest Pill* (http://thebitterestpill.com): Perhaps you like your humor dry, witty, and maybe just a touch smarmy. Dan Klass and his podcast, *The Bitterest Pill,* should do the trick. With his background in stand-up comedy, Dan's delivery is edgy and relentless. He takes a hard, cold look at the world and makes observations that you might think but would not have the courage to express openly. Dan not only gives you his opinions but also podcasts them for the world to hear.

✔ *Bell's in the Batfry* (www.thebatfry.com): One of the best examples of a professional voiceover talent getting into podcasts is John Bell and his podcast *Bell's in the Batfry.* In the world of classic movies, Lon Chaney was known as the man of a thousand faces; in podcasting the same could be said about John Bell and his cast of characters. *The Batfry* is a fun place with a different situation in each show within an overarching story. John isn't just a master of voice; his editing talents really shine with the timing of each character interacting with the others in a way that really makes it believable.

✔ *Calls for Cthulhu* (www.callsforcthulhu.com): If *Ask a Ninja* (http://askaninja.com) still leaves your burning question concerning life unanswered, it might mean time to turn to a higher power, a higher power hidden deep within the submerged city of R'ylah. This is where Cthulhu hosts a call-in show and offers counsel only the Old Ones would have on hand. Created by Brand Gamblin, this video podcast (shown in Figure 18-3) will not only keep you laughing but also show a softer side to this H.P. Lovecraft creation and maybe even enlighten you with a nugget of sage advice. (Or, Cthulhu might just swallow your soul. Hard to know for sure.)

Figure 18-3:
Calls for Cthulhu is the video podcast that always promises helpful advice straight from the cephalopod's mouth.

✔ *Comedy4Cast* (www.comedy4cast.com): Another fun podcast is *Comedy4Cast*. The unpredictability from the host, Clinton, is one of the elements that adds charm to the show. Sometimes you get a tongue-in-cheek review of an electronic gadget, another time you hear a parody of another popular podcast like J.C. Hutchins' *7th Son* Trilogy (www.jchutchins.net). Prepare yourself when listening to *Comedy4Cast* by pulling over to the side of the road so you don't drive in to the ditch, or setting the hot coffee aside so as not to spit it on your keyboard — Clinton is not responsible for damages incurred while listening to his cast.

Slice-of-Life Podcasts

Comedy is prevalent in all the various genres of podcasting, especially with the podcasts that just take a look at life and give it a perspective. After all, sometimes you need humor to deal with loved ones, life's unexpected pitfalls, or the headlines. You can find a variety of podcasts that follow the "something about nothing" approach, and here are a few we recommend:

✔ *Dancing with Elephants* (www.dwithe.com)

✔ *Pizza Go Here* (http://beckwithweb.com/podcast)

✔ *The Dawn and Drew Show* (http://dawnanddrew.podshow.com)

✔ *The Big Show with Aaron and Jenny* (www.bigshowradio.blogspot.com)

✔ *Kulture Kast* (www.kulturekast.com)

These shows are difficult to describe because they change from day to day in their tone and approach to topics. These podcast are windows into the hosts' world. True, most podcasts are, but in these podcasts, it's about the moment, the here and now, and what is happening in their lives. There's really no set subject or guest to interview. There is no burning topic, ripped from the headlines. It's a group of people huddled around a microphone, giving their two cents on a week at work, what's at the movies, and what band is currently dominating their iPods. From this slice-of-life approach comes a podcast that might make you laugh, might make you cry, and maybe — just maybe — make you think.

As it goes with slice-of-life podcasts, the general content can go in any way: G, PG-13, to "What did they just say?!" Always check the podcast's listings (in directories, on their Web sites, or on iTunes for the Explicit tag) to see how "playfully blunt" these podcasts can get. For example, Dawn and Drew give a disclaimer on their homepage, a brief and simple warning that maybe they will dare to tread paths that few choose.

Spiritual Podcasts

In this book, we have referenced a few "critical thinking" podcasts (*Skepticality, The Geologic Podcast*), but alongside realists and skeptics in the podosphere are many podcasts of faith, spiritual studies, and meditation. It doesn't matter what faith you follow or denomination you are a part of, there are all kinds of podcasts (also called *Godcasts*) offering everything from a prayer for the day to soothing music to meditate by.

Here are some examples:

✔ **Catholic Insider** (www.catholicinsider.com): When it comes to Godcasting, Father Roderick Vonhögen stands out as the trendsetter with his award-winning podcast, *The Catholic Insider* (shown in Figure 18-4). He offers up commentary on Catholicism in the modern world, along with thoughts on *Harry Potter, Narnia,* and *Star Wars.* Father Roderick's success inspired others to step into the podosphere, like Father Jay Finelli of *iPadre* (http://ipadre.net), Father Seraphim Beshoner's *Catholic: Under the Hood* (http://catholicunderthe hood.com), and *Praystation Portable* (http://sqpn.com/category/spirituality/praystation-portable) offering divinities to go.

Figure 18-4:
Want the inside scoop on the Catholic faith? Tune in to *The Catholic Insider,* a podcast that looks at life from the Archdiocese's point of view.

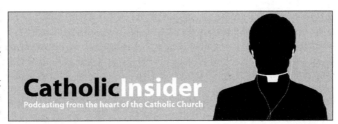

✔ **Zencast** (www.zencast.org): Zen is a study of Buddhism focusing on your present moment in life and how you are handling it. If this quick-and-simple explanation has you curious, have a listen to the *Zencast.* The teachers featured there explore different Buddhist and Zen teachings. There are also episodes featuring new age music artists, techniques in meditation, methods of aligning bio-energies, and spiritual enlightenment.

✔ *The Tarot Connection* (www.tarotconnection.net): If your understanding of Tarot doesn't reach beyond the 007 classic *Live and Let
Die,* you need to know "There's more to the cards than you realize, Mr.
Bond." A podcast like *The Tarot Connection* dispels many of the myths
and misunderstandings of what card readings really mean and how
they work. Host Leisa ReFalo, an author of two Tarot decks herself,
talks Tarot on *The Tarot Connection* but also explores Journeywork,
Astrology, Numerology, and other studies.

Podcasts of the Pen

When Tee stepped into podcasting, no author had yet set out to do what he
was planning: to serialize a novel in podcasts, from beginning to end. Twenty-
two chapters of *MOREVI* and a preview of *Legacy of MOREVI,* over a period of
23 weeks. But would anyone really want to listen?

Wow — people did want to listen and continue to do so months after its conclusion! And now, other authors have discovered the potential of this exciting way to promote their works, their unpublished material, and (of course)
themselves.

Podiobooks are podcast novels with the authors recording their works.
Alongside Tee's swashbuckling epic fantasy, *MOREVI* (www.morevi.net),
many others have come on board, including

✔ *The 7th Son* **Trilogy** (http://jchutchins.net): J.C. Hutchins captured his audience from page 1 with his unpublished techno-thriller
trilogy. From the twists, turns, and surprises, the podcast caught the
attention of St. Martins Press and set the bar for podcast fiction at a new
high.

✔ *Crescent* (www.crescentstation.net): From musician, podcaster,
and author Phil Rossi, this science fiction/horror novel takes the
"spooky, old mansion" and sets it not on Haunted Hill, but in the deepest
corner of space. This podcast is best listened to with the lights on.

✔ *The Immortals* (http://podiobooks.com/title/the-immortals):
Written and read by *New York Times* bestselling author Tracy Hickman,
The Immortals is set in a not-so-distant future where the cure for AIDS
mutates the virus into something far deadlier, and personal triumph
must overcome the society this new disease has created. On listening
to this, it's no surprise Hickman's podiobook won the Parsec Award for
Best Novel of 2007.

Although many podcast titles available are science fiction, horror, and fantasy, many other podiobooks step into other genres free of the scares, the
deep space travels, and the dark magic.

✔ *Jack Wakes Up* (www.sethharwood.com): Movies had Dashell Hammet's Sam Spade. Television had Mickey Spillane's Mike Hammer. Podcasting has Seth Harwood's Jack Palms, a one-hit-wonder of an actor who, after cleaning up his act, finds himself in a load of trouble. This time, there's no stunt double around to take the fall.

✔ *Marwan* (http://podiobooks.com/title/marwan): On September 11, 2001, America was attacked on three fronts. In *Marwan*, we see one of these battlefronts from the *other* point-of-view. This is 9-11 from the terrorist's perspective, and a look at how a terrorist is made.

✔ *You're Hired!* (http://podiobooks.com/title/your-hired): Proving that you can podcast in any genre, *You're Hired!* is a self-help podiobook for both the first-time job seeker and the seasoned professional looking for a change of pace. In these audio podcasts, helpful tips are handed down to help you get one step closer to that dream job.

Passionate Podcasts

There it is again! The *P* word — passion. Yes, yes, yes, there should be passion in every podcast you listen to, but some people do their thing simply as a celebration of something — a salute, dedication, or just plain declaration of love for a sport, TV show, or another interest that (for whatever reason) *matters* to a group of people. Here are some podcasts around such interests:

✔ *The Signal* (http://signal.serenityfirefly.com): This Parsec-winning podcast is a celebration of the prematurely cancelled sci-fi-Western-adventure television show *Firefly*. *The Signal* is a podcast from *Firefly* fans, for *Firefly* fans, and for people curious as to what the fuss is all about. *The Signal* continues to show support for an out-of-this-world Western, its actors, and the crew behind the scenes as well as provide inspiration for other podcasts like the Parsec-winning *ScapeCast* (http://spacecast.org for the fans of *Farscape*) to start podcasting their own passions about the innovative science fiction epic from Henson Studios.

✔ *Steampunk Spectacular* (http://steampunkspectacular.org): Curious about the subgenre where computers existed in the Victorian period, where airships rule the sky, and where incredible gadgets of unimaginable power were complex creations of gears, clockworks, and latches? It's known as Steampunk, and *Steampunk Spectacular* is the podcast for anyone curious about this genre and a Gentlemen's Club (ladies invited, with proper introductions and references, of course) for the hardcore fans. With book reviews, event announcements, interviews, and original fiction, *Steampunk Spectacular* is delightful *camera obscura* for the podosphere.

✔ *Cubscast* (http://cubscast.com): If you are less into achieving inner peace and more into screaming from the cheap seats at Wrigley Field, then *Cubscast* may be what you're looking for. As of the writing of this book, podcasts are available for the Boston Red Sox, the New York Yankees, the Oakland Athletics, and the new kids in the sport — the Washington Nationals. There are podcasts for professional wrestling, football (both American and European), and NASCAR, many of them fan-based, fan-sponsored, and fan-hosted.

Podcasts about . . . Podcasting

It may sound redundant and feel a little odd to listen to a podcast about podcasting. It would be like having an electrician come over to another electrician's house to fix faulty electric wiring. But why not?

- ✔ *podCast411* (http://podcast411.com): On this podcast about podcasting, Robert Walch picks the brains of podcasters from every genre, every recording method, and every work ethic, and asks them "So how do you do it?" and "Why do you do it?" The goal of *podCast411* is to answer just those questions — and to keep podcasters informed about what is currently playing in the podosphere. Featuring these podcasts lets other podcasters tune in, listen, and use what they hear to make their own podcasts grow and improve.

- ✔ *Podcast Junky* (http://podcastjunky.com): Megan Enloe was, once upon a time, a fan of podcasting. Just a fan. Then her iPod started to fill up and so she got herself a larger one. When that iPod filled up, she upgraded again. Megan continued subscribing until her podcasts numbered well over 150 (and continued to climb!). She then discovered many of her favorites were still relatively unknown to other podcast listeners. "What are you listening to?" not only became her personal mantra, but it also became the motto for her own podcast review show, *Podcast Junky,* a show that spotlights new podcasts, laments over the ones that have pod-faded, and talks with the voices that have been there from the beginning. If you want a podcast from the fan's perspective, subscribe to *Podcast Junky* and you too can get hooked on a new media fix.

- ✔ *Podcast Brothers* (www.podcastbrothers.com): This podcast keeps the podosphere informed on the various trends, the experimental, and the really cool developments of podcasting. Tim and Emile Bourquin focus on the monetary side of podcasting — making quality media kits, best practices for calling on potential advertisers, and presenting yourself as a professional. Again, two podcasters keep their attention on their passion of podcasting and keep their listeners and show producers in the know about what people are doing in this exciting medium.

Chapter 19

Top Ten Most Influential People in Podcasting

● ●

*I*f you're reading this book, you're likely new to podcasting and might have missed out on the trials and tribulations that went along with that huge growth spurt. As with any sudden rise, select individuals proved themselves to be instrumental to podcasting, as well as to other podcasters, during those formative times all those long months ago.

This chapter suggests ten (or so) of these individuals who will likely continue to influence the shape of things to come in the podcasting world. As you read these names, try to remember that these are regular people like the rest of us. True, some of them may seem larger than life (even in a field this new), but all of them put their pants on one leg at a time — unless they're wearing kilts.

Although we encourage you to make your own decisions, a wise budding podcaster or future podcast star would do well to take a listen to the wisdom/ information/rants put forth by this group. Often controversial and usually informative, each of these people has a unique outlook on the world of podcasting. We've found these folks to be helpful guides in our own growth in podcasting. But (as we've said probably way too many times in this book for our editors' tastes) your mileage may vary.

Dave Winer

Podcasting really wouldn't be podcasting without the capability to enclose files inside an RSS feed — and Dave Winer is the one who made that happen with the development of RSS 0.92 and then RSS 2.0 specifications. Without that RSS extension, we'd all be downloading files in real time, wondering why anyone would put up a 65MB file.

Dave is one of the more interesting characters in the world of podcasting. In addition to his technical contributions, some would argue that Dave's contributions to the spirit of podcasting are every bit as important.

As of this writing, Dave continues to produce *Morning Coffee Notes* (`http://morningcoffeenotes.com`). This podcast sticks with relatively rough-and-ready production values, but it's worth checking out as a pioneering approach.

Dave's show features Dave, a portable recording device, and his surroundings. Sometimes it's a discussion about a piece of technology; sometimes it's a conversation with an interesting individual. But listeners to *Morning Coffee Notes* are always treated to thought-provoking opinions and ideas from one of the progenitors of podcasting.

Dave is very much a "polarizing" individual with strong opinions he's not afraid to share. He doesn't pull any punches, and you always get the truth as he sees it. As is often true of strong opinions, the result is that some technologists bristle at the mention of his name, while others welcome his ability to look at challenges and conventional wisdom from a new perspective. Yes, he rambles — sometimes in directions that escape our personal interest or clash with our opinions on various topics. But he's Dave Winer, a voice worth listening to. You can decide what to do with the information after that.

Adam Curry

In 1987, your authors were in college, and MTV (the icon of the generation that remembers when they actually *played* music videos) hired a new VJ named Adam Curry. Almost 20 years later, despite life experiences, diplomas, and other strange changes and artistic ventures, it's still baffling to think that the same guy who was introducing the latest Madonna video is now "the Podfather."

Adam Curry's importance to the craft might be the single best example that illustrates the "just-do-it" nature of podcasting. It was Adam Curry, not some highly trained programmer, who hacked together the first podcatching client program to harness the power of the recently created enclosed-media files in RSS 2.0 feeds — and made them downloadable during the computer's off hours.

Since that time, Adam has become the most recognized (and arguably the most popular) podcaster around. He continues to produce the *Daily Source Code* (DSC) at `http://dailysourcecode.com`, which was probably the first "podcast about nothing." Listeners never know quite what to expect;

Adam could take them on a tour of his kitchen or discuss the latest round of talks that his company, BoKu Communications, is having or a content partner that will change the shape of podcasting. It's the proverbial potluck show that contains its own joke.

It's worth making time to listen to "the DSC," even if you fast-forward through the parts that don't appeal to you.

Steve Jobs and Bill Gates

To the best of our knowledge, neither Steve Jobs or Bill Gates have podcasts of their own, and you may be wondering why we're listing them as influential. For those who don't collect the Mega-Corporation Trading Card set, Steve Jobs and Bill Gates are the brains and founders of Apple and Microsoft, respectively. The actions of their companies have a distinct and unquestionable impact on the future of podcasting.

It's not a big leap to assume that without the consumer adoption of the Apple iPod (which arguably has spurred sales of other portable audio-file players), podcasting would not have spread at the incredible rate it has. iTunes is, by far, the most popular podcatching client, making it easy for people to find, subscribe, and listen to podcasts. GarageBand continues to be developed with podcasters in mind, and it still remains an invaluable tool for even the seasoned veterans. When it comes to podcasting, Apple remains out front with the latest innovations with third-party software developers like Ambrosia eager to develop for the platform.

It may appear that Microsoft was late to the podcasting party, but as podcasts originate from, are transferred through, or wind up on a personal computer, the World That Bill Built is involved. Microsoft products are *everywhere* — from cellphones and PDAs to entire media centers and game consoles. In November 2006, Microsoft finally stepped into direct competition with Apple's iPod by unveiling the Zune (www.zune.net), a portable audio and video player that offers many features iPod users have known and loved for years. On the Zune official Web site, The Marketplace — Microsoft's music store where folks can find artists and their music — hosts a podcast directory where downloading podcasts remain only a click away.

Déjà vu, anyone?

This is only the beginning for Microsoft. Look for it to continue to turn out products that not only make use of podcasting technology, but also extend it in directions that directly benefit its bottom line.

Podcasting has been (and still is) a bootstrap movement, but with its popularity, the big guns want to get into the game. Heck, they're already here, changing the game as it's forming. Such is the nature of all technology. Of course, other technology companies will exert their influence as well, but it's worth remembering that market forces are in play already and will continue as podcasting progresses.

Doug Kaye

Doug Kaye is the driving force behind IT Conversations (`itc.conversa tionsnetwork.com`), a collection of podcasts and programs that stay at the cutting edge of technology and innovation. With show hosts talking about everything from blogging to digital rights and new-media trailblazing, it's easy to stay informed (though sometimes a challenge to keep up) if you listen to one or all of the programs Doug helps produce. (Good luck!)

Doug's contribution to podcasting goes beyond simply assembling the best high-tech people to create the latest conversations about IT innovation — and providing them a vehicle for their thoughts. He's actively seeking to capture speakers, panel discussions, and conversations from various events and expositions all over the world. There's a vast amount of knowledge shared in these venues, and Doug's opinion is that too few people get a chance to hear about it. He's working hard to change that by capturing those discussions as they happen and making them part of the IT Conversations family of offerings. In essence, he'll be archiving this knowledge for future interested people. (Should be quite a future.)

It's a great plan; one that takes an incredible amount of dedication. Doug works closely with his show hosts to make sure their podcasts are engaging, sound great, and are a joy for interested people to listen to.

Rob Walch

Every few weeks or so, Rob Walch releases another edition of *podCast411* (`http://podcast411.com`), often referred to as the *Inside the Actor's Studio* for podcasters. His episodes feature an interview with another podcaster about . . . podcasting. Although that may sound a bit like navel-gazing, you might be surprised at how worthy the content is to add to your already overloaded subscription list.

Podcasters should be listening to Rob's show because it's about what they do. Who better to learn new tips and tricks from than the people actually doing the tricks on their shows every week? Most of the conversations stay focused at a fairly high level, avoiding the "detail dump" that would turn off most people.

Rob talks with other podcasters not only about how they podcast but also *why* they do it. For every question about a microphone or particular piece of hardware, Rob digs deeper into the goals of the show, the way the hosts approach their craft, and what their hopes and dreams are.

It's a fascinating show for anyone interested in learning from others who are constantly refining their shows. If you're podcasting, you should be listening to this one.

Mur Lafferty

Podcasting has never been a "Man's World," as female podcasters were blazing trails in 2004 alongside the boys. Some of those leading ladies of the RSS feeds have either *podfaded* — meaning they slowly stopped producing content without any announcement — or moved on to other pursuits, but one remains to this day as an outstanding podcast personality: Mur Lafferty (http://murverse.com). She is referred to (with great affection) as "The Grand Dame of Podcasting."

Mur Lafferty's podcasting career began with *Geek Fu Action Grip,* a show that was commentary about what was going on in her life, what games she was playing, and what bands she was listening to. Each episode of *Geek Fu* ended with an original essay of something that struck her funny bone in that particular way. This podcast spawned *I Should Be Writing,* the 2007 Parsec-winning podcast documenting her own tests and trials in getting her first novel published.

She has never stopped raising the bar for podcasters. Keeping many of her podcasts to the basics, Mur produces quality content from both sides of the brain: the analytical (*I Should Be Writing*) and the creative (The *Heaven* series, *Playing for Keeps*). Mur, with her talent in writing, also raises the bar for other creative podcasters, inspiring many to podcast their own fiction and even return to a writing passion they had stepped away from for many years.

It's hard to listen to podcasts and not hear the name of Mur Lafferty. It's harder still to subscribe to any Mur Laffery podcast and not be completely taken by her. Her personality shines in every episode, with every work, and with every show.

Joe Murphy

April 1, 2007 can truly be called "the best of times, the worst of times" for podcasting. Horror-writer and popular podcaster Scott Sigler took the print version of his podcast, *Ancestor* (print version published by Dragon Moon Press), to number one on Amazon.com's Science Fiction and Horror lists. That success was eclipsed slightly with the death of podcaster Joe Murphy.

Joe Murphy was one of the early voices in podcasting, first providing book reviews for *The Dragon Page's Cover-to-Cover* and an extra opinion on *Slice of Scifi*. Although he was reluctant to create an original podcast, Joe's no-nonsense personality and opinions earned him a fan base of his own, a fan base that followed him between both aforementioned shows and then on to the *Wingin' It!* and *The Kick Ass Mystic Ninjas* podcasts from FarPoint Media. In the winter of 2006, Joe's voice chimed in less and less, and the community noticed. He came on *Wingin' It!* to let listeners know that he had been diagnosed with Leiomyosarcoma, an extremely aggressive form of cancer. Six months later, Joe was gone.

Joe's death galvanized the community of podcasters around the world. Letters of support and donations to FarPoint Media (which later, Leann Mabry used to put together the Joe Murphy Memorial Fund), podcasters like J.C. Hutchins, Philippa Ballantine, and George Hrab gave tributes on their shows, and many podcasts (both FarPoint Media and outside the network) went dark in Joe's memory. Although many people in this international community had never met Joe, they "knew" him, and his loss is still felt.

Along with the memorial fund, the podcast *Give Us a Minute* (www.joemur phymemorialfund.org) and the Joe Murphy Memorial Award (presented at the Parsecs for community outreach and awareness through the medium) remain as his legacy to a community that still misses him.

Brian Ibbott

We put Brian Ibbott on this list for two reasons. First, he's one of the original music podcasters, and you might be thinking of starting a music podcast of your own. (Hey, lots of us wanted to be DJs when we were kids.) More importantly, Brian is a music podcaster who is doing it right — the legal way.

As mentioned in Chapter 4, podcasting licensed music legally is a challenge. With his podcast *Coverville* (http://coverville.com), Brian works directly with ASCAP, BMI, with the musicians, and other organizations that hold the rights to major-label music and songs. Although many music podcasters are just a process server away from a major lawsuit, Brian is sitting pretty.

Brian also serves as an example of how to create a niche podcast out of the music you love and fill a void not covered by the traditional outlets. Brian has a passion for cover songs and has built a show completely around songs that fit that bill. Not only that, but he's taken it a step further, featuring groups of cover songs that have a common thread and producing *themed* episodes of his podcast. Simply brilliant — we don't know of any radio stations or programs that provide this service.

So before you rush out to make the next hot music podcast, consider the legal ramifications. And while you're pondering that, also ask whether your future podcast sounds like the same stuff people can listen to over their radios. Follow Brian's lead and give the world something *different* with your podcast.

Grant Baciocco

If you were a child of the '70s, you probably remember *Schoolhouse Rock,* ABC's series of educational vignettes in between cartoon features that taught you something about American History, grammar, math, or science. These animated shorts were out to entertain as well as educate; and thanks to *Schoolhouse Rock,* a generation not only can recite the Preamble to the United States Constitution, but can *sing* it.

Grant Baciocco has created his own version of *Schoolhouse Rock* with *The Radio Adventures of Dr. Floyd* (http://doctorfloyd.com); and just like Bill on the steps of Capitol Hill, Naughty Number 9, and Interplanetary Janet, the cast of characters on this podcast are making impressions on their listeners, young and old.

Taking the approach of *Schoolhouse Rock* and throwing in a touch of *Rocky & Bullwinkle* for fun, show creators Grant Baciocco and Doug Price continue to produce a podcast that shows exactly how much you can accomplish in five minutes. Featuring original music from Jody Whitesides and the talents of guest actors like Lani Tupu (*Farscape*), Jeffrey Tambor (*Hellboy*), June Foray (*Rocky & Bullwinkle*), and Joel Hodgson and Frank Conniff (*Mystery Science Theatre 3000*), *The Radio Adventures of Dr. Floyd* keeps its delivery sharp and the content family-friendly, reaching audiences everywhere of all ages.

Don't underestimate the influence of *Dr. Floyd.* As a testament of how much impact you can have in a short amount of time, *The Radio Adventures of Dr. Floyd* is bringing mom, dad, and the kid(s) around the iPod for a bit of the old-school radio drama with a high-tech sound. This podcast has become such a hit with parents that it's being replayed in classrooms from coast to coast, laying down the groundwork for other podcasters to explore the educational application of the media. It's likely that many other educational entertainment podcasts will follow.

Dave Chekan, Matt Hoopes, Marty Mulligan, and Dave Mansueto

Podcasting sucks. Bandwidth, that is. A lot of it, as we discuss in Chapters 3 and 10. Without Dave Chekan, Matt Hoopes, Marty Mulligan, and Dave Mansueto (DMMD, as we like to call them), many podcasters would have folded up shop long ago because they couldn't afford to pay their hosting bill.

DMMD gave the podcasting world Liberated Syndication (`http://libsyn.com`) — now part of Wizzard Media — providing unbelievably cheap hosting and serving of podcast media files at a time when subscribers were flocking toward podcasts like lemmings off the cliff.

LibSyn is helping to change the paradigm of bandwidth and media-file delivery systems. Okay, nontechnical types may find it boring, scarily technical, and incredibly complicated — but it's a complete necessity for any podcaster who receives a modicum of popularity. Luckily for everyone, these four guys make it a breeze to keep your podcasts going when the wave hits.

As with any small company, they've weathered some rough spots along the way. But DMMD are committed to sticking it out, and we hope podcasters continue to stand by them or other companies like theirs. Because the thought of paying for incremental bandwidth is simply too scary to consider unless you win the lottery.

Chapter 20

Top Ten Reasons Why Podcasting Won't Kill Radio

· ·

Do you remember when you tuned in to MTV and actually saw music videos? Good times, good times. If you ever want to throw out some fun trivia, ask, "What was the first video to ever play on MTV and what group performed in it?" The answer is the video for the song "Video Killed the Radio Star" by the Buggles.

As goofy, chintzy, and utterly new wave as that song is, there was a bit of a panic when MTV went on the air. Radio stations suddenly had to compete with television over rock stars! Listeners were listening to music on their TVs! What will become of the music industry as we know it?!

Well, radio is still here. MTV now shows a variety of programming, and very little of it includes music videos. Radio — much to the contrary of what bean counters and consultants convince program directors — has survived MTV, Napster, Internet radio, and Howard Stern's jump to satellite radio.

Now comes podcasting, and what many in the broadcasting industry dismissed as the next wave of Internet radio. Even though podcasting is a new medium that's easily disregarded, the radio industry is taking notice. Although it would be neat to think that podcasting is the people's radio and will bring about the downfall of the radio, the radio industry won't be closing its doors. No, the corporate radio business will continue to stand strong and still smell as pretty as a red rose in full bloom.

The Undiscovered Country: Podcasting Awareness

Podcasting has certainly come a long way since 2004, and yet it isn't uncommon to hear this question: "What's a podcast?"

Something like this happened to Evo when a mechanic at his local auto body garage spotted his license plate, which reads, simply enough, *PODCAST*. The mechanic asked, "What's a podcast?"

When you use the word *radio,* even with the word *satellite* tacked in front of it, people understand the concept and know what you're talking about. For some, podcasting sounds too much like something geeks do for fun, but we're here to tell you that even geeks don't know what podcasting is!

Radio has decades of history, ranging from Orson Welles' *War of the Worlds,* to Abbott and Costello, to FDR's Fireside Chats, to Edward R. Murrow bringing the news from London during World War II. In contrast, podcasting's history includes socialite Paris Hilton, a technical writer named *Grammar Girl* who helps the world communicate clearer, and Adam Curry, a former MTV VJ who refers to himself as "The Podfather."

It's the newness of podcasting, along with the comfort level and familiarity of the general public (geeks included), that will keep radio in the forefront of broadcasting audio content. Perhaps marketers see a potential here, and so they should, but it'll be a few more feeds, a few more articles in print media, and a little more innovation before podcasting can truly unhinge radio.

Are You Sure You Want to Say That?: Benefits of the FCC

The origins of George Carlin's famous rant "The Seven Dirty Words You Can Never Say on Television" stems from a routine appearing on the album *Indecent Exposure.* The monologue was played on Pacifica radio station WBAI-FM, bringing on the wrath of the Federal Communications Commission. Since then, the FCC has kept a watchful eye on what is said and done on the public airwaves of both television and radio.

The lack of restraints and restrictions of the FCC, allowing podcasters to go far beyond what is considered by the government as decent, is not only podcasting's greatest strength but also its greatest weakness. Part of the appeal of on-air personalities like Howard Stern is watching how far they're willing to go in order to challenge the FCC. However, without the restraints of the FCC, Stern can now cuss like a sailor, go way above and beyond what can be heard on conventional radio, and not care what he does or who he offends. Does this mean he loses some of the appeal he had on terrestrial radio? Perhaps.

But here's a more obvious way the FCC gives broadcast radio an advantage over podcasting: You know that what you'll listen to is deemed free from profanity and (generally) safe for various age groups. That can't always be said for podcasting. On your podcast, if you're swearing and producing content that's nothing better than prerecorded locker room talk, you're probably in the clear because people know what to expect. However, if your podcast is on hobbies, politics, or sports, don't blindside your audience with profanity just because you can.

So Many Podcasts, So Many Choices

An incredible thing about podcasting is how many choices listeners have in the way of content. Podcasting offers thousands of feeds, ranging from general topics of interest to narrower topics that appeal to more specialized audiences.

Conventional radio, however, has to vie for available airwaves and signal strength as well as fulfill a specific demand in the area. Sure, you may have choice in your listening area. For example, in the Washington, D.C. area, Tee can listen to either DC101 or Arrow 94.7 if he wants to hear classic rock. If both stations are playing music he's not keen on, Tee must weather the storm and wait in the hopes of better programming. Podcasting, on the other hand, grants the freedom to choose from a variety that radio, be it public airwaves or satellite, could never deliver.

But is it possible to have too many choices? From a marketing perspective, yes, there can be so many choices offered to a consumer that the brain can't process that much information all at once. Then there's an issue of time. Do you have that much time in the day to listen to however many podcasts you register for? When you're searching for the right sports channel, you can more easily narrow down which show is best suited for your interests if you have 20 sports shows to choose from on satellite radio, as opposed to 188 various sports podcasts.

So even though choice and variety are good things, too much can be a little overwhelming.

Quality versus Quantity

Someone once said, "Just because you own a camera doesn't make you a photographer." The same can be said for podcasting. Because of the low cost of entry to podcasting, a lot of people give it a try. Some have talent, and others — well, let's just say they're not *photographers*. With radio or TV, you have some baseline expectations of quality:

- **Audio and video quality:** Broadcast radio and TV stations hire people based on their qualifications, such as journalism, meteorology, communications, and so on and they invest in their equipment. Podcasters on the other hand need none of these qualifications to get started — only a $20 microphone. As a result, you get a wide variety of audio/video quality. Some podcasts sound and/or look like they were recorded in an expensive studio (which may be true), and some sound like they were done on a garage sale walkie-talkie. You never know what you'll get.

- **Delivery quality:** Remember, the people on radio or TV are trained professionals — at least that's what they want you to believe. Most went to school and studied, apprenticed, and competitively worked their way to the positions they hold. In general, they know how to deliver a message about politics, sports, tech, music, comedy, or a variety of other topics. If the world doesn't like them, they're out of a job. Podcasting? Again, it's hit or miss. To be fair, most podcasters are genuine. They have a passion — they get an A for effort. Some are good at delivering their messages, and others make Ben Stein sound like a caffeine addict.

- **Content quality:** In many cases, radio and TV have writers and editors to make the content rich. Trained professionals know how to direct an interview or change subject if it's leading nowhere. Even the authors of this book wish they had writers and editors for their podcasts! That's not to say that all podcast content is lacking for quality. Some of it is excellent, insightful, thought provoking, and controversial, but you're going to have to search for it.

I Can't Name That Tune: Music in Podcasting

Music is a popular topic in podcasting. In fact, it's the most popular podcast topic. At the time of this writing, over 7,000 podcasts are listed on Podcast Alley (http://podcastalley.com) in the Music/Radio genre. As impressive as this may sound, hold your applause. As it was said in *The Hitchhiker's Guide to the Galaxy,* "Things are not always as they seem."

The Recording Industry Association of America (RIAA) is about as happy about podcasting as it was about Napster. With recent lawsuits following file-sharing technologies and the swapping of music files, legal teams are merely waiting to hop into their fleet of Tumblers (thank you, *Batman Begins*) and hunt down copyright offenders, and podcasting (in particular, music podcasts) has the potential to be a favorite target of the RIAA.

If you want to podcast a tribute, for example, to Billy Joel — call it the Big Shot Podcast: All Billy Joel; All the Time — you have to pay licensing fees to the RIAA just as radio stations across the country do. These licensing fees can be costly to the average podcaster.

If you want to play the new releases from Coldplay, Switchfoot, and U2, you won't be able to do it for free. Because radio stations have the backing of corporate entities like Viacom, these fees are simply chump change for them. For the podcaster, that fee could be spent elsewhere . . . like rent.

A Prerecorded Show, Recorded Live: Live Remotes versus Remote Podcasting

Some podcasts are slice-of-life podcasts, recording a day in the life of the podcaster. These remote podcasts can be anything from a trip to the super-market to the more-popular (and quite-fun-to-participate-in) *beercasts,* where friends just sit around and sample the beers of whatever establishment they're visiting. However, this is what separates podcasting from traditional radio/TV: Podcasts are all prerecorded.

Radio will always have the advantage of *immediate* content. Radio broadcasts bring live concerts, sporting events, and news to listeners. Sure, podcasting can serve as an archive for legendary moments of sports or history, but — while it's neat to hear Al Michaels scream, "Do you believe in miracles!?" — nothing can beat the moment itself, whether you're watching it on television, listening to it on the radio, or fortunate enough to be there. The same can be said for the climax of Roger Waters's *The Wall Live in Berlin* concert or the 2004 Boston Red Sox breaking the curse.

Radio will always have the advantage of transporting audiences to history as it happens, keeping listeners in the know of current events, and deliver-ing content at that very moment. Satellite radio now solves the problem of limited reception. Subscribers to satellite radio never have to worry about losing a signal, staying with the live coverage from the beginning to the end.

Some may argue that streaming and conferencing technologies like TalkShoe (www.talkshoe.com), Skype (www.skype.com), and UStream (www.ustream.tv) allow the podcaster a sense of "live" reporting. However this requires the podcaster and the listener to be on a specific schedule. What's more, only a very small percentage of the overall listeners "tune in" at the right time to hear the show being streamed live. Don't get us wrong: This is a cool way to interact with your listeners. It just doesn't compare with the con-venience radio has.

Advertising: Show Me the Numbers

Potential advertisers will ask podcasters the same question they ask a radio station's sales representative: "So, what kind of numbers does your show pull in? How can I justify the cost of running ads on your show?"

The radio executive can pull out a ratings chart for his or her morning show and tell the perspective advertiser that the show pulls in a 12 share, which means 24,000 people are listening to the show. He can also break down the ratings points into age and gender groups, to give the executive an idea of what kind of listener tunes in.

The podcaster says, "We measure by bandwidth and downloads." Already, the podcaster has probably lost the potential advertiser with the word *bandwidth*. So the advertiser asks, "How many downloads do you have a month?" He looks at the numbers and asks, "Is that men and women, 18–25?" The podcaster doesn't really know for sure.

Advertisers want to know who your audience is and how your podcast can make a difference in getting people to their business. True, a podcast — unlike radio — reaches a much wider audience. A global one, in fact. But for many local businesses, reaching a global market is less important than reaching their "closer" clients. You can measure your podcast's downloads many different ways, but when it comes to target groups (also known as *demographics*), radio holds an advantage with the ratings system in place.

Podcasting will eventually refine the various methods of measuring listenership and subscribers, and there are various scripts available that can be downloaded and incorporated into feeds and Web pages that can produce accurate numbers. But they're a far cry from the sophisticated ratings books generated for radio stations and their programming. Until computer programmers can come up with something more in-depth and easier for nontechnical types to understand, it will be radio's ratings shares trumping the podcast downloads.

My Corner of the World: Local News

It's early morning rush hour and time to head out with a cup of joe, a breakfast burrito, and your newspaper. You get into the car and plug in your MP3 player and listen to the latest installment of *The Daily Source Code,* a change of pace from the local news station that is your usual morning fare. Only ten minutes into your commute, you run into a traffic jam. Thirty minutes later, you haven't moved. So you switch to your radio and hear:

> "And as we have been reporting all morning, the trailer spilling biohazardous waste has caused a strange mutation to spread from car to car now trapped on the interstate. And it appears that some of the drivers closest to the tanker are eating the other commuters . . ."

You look up, just in time to see a small group of grey-skinned commuters with freakily glowing eyes walking toward you. What a different morning it would have been if you had listened to the radio. Broadcast radio can keep listeners informed with up-to-moment local news, a distinct advantage that podcasting falls short in fulfilling.

If you want to entice listeners to visit your community, traffic reports and local headlines might not be what you want to use. Add the problem of being unable to perform true live reports, and the immediacy and urgency of local issues, traffic reports, and weather forecasts are lost. Local commercial- and community-sponsored radio continues to fill a demand that podcasting cannot: late-breaking news in the area.

So before plugging in your MP3 player for your morning drive, you might want to plug in to your local news radio station first, just to avoid any apocalyptic backups on the interstate.

10-4, Good Buddy: Satellite Radio versus Podcasting

Satellite radio (XM and SIRIUS leading the charge) exclusively holds one advantage over podcasting: continuous content. Satellite radio also solves the problem of traditional AM/FM radio in that the signal is clean, clear, and constant from one coast to the other. It is 24 hours of content that continuously refreshes itself.

In a 14- to 16-hour nonstop trek across the country, satellite radio can offer new and original programming. To achieve the same thing with podcasting, you would have to program into a podcatching client at least 28 podcast feeds (provided the podcasts are an average of 30 minutes in length), download them, sync them with your portable MP3 player, and then take it on the road.

It isn't impossible to have podcasts take you from one coast to the other and back again, but as far as keeping the content original and new from beginning to end, you're looking at an impressive collection of feeds numbering in the 30s to 40s. There's also a bit more work involved with podcasting in programming in the feeds, downloading, and then syncing the casts. With satellite radio, you simply have to turn on the unit.

Audio for the People, by the People, but Not Necessarily Embraced by the People

To listen to a radio broadcast, you need a simple transistor radio, a power supply, and a strong signal. Anyone can tune in, and you can listen anywhere within range of the transmission signal.

To listen to a podcast, you need the following:

- ✔ A computer
- ✔ A power supply
- ✔ An Internet connection
- ✔ An aggregator/podcatching client to subscribe and automatically download the audio content
- ✔ An MP3 player on the computer for listening at home or a portable MP3 player for the road.

The sad reality of a podcast is that you can tell your family about it, but that doesn't mean that they'll listen. Your grandmother might download and have a listen, but that's if she's up on the latest Internet trends. Otherwise, she'll miss your podcast.

An advantage of radio is that you tell your family about your radio show. You give them the station and broadcast time. They tune in.

Listeners need to have some familiarity with technology and some Internet know-how to be able to set up their computers to receive feeds. Although iTunes has opened the door for podcasting to reach the general public, podcasters are still working against the technophobia in receiving a podcast versus turning on a radio, tuning in, and listening.

Chapter 21

Top Ten Reasons Why Podcasting Will Kill (Or Seriously Dent) Radio

• •

*P*odcasting is just a fad."

"This is nothing more than streaming audio, and that didn't go anywhere."

"I've listened to a few podcasts, and I'm not impressed."

The nay-sayers of podcasting (especially those who have no idea what it is, have never listened to one, but are the first to dismiss it) have a plethora of reasons why podcasting will fail or never catch on in mainstream media. Even with the thousands of podcasts available, their listenership steadily rising, radio and other traditional media outlets have nothing to fear.

Or do they?

Chapter 20 gives you a few reasons why radio will continue to be radio for the foreseeable future. Here, we take the opposite vantage point. Although the chapter title may be a bit — okay, a lot — of blue skies and optimism, we believe the powers-that-be in charge of the large corporate media conglomerates have been observing the podcasting phenomenon for the past few years with a wary eye.

Here are a few (ten, to be exact) reasons why.

Podcasters Don't Need No Stinking Transmitters

The distance a terrestrial radio station can transmit a signal is dependent on three things: tower height, transmitter strength, and government regulations (which in the case of the United States is designated by the FCC). The first two are physical limitations that control how far a signal can travel. At some point, geography gets in the way or the signal-to-noise ratio simply gets too low to allow for continued reception. The latter serves as the rules and guidelines needed in order to control the competitive environment, ensuring that stations in different cities transmitting on the same frequency don't have to worry about their signals crossing over one another.

Podcasting is free from all those trappings. Instead of traveling in relation to the topography of the land, podcasts travel along the topography of the Internet. A show released as a podcast in Arlington, Virginia, is just as easy to pick up in Perth, Australia, as it is for someone 20 miles away in Washington, D.C.

Syndicated radio programs rely on network relationships with various radio stations, each one picking up and rebroadcasting the program to its local area to achieve nationwide or sizeable regional coverage. Satellite radio doesn't have those same limitations, but even it can't boast of global coverage unless it adds a few more multimillion-dollar satellites to its arsenal.

Syndicated and satellite radio have nothing on podcasts. A podcast of exceptional quality and high personal appeal produced out of northern Scotland, for example, can (and occasionally does) enjoy worldwide distribution via RSS the moment the podcast is available online. Even the most popular programs on the largest radio networks in the world cannot make this claim.

Reality check time: Just because folks all over the world can listen to your podcast doesn't mean that they will. Provided they can get your show, they first need to understand what language you're speaking. And even if they all decide your program is the best thing since sliced baklava, listening to your program still requires a computer connection (high speed, preferable) and a player of some kind, be it on the computer or a portable one. So simmer down and get your head out of the clouds.

Podcasting Is Outside of 88.1 and 107.9 (And 530 and 1690)

The FCC (or similar government agencies worldwide) allows a radio station to transmit on a specific frequency. That frequency falls somewhere between the end points of the AM and FM radio dial (88.1–107.9 for FM and 530–1690 for AM). In other words, you can't tune in to 87.3 or 108.7 FM, nor could you hear anything if you could get your little orange stick to move to 450 or 1710 AM. (Yeah, okay, that dates us, doesn't it?)

Really boring physics that you probably didn't pay attention to in high school tells you that there's a limited number of frequencies between those two end points of the spectrum. Rather than make you do the equations, trust us that fewer than about 200 radio stations are in any given area, split between the AM and FM spectrum. Two hundred may sound like a lot of radio stations, and it is. But due to a host of other incredibly mind-numbing physics issues and the hard facts of economics, you're unlikely to find that many choices in your area. True, satellite radio differs from this. However, while satellite radio allows for many more channels than terrestrial radio, it still has very real limits.

But pretend for a moment that money and physics weren't an issue and that station owners were willing to take any slot they could get on the spectrum. Two hundred stations is a drop in the bucket when you consider how many podcasts you can access with a click of the mouse.

Can you say "unlimited"? Seriously. The Internet wasn't designed with a hard limit on the number of connections. When network traffic gets slow, the companies that rely on those connections find ways to add more capacity. As the Internet has no end in sight (unless you go to www.shibumi.org/eoti. htm), we aren't in danger of filling it up anytime soon.

The Rats Are Leaving the USS Commercial Media

Though the mega-corp media companies will squirm to hear us say it, the populous is spending less time with their radios, televisions, and newspapers. It's not that these staples of news and information are somehow less effective than they were 50 years ago. People are discovering new, improved, and more interactive ways to get their content and are making the switch.

Do a quick Web search (hey look! another interactive media), and you can find all the supporting documentation you need. Blog posts, podcasts, and news articles both online and even in print talk about Web 2.0 and how consumers are turning to interactive television, online vendors (such as YouTube, iTunes, and Google News), and video games for their news, information, and entertainment. A 2006 study from the Forrester Research, Inc., found that one-quarter of all online consumers (the people who log on to the Internet) subscribe to podcasts because they can access the audio and video on their schedule, not someone else's. Traditional media, if not on a serious decline, has hit a plateau at best.

We can toss out a host of reasons for this exodus, but it all boils down to one thing: convenience. You're still stuck with a 24-hour clock, and try as you might, you just can't cram any more hours in the day. Leisure time for most people is decreasing, so the ability to consume media on the go is critical to many. With new devices like the iPhone, the iPod Touch, and cell phones that can do everything but cook your breakfast (but can they take a call and keep you connected, we ask), podcasting has become even easier for people to subscribe and listen. Podcasting offers audio and video on your time, wherever you may be, leaving the other forms of media consumption contemplating innovative ways to become more portable. Maybe that's why so many media outlets (CBS, ABC, CNN, Comedy Central) are entering the podosphere.

Podcasters Don't Have to Care That Most People Don't Care

Because of the physical, legal, and economic limitations on traditional broadcasters, they have to make every second of their programming day count. How well they perform this task is in the ratings, and the all-important ratings share becomes the only thing that counts. When you try to appeal to the greatest number of people, the content often gets watered down. You trade intensity for density, and you sacrifice important and compelling programs for those that require a little less thought and are easily digestible.

As a natural result of this homogenization of radio, specialty and niche programs get pushed to the fringes of the clock, when listenership is already low due to the human body's sleep requirement. The station owner needs to fill the time with something, and it's a convenient way for him to say, "See? I carry cutting edge and meaningful content." He leaves out the ". . . at 4 a.m." part, though.

But podcasting is all about the niche because the podosphere has no prime time. No one has to make hard decisions about putting great, but laser-focused, programs in a bad time slot. Whether a show has hundreds or thousands of listeners, it makes no difference to the non-existent programming lineup. It's a matter of personal preference in the hands of the people listening, and no sacrifices are required to appeal to anyone more than those who are interested in tuning in.

We'll Be Right Back after a Brief Word from Our Sponsors . . .

Podcasters, by and large, are more sensitive to the perception of too much commercialization. Many prefer to do it for the passion and the love of producing something very personal; they prefer not to make money or "work for the man." On the flip side of this very important coin, some podcasters want to run commercials to not only pay the bills but also to make money. (Getting *paid* to podcast! How cool is that?!) As podcasting works to try and come up with a reliable and standardized approach to measuring listenership (like The Nielsen Ratings), it's a challenge to sell a podcast to advertisers.

So why exactly is the advertising dollar turning to podcasts?

- ✔ **Podcasts can create a ready made target audience.** Many advertisers *hope* that consumers are watching or listening to the commercials on TV or radio. People who subscribe to a podcast are there because they are choosing to be there. Consumers are demanding this podcast, so if you're advertising Mac accessories in a podcast about Macs, your audience is receptive.

- ✔ **Portable devices have proven themselves a popular means of consuming media.** With iTunes carrying television and movies and the prevalence of iPhones (with the one millionth iPhone sold within three months of its premiere) and PlayStation Portable devices, you can now expect your media to be as mobile as you are. Advertisers now have an even more direct way of reaching consumers through such devices.

- ✔ **The podcast audience is a captive audience.** Advertisers have tried to get consumers attentions by boosting the volume of commercials (pretty annoying) or offering "bonus content" that can be seen only during the commercials (pretty silly). With a podcast, people are listening because they want to listen. A captive audience is the advertiser's dream.

The podosphere still harbors a less-is-more approach and is very cognizant that over-commercialization can have a detriment on a podcaster's ability to reach a wider audience. Also, as podcasting remains an undiscovered country of media, you won't get rich quick with it. Still, why not get paid doing something you love?

Podcasting Can Extend Public Radio

Mention public radio to many people, and minds immediately turn to endless classical music, bluegrass and dry humor courtesy of *The Prairie Home Companion,* and in-depth analysis of the current political situation in Uzbekistan. It seems that public radio is acting as a counterbalance to the extreme sensationalism that is commercial radio by being anything but.

Say what you want about public radio, but we happen to like it. Unfortunately, much of the special-interest programming we would enjoy isn't on at a convenient time. Similarly, we've heard great programs on other stations while traveling around the country that simply aren't available in our local area.

Podcasting extends public radio beyond its airwaves' limitations, whether you take that literally or figuratively. National Public Radio (www.npr.org) is often the first experience for listeners new to the podosphere, and NPR continues to repurpose its programming in podcasts, allowing listeners the freedom of time-shifting. Additionally, many NPR-esque podcasts (art magazines, yoga tutorials, political discussions, and so on) are appearing, again spreading the feeling and spirit of public radio, minus the radio.

Of course you can find plenty of sensationalistic and commercialized podcasts in the mix, and these over-the-top podcasters go head-to-head (whether consciously or not) with the sensationalistic and commercial radio programs already on the airwaves. Because public radio is less about competition and more about cooperation, mutually beneficial relationships are developing between public broadcasters and podcasters.

John Q. Public — Program Director

Program directors are the people responsible for setting what you hear on a station. The program directors pick the content, sometimes with lots of help and guidance from the larger corporate body or from a computer keeping track of album sales and Billboard charts. If it's a music station, the program directors pick the genre of music that's played, the individual tracks, and the artists, which are usually in track with the station's chosen market (country, jazz, contemporary hits, and so on). The same goes for talk and sports radio. In a nutshell, if something makes it on the air, it passed across the director's desk for approval.

We've known a few program directors. Many have an uncanny knack for selecting the hosts, programs, and style of entertainment that resonates to the listeners in their community. But so far, none of them have made a station we can listen to for more than a few hours straight.

This isn't a negative comment about program directors, mind you. This is merely an observation about programming for one versus programming for many. Although podcasting networks — such as FarPoint Media (http:// farpointmedia.net) and SQPN: The Best in Catholic Podcasting (http:// sqpn.com) — have developed to provide listeners and subscribers with similar or related content, most podcast listeners create their own programming lineup by way of their subscription lists while the podcast hosts themselves provide the content based on what they want to do and what their audience might enjoy.

The Niche Shall Inherit the Podcast

All the specialty and niche content radio shows that are currently beating themselves up and doing everything they can to get that 4 a.m. time slot will discover and embrace podcasting sooner or later. We're not saying they'll stop airing their programs over the radio, but they will find a bigger and more dedicated audience via podcasting. Sure, you can likely still catch the show at 4 a.m., but on the very good chance you're still catching some shut-eye, you'll be able to listen to it later, as a podcast.

Producing an independent syndicated radio program is hard work, but producing a quality podcast is easy — at least it is with the help of this book. The latter has some benefits. The first is freedom: freedom from the FCC, freedom from a preset format clock that tells you exactly how long your show can be, and even freedom from the real clock and calendar in the time-shifted world.

Podcasters also don't have to worry about keeping stations happy, nor do they have to spend countless hours on the phone trying to convince new stations to carry their programming. We know more than one independently produced syndicated program that has ceased all attempts at gaining new stations simply because their listenership expands greater with podcasting. At least one has taken it a step further and canceled its relationship with its previous network of stations. And why not, when podcasting allows you to dump those burdens and focus on building the best show you can? Sounds like a good plan to us.

Welcome to Your Own Reality

Everyone lives in a customized version of reality, even though you may not be conscious of it. Every day, you make choices that reinforce that reality. You select one particular grocery store as the best even though you could likely go to five different stores. You choose a particular model of car to buy based on who you want to be as much as any other choice. Your hair styles, the clothes you buy . . . it's human nature.

Whether you do it for status, frugality, or to be good to the environment doesn't matter — just as whether it's a good or bad choice doesn't matter. Unless you behave in a completely random pattern, you're reinforcing your own reality with the choices you make.

Podcasting gives you one more thing to add to the inventory of *you* and who you project yourself to be. We're sci-fi fans, and we listen to lots of sci-fi podcasts. Sure we like them, but they also help to reaffirm who we consider ourselves to be. Evo is into holistic health, thinks of himself as environmentally responsible, and he digs trippy world music with lots of freaky drums and weird time signatures. Guess what sorts of shows are in his playlist? Tee loves thriller fiction, new gadgets, and true-life stories centered around espionage. It is no surprise that his iTunes is waiting for new episodes of The International Spy Museum's *SpyCast*. And Chuck? He's an IT guy who needs to keep up with the latest trends in tech. He also has a lot of friends over at Friends in Tech (http://friendsintech.com), producing podcasts that do just that.

Radio can't do this. Oh sure, you can make the assumption that all NPR listeners are democrats and everyone who tunes in to the local classic rock station used to have a mullet. While that may be true in some cases, it's likely not universally true, simply due to the complexity of the human psyche. We're complicated guys, and we haven't found a station that gets anywhere near summing us up. But take a listen to some of the podcasts in our playlists, and you're a few steps closer to understanding where we're coming from.

You Bought This Book, Didn't You?

We end on the number-one reason podcasting will put a dent in radio: *you*. The three of us are betting you've listened to the radio at least once in your life. We'll go out on a limb and say it was even more than that — a *lot* more. Yet here you are, reading a book that teaches you how to podcast. Even if you're just curious, your actions speak volumes.

Hey, don't get us wrong. We're not assuming this book has some magical power or that you're so stunned by the stellar quality of the writing that you'll rip the radio out of your car. But you must be looking for something that radio is not providing, or by your perception cannot provide, to *you*.

Maybe it's one of the reasons outlined in this chapter. Perhaps podcasting just sounds really fun, and you'd love to try it out. You sure can't do that in radio. But whatever the reason is, we hope you enjoy the journey of finding your own voice in podcasting.

Index

• N •

• O •

• **X** •

• **Y** •

• Z •